The Olympian Dreams and Youthful Rebellion of René Descartes

Portrait of René Descartes; engraving by Gérard Edelink
from a painting by Frans Hals.

THE OLYMPIAN DREAMS AND YOUTHFUL REBELLION OF RENÉ DESCARTES

JOHN R. COLE

UNIVERSITY OF ILLINOIS PRESS
Urbana and Chicago

This book is printed on acid-free paper.

Library of Congress Cataloging-in-Publication Data

Cole, John R. (John Richard), 1941–
    The Olympian dreams and youthful rebellion of René Descartes /
John R. Cole.
        p. cm.
    Includes bibliographical references and index.
    ISBN 0-252-01870-2
    1. Descartes, René, 1596–1650. 2. Dreams—History—17th century.
I. Title.
B1873.C65 1992
194—dc20   91-25999
                                                                       CIP

Contents

Preface

Gérard Edelinck's engraving after Frans Hals's portrait served as the frontispiece for Adrien Baillet's *Vie de Monsieur Des Cartes* (1691), the first great biography on this subject. In the engraving, the philosopher's torso is oriented three-quarters left, while his head turns back to face forward. This orientation reverses that of the painting but represents its subject rather better. The conventional trappings are another matter.

At the base of the oval frame are the helmeted arms of the Descartes family, signifying the nobility that their magistracies in the sovereign courts had assured for his father, his brothers, and his brothers' descendants. Around this oval we read, "René Des Cartes, *chevalier*, seigneur du Perron." The term *chevalier* qualifies our hero as a *gentilhomme*, or old nobleman, although legally he was a *roturier*, or commoner, having turned away from his own training in the law and the quest for status, wealth, and power in judicial offices that motivated others in his family. To his contemporaries, the name of this *seigneurie* would have recalled the eminent churchman, courtier, and statesman Cardinal du Perron, although there was no historical relationship between the two men. To moderns, it suggests significant landed estates, although Descartes's le Perron was only a small, nonnoble *métairie* that he sold quickly on coming of age.

This Descartes chose to spend his life as a voluntary exile searching for truth, eventually writing the Great Books that were to make him a king in the world of minds. The engraving makes no reference to any of this, but no matter. The bust in its oval rests on a pedestal inscribed with a motto that the reclusive intellectual had taken from the Latin poets: "He who hides well, lives well." The public Descartes did hide well, even in the nominally historical parts of the *Discourse on Method* (1637), wherein he omitted his family, friends, emotional life, and all experiences other than his own thinking. The single event that he did include was an epochal day of thinking in a heated chamber "at the beginning of winter" in 1619, when he declared his intellectual independence from the past and from all other persons. To a culture in which tradition, authority, and community ruled, the hero of the heated chamber was a youthful rebel. Whence his rebellion?

In the *Olympica*, his contemporaneous manuscript record of three dreams from the night of 10 November 1619, this rebel thinker bared more of himself than he or anyone else has ever known. Descartes himself could never have imagined a methodical analysis of what he preferred to regard as heaven-sent visions, and even Freud, who considered the dream reports as such, did not believe that the associations necessary for any informed interpretation could ever be recalled from the dead dreamer. That is my challenge.

I want to try to understand the dreams and the dreamer, to use the irrational narratives and enthusiastic interpretations emerging from the heated chamber as the basis for a new inquiry into the mind of the archrationalist at the very moment of his epochal break from the past.

Acknowledgments

Although they are long past caring how much or how little I have taken from their work, or what I have done with their leavings, Adrien Baillet and Charles Adam merit pride of place in this list of my creditors. Among all the students of Descartes's life and thought, they have given me the most, without expecting anything in return.

The same might be said for Sigmund Freud as a student of dreams in general and these dreams in particular, were it not hard to imagine that mere death can have lessened his heroic determination to define his new "science," its limitations as well as its powers.

Richard Wagner, a good friend and colleague at Bates College, shared his understanding of Freud and Jung without discouraging me from a project that must still seem venturesome to him. Another friend and colleague, Thomas Hayward, gave me a great deal of his time, putting at my disposal his mastery of the Latin language. I am very grateful to both.

Allan Rechtschaffen, director of the Sleep Research Laboratory at the University of Chicago, obliged my request to examine the Olympian dream reports (or more properly, my translation of Baillet's version of Descartes's dream reports) in the light of Henri Gouhier's exaggerated suspicions.

George Bournakel set aside a busy practice to share his expert knowledge on technical points of ophthalmology related to Descartes's Interpretation II, wherein the awakened dreamer lightened the burden of his guilty conscience by "scientific experimentation" in the darkness of his heated chamber.

Great universities gave me access to their research collections. At Harvard, many persons from the staffs of the Widener, the Houghton, the Law School, and the Medical School libraries helped me. At Yale, others at the Sterling, the Beinecke, the Divinity School, and the Medical School libraries extended services and courtesies. All deserve my thanks.

The Boston Public Library, the New York Public Library, and the Library of Congress all hosted me on occasional visits. The same is true for the Hôtel de Ville at Sucé, the Musée Descartes in La Haye-Descartes, the Bibliothèque Municipale et Universitaire in Clermont-Ferrand, and the Bibliothèque Nationale. Thank you, *merci*.

I bow more deeply to the staffs of two fine college libraries, the Hawthorne-Longfellow Library at Bowdoin, with its rich collections, and the Ladd Library at Bates, with its riches in people. I am particularly indebted to Laura Juraska and LaVerne Winn.

I can never hope to express adequately my gratitude to persons who have had confidence in me and my work. They include teachers at Haverford, Wallace MacCaffery and John Spielman, scholars at Harvard, Crane Brinton and Franklin Ford, and administrators at Bates, Thomas Hedley Reynolds and Carl Straub. Most importantly, they include Margaret Cole, Donald Fennessey, Neil Fennessey, and the woman who said yes both to the law and to me, Joanne Fennessey Cole.

By far the greatest obstacle to the progress of science and to the undertaking of new tasks and provinces therein is found in this—that men despair and think things impossible. For wise and serious men are wont in these matters to be altogether distrustful, considering with themselves the obscurity of nature, the shortness of life, the deceitfulness of the senses, the weakness of judgment, the difficulty of experiment, and the like, and so supposing that . . . when they [the sciences] have reached a certain point and condition, they can advance no further. If, therefore, anyone believes or promises more, they think this comes of an ungoverned and unripened mind, and that such attempts have prosperous beginnings, become difficult as they go on, and end in confusion.

Now, since these are thoughts which naturally present themselves to grave men and of great judgment, we must take heed that we be not led astray by our love for a most fair and excellent object to relax or diminish the severity of our judgment. We must observe diligently what encouragement dawns upon us and from what quarter, and, putting aside the lighter breeze of hope, we must thoroughly sift and examine those which promise greater steadiness and constancy. Nay, and we must take state-prudence, too, into our counsels, whose rule is to distrust, and to take the less favorable view of human affairs.

I am now therefore to speak touching *hope,* especially as I am not a dealer in promises and wish neither to force nor to ensnare men's judgments, but to lead them by the hand with their good will. . . . The strongest means of inspiring hope will be to bring men to *particulars.*

—Francis Bacon, *Novum Organum,* 1:xcii

INTRODUCTION:
DESCARTES'S *OLYMPICA,*
HISTORY, AND PSYCHOLOGY

This book concerns René Descartes's three dreams from the night
of 10 November 1619 and his youthful rebellion against both the
ways of thinking dominant in French culture and the ways of life
dominant in his father's family. We know about these dreams because
the awakened dreamer recorded them in a "little notebook bound in
parchment," grandly entitling his dream record the *Olympica*. Descartes's Little Notebook has been lost since the seventeenth century,
but the detailed inventory made by Hector-Pierre Chanut in 1650 still
exists, as do the substantial excerpts from its several dossiers copied
by Gottfried Wilhelm von Leibniz in 1676 and, most importantly, the
very extensive paraphrase-translation of the *Olympica* published by
Adrien Baillet in 1691.[1] No body of evidence, not even the *Discourse
on Method,* is potentially more significant for historians curious to
understand the formation of Descartes's personality as a thinker. In
the *Discourse,* the philosopher swings the "history" of his life on the
pivot of one event, just one, his day of thought in a heated chamber
at the beginning of winter, 1619: "I was then in Germany, where I had
been called by the wars that have not yet finished. While I was returning
toward the army from the coronation of the Emperor, I was halted
by the beginning of winter in a quarter where no conversation diverted
me and neither cares nor passions troubled me. I remained the whole
day shut up alone in a heated chamber, where I had uninterrupted
leisure to consider my thoughts."[2] Descartes's recapitulation of these
thoughts leads directly to his enunciation of both the rules of the

1

method by which he hoped to discover everything knowable and the maxims of the morality by which he proposed to govern his behavior.[3]

With all the wisdom of his twenty-three years, the restless genius decided on this memorable occasion that he could rely exclusively on his own thinking, rejecting all others'. He would think for himself, not just on this topic or that but on everything, and though in his published account he excepted both politics and religion from this program,[4] this was still to defy the principles of a culture in which individuals were expected to defer to tradition, authority, and community. As importantly, he would go his own way, without regard for the status and income of a professional career.[5] To do this was to break decisively from the norms of a hierarchical society in which the Descartes were rising into the nobility by means of judicial offices.

What inspired this youthful rebellion? In the retrospective *Discourse,* an older Descartes offers no answer more satisfactory than his mature "thoughts." He had negative thoughts on what he had been able to learn from books, even as a favored schoolboy, or from experience, even as an observant traveler.[6] And he had positive thoughts on the great virtues of thinking for himself. In the *Discourse,* this is the more or less logical conclusion of a quintuple analogy: like the architect, like the town planner, like the law giver, like the scholar, and like the emancipated youth, just so, he, René Descartes, would do better to think for himself.[7]

Descartes's youth has always been a closed book, barely cracked in the philosopher's own quasi-historical account. In the *Discourse,* he seems always to have been a detached intellect, never a developing personality. He lacks a past other than his schooling and his travels; he lacks a family or friends worth mentioning; and he lacks anything like passions or conflicts. Historians have discovered other documentation that adds some information—for instance, the significant fact of his own legal training at Poitiers and the births, marriages, offices, and deaths of other family members—but there is little or nothing in the *Discourse* that can help relate these bits and pieces of data to the story of the great philosopher.

Paradoxically, it is Descartes's account of his youthful dreams that can help explain what he himself took to be the decisive stage in his formation as a thinker. What survives from the *Olympica* confirms that the younger man, too, had been convinced at the time that there had been a particularly important day of intellectual discovery at the be-

2

ginning of winter, 1619. He wrote: "10 November 1619. When I was full of enthusiasm and I was discovering the foundation of the wonderful science . . ."[8] After his narrative of the third dream, he concluded that "it was the Spirit of Truth [God] that had wanted to open unto him the treasures of all the sciences by this dream."[9] Finally, in a marginal note that he added on the first anniversary of his awakening, he echoed his own first words: "11 November 1620. I began to understand the foundation of the wonderful discovery."[10]

These three passages are all well known, but the first, on "the wonderful science," and the third, on "the wonderful discovery," puzzled even the savants who still had full access to the manuscripts.[11] Descartes must have said nothing more about his "foundation(s)," and the most learned scholars have added little more than their own speculations. The second passage has been even more troublesome. Properly respectful but inevitably skeptical students of the great thinker can hardly credit his enthusiastic claim that God revealed to him the secrets of all sciences in a dream centering on two books, the first a phantom dictionary that mysteriously appears and disappears, then reappears and disappears once again, and the second a schoolboy anthology most notable as a source for the wisdom of Ausonius![12]

How can I justify the claim that the evidence on Descartes's *dreams* can have such significance for students of his *thought?* It cannot be done by claiming that the dream narratives themselves have much to offer to anyone but the enemies of Cartesianism, who have been delighted to ridicule the dreamer as a way of attacking the thinker.[13] In Dream I, young Descartes stumbles dizzily through the streets, as if drunk. In Dream II, he cowers fearfully in his bed, as if thunderstruck. Finally, in Dream III, he boasts emptily of knowing the anthology perfectly, only to lose his way from one bad poem to another on the pages open before him.[14] It is hard to imagine how the rationalist's rationalist could ever have taken these dreams very seriously — or why anyone else should ever do so.

Nor can Descartes's waking "interpretations," read as such, justify any claim that the dream materials are much more than an occasion for anti-Cartesian derision.[15] The heroic discoverer of methodical doubt and critical reason concluded that his dreams had not come from "his human mind." Before sleeping, he had anticipated some sort of celestial visitation; while sleeping, he pondered whether to call his last dream a "vision"; after awakening, he finally concluded that "the Spirit of

Truth" had descended "to take possession of him."[16] In Descartes's *waking judgment*, this dreamy nonsense had been *visionary truth*. It had been *the Holy Spirit*[17] who had descended to illuminate his mind and to foretell his future. So enlightened, the visionary explained that a melon promised in his first dream must have meant "the charms of solitude" and that a wind that had blown him toward a church for prayer had been "nothing other than the Evil Spirit."[18]

Nevertheless, the sources on Descartes's Olympian dreams are potentially the most significant evidence on the development of his personality as a thinker. This grand claim is based on three lesser judgments: first, an ordinary historical judgment concerning the relative quality of the sources on 10 November 1619; second, psychological judgments concerning the meaningfulness of dreams and the existence of regular methods of interpretation; and third, psychohistorical judgments concerning both the adaptability of these clinical methods to historical inquiry and the capacity of passions aroused in the course of past relationships to affect the formal thinking of even the greatest mind working in the most perfect isolation.

The historical judgment is that the surviving sources on the Olympian dreams are remarkably good. This judgment controverts the most influential opinions of the most authoritative scholars. Charles Adam denies (or seemes to deny) the reliability of Baillet's paraphrase-translation; Henri Gouhier denies the accuracy of Descartes's own waking dream report; and Paul Arnold denies the very historicity of the dreams themselves.[19] In the course of these successive denials, the scholarship of the twentieth century has actually retrogressed from the point at which the Cartesians from the seventeenth century set aside the evidence that they could not comprehend.[20] Even in the form of Baillet's paraphrase, Descartes's private *Olympica* is superior to the public *Discourse* in the following important ways: it was contemporaneous with the events, inclusive with respect to nonrational aspects of experience, unsystematic by the standards of any formal metaphysics, and absolutely unembarrassed by persuasive or defensive purposes.[21]

The psychological judgment is that dreaming is a form of thinking, and as such, it is meaningful. This judgment controverts some of the most familiar tenets of Cartesian philosophy. Descartes begins and ends the informal metaphysics of his *Discourse* claiming his thought to be self-conscious and rational and emphatically distinguishing all true thoughts from delusive dreams;[22] in the more formal *Meditations*, he again makes these two points his alpha and his omega.[23] In lieu of a modern dream psychology, this dream philosophy was perfectly defensible, although now, nearly a century after Freud's *Interpretation of Dreams* (1900), it is archaic.[24] In his very first sentence, Freud proclaims that *he has discovered a regular method of dream analysis* by which he can recover a more deeply coherent and relevant latent dream from beneath the superficially incoherent and irrelevant manifest dream.[25] In his very last paragraph, he reflects that *dreams are properly historical,* insofar as "they are derived from the past in every sense" and their interpretation provides deeper understanding of this past than would otherwise be possible.[26] Between this beginning and this end he ventures many more dubious claims, but these two points are still credible, even fundamental.

The primary psychohistorical judgment is that the method of dream interpretation discovered by a clinical psychiatrist can be adapted by a disciplined historian. This judgment controverts that of Freud himself, as expressed in his classic book, technical papers, and nontechnical lectures. His method comes down to two rules, which he called "an essential rule" and "the fundamental rule." The essential rule requires only that the analyst focus severally on the parts or elements of the dream, disregarding whatever narrative continuity there may be.[27] That is easy enough for a historian. The fundamental rule requires that the meaning of each part or element be determined by the associations of the analysand.[28] That has been the great difficulty. Yet difficulty is not impossibility, and we can still hope to recover particulars concerning even a dead dreamer.[29] Disciplined inquiry into the particular significance of the particular dream date orients the analysis, and further inquiry into the particular social relations of the particular dreamer gives it substance. So informed, we can seek—and find—particular associations for the particular dream elements. These associations exhibit a coherence and relevance sufficient to satisfy Cartesian as well as Freudian standards for the meaningfulness of dreams.[30]

Historically analyzed, Descartes's Olympian dreams offer a wholly new perspective on the personal rebellion that began the Cartesian Revolution. The dreams of 10 November 1619 at once reflected and helped resolve what we might very loosely call an identity crisis. René was the second son of a provincial judge, Joachim Descartes. He himself had been trained in the law, but he rejected this vocation. Instead, he chose to become a "searcher for truth," a way of life quite like that of his beloved friend, Isaac Beeckman. This choice was apparently complicated by ambivalent relationships with both his father and his friend. He rejected the ways of the former to embrace those of the latter, but this rejection could not have been simple, because he knew that the former was his father, and he seems to have feared that the latter was not his true friend.

None of this is strictly philosophical, of course, but all of it contributed to the formation of the philosopher, so we must consider its relationship to a philosophy that is most notable for its egocentric rationalism. For the purposes of this introduction, it is enough to remark that the first rule of Descartes's method, the rule of *evidence,* and the last maxim of his morals as a rational thinker serve to legitimate his denials as an intellectual rebel and his affirmation of an idiosyncratic vocation. Furthermore, his evident determination to identify himself metaphysically as nothing other than his rational thought reflects his earlier determination to identify himself psychosocially as nothing other than a searcher for truth.

In the twentieth century there have been two quite separate literatures on the Olympian dreams, one broadly Cartesian and the other broadly Freudian. Unfortunately, none of Descartes's historians has ever seriously attempted to learn the relevant psychology, whether Freud's or his successors', and no psychologist, least of all Freud himself, has ever attempted to master the relevant historical sources. Therefore, even the best of the former have been naive with respect to dreaming and the interpretation of dreams, and even the best of the latter have been ignorant with respect to the scattered evidence on Descartes's life and thought.

The Cartesians: Rationalized History but No Psychology

Cartesians (I use the term here broadly for sympathetic students of the philosopher's life and work) have always known these facts: Descartes himself left a perfectly reasonable theoretical basis for the rejection of all dream experience as meaningless when he noted its internal incoherence and external irrelevance; furthermore, he also left a canonical history of his thinking in the heated chamber in which there is no mention of revelatory dream visions and no apparent place for anything of the sort. It cannot be surprising, then, that latter-day Cartesians have tried to defend the hero Descartes and his thought against the fool Descartes and his dreams by strategies of exclusion, compartmentalization, and, for the lack of a better term, rationalization.

Excluders have simply stricken the Olympian dreams from the record of the philosopher's life and thought. In his notes on the *Olympica*, Leibniz is an excluder. He had before him the still-extant Little Notebook, and had he chosen to do so, he could have copied out its contents, including the three dream narratives. He chose not to do so. The notes that he did make on more thoughtlike materials are invaluable, because they provide reliable information on at least some of Descartes's concerns just before and just after the Olympian dreams,[31] but the otherwise respectful note taker lost patience when the heroic rationalist "deviated" from the record of his thinking to recount his dreaming. Leibniz was fascinated by the "wonderful science," but he was not interested in dreams, even Descartes's Olympian dreams, and he or his scribe did no more than simply note the fact of the dreaming and one element from one dream.[32]

Charles Adam has been the most influential Cartesian of modern times. His edition of Descartes's works and his history of Descartes's life are still the standard references for serious scholars. As editor, Adam included the surviving sources on the lost *Olympica*.[33] However, the critical remarks with which he prefaced his edition of the material from Baillet betray his suspiciousness about the dream narratives and interpretations themselves and his willingness, perhaps even his anxiety, to rule them out.[34] By ejecting the text from the canon and relegating it to a sort of apocrypha, he effectively solved the problems this material presents (see appendix 1).

As historian, Adam excluded ruthlessly. In his magisterial *Vie et oeuvres de Descartes* (1910), he salvages only one classically respectable element from the wreck of the dreams, Ausonius's "Quod vitae sectabor iter?" The rest of the offending material has disappeared.[35] Adam's history of Descartes's life is still the best, but the remarkably pervasive rationalism in this best Cartesian scholarship exacts a cost for any understanding of Descartes's youthful rebellion and so of the Cartesian Revolution itself. The most learned, most patient, and most authoritative historian acknowledges that the three dreams constituted a "decisive" event, but from the extensive dream narratives he retained only the one classical tag and the elliptical *preliminary* reference to the *prior* discovery of "the foundation of the wonderful science."[36]

Adam himself would not deign to consider the dreams as dreams, but he did accept that there had been a "capital," even "epochal" event. What had it been, though, if not the dreams? Adam makes an apologetic bow to Descartes's characteristically "stable mind"; he recalls that both Leibniz and Huygens censured the (unstable-minded) dreamer; he declares that "the philosopher [our twenty-three-year-old] obviously [a trouble sign] had a fit or a mystical crisis [which seem to be equivalent terms]"; and he speculates desperately that such fits or crises may be "the condition of every great discovery: to see a new vision of truth, the man must be raised outside himself, above himself."[37]

Adam then turns from the good evidence on Descartes the dreamer to speculate at great length without good evidence on Descartes the thinker. After five pages of *Adam's* reasonable thoughts about what might or might not have been *Descartes's* reasonable thoughts, there comes the truly Olympian conclusion: "The winter of 1619–1620 thus marks the decisive date and the culminating point in the intellectual life of the philosopher. In a bound, he leaped to the summit from which, as if by the illumination of a stroke of lightning, the whole distance that he would travel thenceforth appeared momentarily before his dazzled eyes."[38]

Compartmentalization provides an alternative to exclusion. Compartmentalizers incorporate substantial paraphrases of the dream narratives and interpretations into their histories, but they also diminish the importance of the episode by detaching it from what preceded it and what followed it. Baillet began this venerable tradition. He included a French version of Descartes's Latin *Olympica* in his *Vie de Monsieur Des Cartes,* but as I explain later, he did not so much as attempt to comprehend the dreams. He apparently considered the material to be too important to omit but also too nonsensical to explain as anything more than a momentary consequence of intellectual exhaustion (too much thinking beforehand) and an undisciplined imagination (too little thinking at the time).[39]

In our century, Gustave Cohen kept this tradition alive, including but also compartmentalizing the dreams in his *Écrivains franaçis en Hollande* (1920). After Adam's life, this is the single most important biographical work. For Cohen, too, the *Olympica* betrays an exaltation that is "strange" and "mystical." That Descartes took his dreams so seriously makes him "the most positivistic and the most rationalistic of our philosophers," at least momentarily a "visionary."[40] "As for the nighttime dreams, they are so crazy that we would have preferred for Descartes not to have attached such importance to them that he took notes on them and wrote them out."[41]

That is, Cohen would have preferred not to have had this evidence. There it was, however, and what could he do? He recited, following Baillet at a distance, and he laughed, rather unhappily echoing the anti-Cartesian Daniel-Pierre Huet. Finally, he concluded that the dreams provide a deep source of great thoughts, but that these "depths" are too "troubled" and too "fantastic" for study: "What a strange mixture of rationalism, religion, and mysticism! But it is too much to pause to fathom the troubled depths from which sprung up the so-pure clarity of the [rule of] évidence. It's time to ask ourselves what was the wonderful daytime discovery of 10 November 1619, we repeat, the daytime discovery, distinguishing it from the fantastic dreams of the following night."[42]

Descartes himself attached extraordinary significance to the episode, calling it "the most important affair of his life";[43] thus, he confronts sympathetic historians with a dilemma. If, as is only reasonable, they choose to pay close attention to the one contemporaneous report from within the heated chamber, then they dignify *dreams,* seemingly incomprehensible dreams. But even if, as is also only reasonable, they choose to ignore the better evidence on these dreams, then they leave themselves with only the worse evidence on the thought, namely, copies of the juvenile cogitations, of the problematical *Regulae,* and the late rationalizations in the public *Discourse.*

In more recent years, two prominent Cartesians have boldly taken this dilemma by the horns, rationalizing the dream narratives and interpretations. Henri Gouhier alone has transmuted leaden dreams into golden thoughts in two contrary ways. First, citing a now-shelved review of the work of pre-Freudian philosophical psychologists, he adduced support for the proposition that Descartes could not have recorded his own dreams accurately.[44] As he awakened, he must have ceased dreaming and begun thinking, so that what purports to be a narrative record must be an interpretive construct. This argument effectively rationalizes the dreams, which thereby become so many thoughts. Gouhier's work on the subject, first presented in his *Pensée réligieuse de Descartes* (1924),[45] is much too important to dismiss lightly. No other qualified Cartesian has ever made any reference to any dream psychology as such. Unfortunately, his argument is flimsy. It misrepresents what long-surpassed dream psychologists actually thought, and it also distorts what Descartes actually wrote. It pays no heed to the dominant schools of twentieth-century dream psychology, psychoanalysis and psychophysiology, and it tempts us to pay no heed to the dream records themselves (see appendix 2).

Second, Gouhier endorsed and extended the arguments of Paul Arnold, who first ventured the ultimate rationalization of Descartes's dreams in 1952.[46] Arnold's own subject was the history of Rosicrucianism and Freemasonry, but in an informal paper spun off from this larger project, he claimed Descartes's *Olympica* to be allegorical fiction in the Rosicrucian manner, its apparent dreams only pseudodreams. Nothing favorable can be said about this line of argument, or rather commentary, which rests on the gravest misrepresentations of the texts and on fundamental misconceptions of the nature of allegory itself (see appendix 3).

Gregor Sebba is the other prominent Cartesian to have attempted a rationalization of the dreams. During his own lifetime he was rather uncritical in his bibliographical summaries of Arnold's and Gouhier's arguments;[47] then, in a few informal papers that he left at his death and his admirers collected and edited posthumously as *The Dream of Descartes* (1987), he sketched yet another form of rationalization. Briefly, Sebba's thesis is that dream thought creatively anticipates waking thought, the movements of the dreamer prefiguring the concepts of the thinker. The Olympian dreams, once again reestablished without argument as real dreams, can be rationalized and so redeemed, if only we see them as anticipations of the vortices, the *cogito,* and so on.[48]

Unfortunately, this approach invites a psychologically unmethodical interpretation of the dreams and a historically anachronistic preoccupation with the dreamer's later thought. In practice, Sebba made no use of dream psychology as such, although he did lean heavily on Freud's one letter to Leroy, to which I turn in the following section.[49] More surprisingly, he made only a very few brief, informal, and unsystematic references to Beeckman's *Journal,* Leibniz's *Cogitationes,* and the earliest strata in the *Regulae,* which are the principal historical sources on the young Descartes's formal thought.[50] This will not do. Without any dream psychology and without enough history, the Cartesian schools of thought on the Olympian dreams have come to a dead end.

The Freudians: Dream Psychology but No History

Maxime Leroy, a prolific student of French social thought who also wrote on Descartes's life, was bold enough to present the historical problem of the Olympian dreams to Sigmund Freud and to publish the psychoanalyst's gracious but discouraging response.[51] This published letter then aroused the curiosity of lesser Freudians[52] and lesser Jungians.[53] However, these two groups neither mastered the historical sources nor solved the problem of adapting clinical methods, so that their work fails on both counts. It is mere commentary, not analysis, of little interest to anyone who does not share their theoretical orientation.[54] Freud's letter is another matter. The dream doctor has looked at the problem and pronounced it unsolvable.

The fact that *Freud* ever wrote anything on the Olympian dreams raises the highest expectations. Freud and Descartes — what an encounter! Old Freud, disillusioned at the end of the Age of Reason, confronts young Descartes, enthusiastic at its beginning. On the one hand, there is the psychiatrist who first systematically explored the irrational and unconscious mental life of our everyday errors, everynight dreams, and all-too-common neuroses.[55] On the other, there is the self-conscious rationalist whose philosophical first certainty was that personal existence itself is a matter of thinking, only thinking.[56] Just imagine what the disillusioned doctor might have had to say about the crazy dreams and crazier thoughts of the Thinking Thing who claimed to have found the way to avoid all errors, all bad dreams, and all disruptive passions![57]

Whatever we might prefer to imagine, there was in reality no titanic struggle of gods and giants. The year 1928 was a very bad one for Freud either to fight the good fight against Cartesian pretensions or to offer substantial help to Descartes's biographer. In preceding years, he had already complained about the burdens brought on him by his increasing fame and the correspondence that he insisted on handling himself.[58] His time was occupied increasingly by his caseload, his editorial responsibilities, and his heroic determination to continue with the sort of writings that could turn psychoanalysis into something more than a merely personal style of medical psychiatry.

In 1928, Freud's old age and ill health further complicated matters. He passed his seventy-second birthday, which he no longer cared to celebrate, and the fifth anniversary of his cancer, which he survived with increasing suffering. His heart was bad, and he complained of severe tiredness. In late winter, severe conjunctivitis in one eye made it very difficult for him to read. The spring, too, was difficult, and he openly yearned to cease working, for him a remarkable concession to physical limitations. From his summer holiday, when in better years he would have been freer to attempt the substantial research necessary for an adequate response to Leroy, he reported home on his "enormous talent for laziness." In the fall he endured a long period in the Tegel Sanitarium, where visitors found him almost unable to talk. Indeed, "Freud seems to have written nothing at all in this year."[59] Even in 1929, a somewhat better year, Freud rebuffed colleagues who urged him to commit himself to a paper on a subject of his own choosing, to be read for him to the members of the psychoanalytical movement of his own making.[60]

The point of this dreary chronicle of infirmities is to limit our expectations and to prepare a critical evaluation of Freud's contribution. Given his personal situation, it is remarkable that he even attempted to assist Leroy, who seems to have approached him as if he were some sort of dream diviner. After all, Leroy was only an otherwise unknown correspondent who was making a somewhat naive request for assistance in the preparation of an otherwise undistinguished book on a subject otherwise remote from Freud's broad interests. The psychoanalyst evidently intended to explain to a layman why neither he nor any other dream doctor could interpret a dead man's dreams, but his explanation awkwardly included three quite different responses.

Freud's first response is still by far the most important contribution to Descartes's history from any psychologist or psychiatrist:

As I considered the letter in which you asked me to examine a few of Descartes' dreams, my first impression was one of dismay, because, [proposition 1] *as a general rule, we can expect only meager results from working on dreams without being able to obtain from the dreamer himself* [associations or] indications on the relations that can bind them together or attach them to the external world—and [proposition 2] *that is surely the case when the dreams of historical subjects are in question* [emphases added].[61]

In a sentence, Freud seizes on the psychological prerequisite and *the* historical problem: his method of interpretation depends absolutely on the dreamer's associations, and Descartes had not known to supply them along with his dream narratives. Freud had to disappoint Leroy, but he deferred in form if not in substance, adopting the philosophical language of the *Meditations*[62] to express the psychoanalytical wisdom of the *Interpretation*.[63]

Freud's combination of gracious civility and rigorous discipline is very impressive, yet his best sentence is also monstrous in its couplings, mating as it does different species of propositions. Proposition 1 (the need for associations) is a professional judgment based on long years of experience in the consulting room and reflection in the study. The dreamer's associations are necessary for methodical interpretations. Proposition 2, however (the living dreamer as the sole source of associations), is only an incidental remark based on negligible historical experience and avowed "first impressions." The death of a dreamer does prevent him or her from volunteering associations in the clinically prescribed manner, but it does not preclude historical inquiry in search of a functional equivalent. In Bacon's wonderful terms, Freud's sentence asks the historian to bow down before the Idols of Sigmund's Cave and the Idols of the Psychoanalytical Theater.[64]

Freud's second response in the same letter is quite different and much less important. His previously quoted "first impressions" were based on the initial supposition that the Olympian dreams, like most others, had been "dreams from below" the threshold of the preconscious mind. Then came reconsideration: "The dreams of *our philosopher* [emphasis added] are what we call 'dreams from above,' that is, formations of ideas that could have been created as well during the waking state as during the sleeping state and that have drawn their material from deeper levels of the mind [the unconscious] only in certain parts."[65] Freud went on to assert that any *analysand* can interpret such dreams "immediately and without difficulty, given that the content . . . is very close to his conscious thought." But the *analyst* cannot employ associative methods on these thoughtlike dreams, which are formally "abstract, poetic, or symbolic." According to the logic of this second response to Leroy, we must accept Descartes's dream interpretations, although we may qualify this acceptance for "certain [deeper] parts."[66]

However, the Olympian dreams as we know them simply do not fit Freud's category of "dreams from above."[67] They are dreamlike and not thoughtlike in any sense implying abstraction, poetic composition, or consciously symbolic expression. There is no need to argue the point in the case of Dream I or Dream II, which no one could consider thoughtlike. That leaves only Dream III, the Books Dream. There is no critical analysis of the poetry in this dream, let alone anything scientific or philosophical, nor is there anything properly artistic about the incorporation of the verses themselves, which are found and lost as fragmentary memories, not poetic embellishments. And there is nothing intentionally symbolic within the narrative, as opposed to the interpretation, where the awakening dreamer immediately begins to pair particular dream elements with portentious thoughts in the manner of an antique oneiromancy.[68]

The notion that the Olympian dreams are "dreams from above" and, as such, quickly and easily comprehensible to the awakened dreamer has the bizarre effect of providing Freud's sanction for Descartes's enthusiastic interpretations, but how could this unrepentant atheist have blessed the believer's credulous overvaluation of dream visions? His own most recent book had been a disbeliever's tract, *The Future of an Illusion* (1927). Old age and infirmities alone cannot account for his apparent willingness to credit past illusions. The best explanation is that, despite Leroy's statement that he had "read Baillet's text," Freud may never have seen the full dream narratives. In fact, the unscholarly biographer may have submitted only his own inadequate version of that text,[69] and the old psychoanalyst may not have bothered to look any further. If he saw only something that skimped on the narratives and emphasized the afterthoughts, his misjudgment that the dreams themselves had been thoughtlike would have been an easier error. Freud also may have succumbed to the rationalized persona of the Thinking Thing, whom he called "our philosopher."

Freud's third response in the letter to Leroy singles out "certain [deeper] parts" of the dreams. He had come to believe that some dream elements, wherever found, can be interpreted even without the dreamer's associations. Wilhelm Stekel had convinced him that everyone shares a universal symbolic language. So-called Freudian symbols are more properly Stekelian, although, with "qualifications and reservations," the master did endorse this "auxiliary" method of interpretation.[70]

Freud found two such symbols in Descartes's Dream I, its left-sidedness and its melon. Stekel had "discovered" the left side of the body to be the symbol of sexual deviance, as well as sin, crime, and wrongdoing more generally. In later editions of his great dream book Freud endorsed these intuitions;[71] in his letter to the supposedly innocent layman Leroy he let it go at "wrong or sin." Elsewhere, the psychoanalysts had also made much of fruits as sexual symbols, especially apples, pears, or peaches as images of breasts, of what Freud modestly called "the larger hemispheres of the female body," or even, as Stekel had immodestly announced, of the vagina *or* testicles.[72] Addressing Leroy, Freud hinted darkly at some such explanation for that most obscure element from Dream I, the gift melon promised to the dream Descartes: "As for the melon, the dreamer has had the (original) idea of explaining it as 'the charms of solitude, but presented by purely human solicitations.' That cannot be exactly right, but it could be an association that would get us on the right track. Combined with his sense of sinfulness, this association could represent a sexual fantasy that occupied the imagination of the young solitary."[73]

What historian would presume to pass judgment on such matters? None of us can claim to know much more about the sexual symbolism of fruit than did that first historian, Moses, who placed the apple at the core of the first great catastrophe. But a *melon* as the juicy secret of Descartes's heated chamber? It is no wonder that Freud discreetly veiled what seems to have been his tentative sexual interpretation: the dream Descartes's left-sidedness, the dream promise of a gift melon from a Mr. N., Descartes's waking sense of sinful wrongdoing, and his waking commentary on "the charms of solitude, but presented by purely human solicitations" — all this, viewed from a psychoanalytical perspective, suggests something homosexual.

Freud was not necessarily wrong in substance when he alluded vaguely to a "sexual fantasy," by which he probably meant a homosexual fantasy, but he was doubly wrong in method. It was an error of commission if he thought that appeal to a supposedly *universal* code of sexual symbols (any dream melon = a fantasy breast, a fantasy larger-hemisphere, or whatever) could explain the meaning of a *particular* individual's *particular* dreams. More importantly, it was an error of omission if, on psychological principle and without historical experience, he gave up on the possible fruitfulness of directed inquiry into surviving sources.

Freud might have been pleased to learn the following particulars, among others: The dream date was the anniversary of Descartes's first known meeting with Isaac Beeckman. The former had come to love the latter. He awakened from his dream to ponder friendship and opposed passions, among other things. In French, Dutch, and German culture, the uncut melon was a favorite early modern image of uncertainty in the choice of friends and lovers. . . . The point is not that Freud was right in substance about the supposed "sexual fantasies." The point is that he was wrong in method not to have considered the possibility of recovering substantial evidence from surviving sources. To find, we must seek. Freud could not well have done so in 1928, and none of the many younger psychologists who followed him to this subject ever made a disciplined study of the relevant sources, starting with Beeckman's *Journal* and Leibniz's *Cogitationes Privatae*.[74]

This is the problem and the opportunity. Descartes was his own first historian, and his *Discourse* has been the regulative account of his life and thought, particularly the decisive day in the heated chamber at the beginning of winter, 1619. But this account simply does not allow for development in more modern senses. Although the historical dependence on the *Discourse* to the virtual exclusion of evidence from the *Olympica* has seemed reasonable, it has been only rationalistic.

It is our great good fortune that we should have such extraordinary evidence on Descartes's dream life at this most crucial period, for the interpretation of dreams offers at least the potential for new insights into personal experience, social relationships, and psychological complications. That this potential has not been realized is due to the understandably—but unfortunately—opposed limitations of the two relevant traditions: first, the Cartesians' suspicion of dreaming, of the irrational, and even of psychology itself; second, the Freudians' ignorance of historical particulars, coupled dangerously with a little knowledge of later Cartesian thought and a great commitment to the dictates of psychoanalytical theory.

Since the day of Chanut's Stockholm Inventory in 1650 we have had good evidence on one of the great turning points in the history of Western civilization, but apparently no one has ever known what to do with it. What we need is both good history and good psychology—in that order. No qualified Cartesian has ever thought to make a systematic study of dream psychology, however, and no one well schooled in dream psychology has ever troubled to make a disciplined inquiry into the historical evidence on the young Descartes. In all the years since 1650, there has been no progress among students of the *Olympica*. Indeed, they have retrogressed, discrediting the evidence on the dreams as dreams.[75]

Progress is still possible. There is hope for the Baconian. It is a matter of particulars. First, we must gather the evidence on the contents of Descartes's Little Notebook, especially the *Olympica,* and reconsider its worth. Second, we must learn what we can about the dream day, obeying imperatives of conventional history as well as of dream psychology. Third, we must reconstruct the social relations of the young man whose rationalistic conceit was to think for himself. And fourth, we must seek the functional equivalent of free associations from the remains left by this dead dreamer and his dead world.

PART ONE

THE SURVIVING EVIDENCE ON DESCARTES'S LOST LITTLE NOTEBOOK

he fundamental fact about the evidence on Descartes's dreams is *not* that his "little notebook bound in parchment" and its Olympian record of dream narratives and interpretations are lost. The fundamental facts are these. First, despite the evanescence of all dream experience and what may have been the passing enthusiasm of his interpretations, *Descartes did record his dreams,* along with immediate reflections on them. Second, despite his mature relegation of dreaming to the philosophical status of subrational nonthinking, *he did preserve this record,* referring back to it and carrying it with him even to his last and most distant relocation. Third, despite his characteristic secretiveness, the apparent indifference of his natural heirs, and the evident incomprehension of philosophical followers, his *friends and admirers did recover this most intimate record* after his death in Sweden, bringing it back to France, *and bequeathing to later scholars complementary source materials,* including a remarkably extensive and apparently reliable paraphrase-translation.

Chapter 1 presents English translations of the Stockholm Inventory and the *Cogitationes Privatae* with minimal commentary. Chapter 2 presents an English translation of Baillet's version of Descartes's *Olympica* and introduces this remarkable copyist, whose bad history is our good fortune.

1

THE STOCKHOLM INVENTORY AND THE
COGITATIONES PRIVATAE

The Stockholm Inventory (1650), a posthumous catalog of Descartes's papers, permits us to date the Little Notebook and to authenticate the *Olympica* beyond any possible doubt; it also provides the earliest evidence on such questions as the length of the document, its place in the sequence of materials from 1619, and the date and content of Descartes's elliptical annotation from 1620. Generally, it gives the best evidence on the form of the Little Notebook but includes no content other than a marginal annotation and an epigraph that particularly caught the cataloger's eye. The *Cogitationes Privatae* (1676), Leibniz's notes on these manuscripts, has complementary strengths and weaknesses, preserving detached and excerpted Cartesian *pensées* without identifying their provenance—the several dossiers that together made up the Little Notebook. This is content without form. It is our great good fortune that these two sources thus complement each other, even if they do not provide anything like either the dream narratives or interpretations that are my focus in this book.

Chanut's Stockholm Inventory

Hector-Pierre Chanut (1601–62) was a French savant, magistrate, and diplomat who in 1650 served as ambassador from the child-king Louis XIV to the philosopher-queen Christina. It was Chanut who enticed Descartes to come to Sweden, and it was in the ambassadorial residence that Descartes lived after arriving in October 1649 and died after a short illness on 11 February 1650.[1] Chanut understood that the "writings concerning the sciences" from Descartes's strongboxes were the real "treasure," the "inestimable inheritance."[2] He acted accordingly. First, he meticulously cataloged the twenty-three items that he discovered, many of them composite, like the notebook cataloged as "Item C." This Stockholm Inventory still exists. Second, he took the papers themselves "under his particular protection." When the Descartes family showed no interest in them, he passed them on to his brother-in-law, Claude Clerselier (1614–84), the great editor of three volumes of letters and of major scientific works.[3] Although neither Chanut nor Clerselier thought to publish the contents of the Little Notebook, they did preserve it for Leibniz's and Baillet's use.

The catalog of Item C from the Stockholm Inventory follows, in a translation based primarily on the Paris copy (B.N., mss. fr., n.a., 4730), with minor corrections:[4]

A little notebook [bound] in parchment, inscribed on the inside of the ["front"] cover: "1 January 1619." First, we find eighteen sheets of mathematical considerations under the title, the *Parnassus*.

5 After six sheets left blank, there is a writing that contains another six sheets written. Holding the book in another way [having turned it "upside down" in order to catalog a text written from "back" to "front"], the discourse entitled the *Olympica* and in the margin:
10 "11 November [1620]. I began to understand the foundation of the wonderful discovery."[5]

Turning the book right side up again, [there] are two sheets written, [consisting] of a few considerations on the sciences; then half a page of algebra.

15 Then [still holding the book "right side up"], twelve pages left empty; then seven or eight lines entitled the *Democritica*.

After eight or ten sheets left blank, five and a half written sheets follow, but turning the book ["upside

20   down" again], under this title, the *Experimenta*.

Then, [still holding the book "upside down,"] twelve sheets left blank, and finally four pages written under the title *Praeambula.* "The fear of the Lord is the beginning of wisdom."

25   This entire book, Item C, seems to have been written in his youth.

The internal evidence of the Stockholm Inventory on the length, content, and orientation of Descartes's written materials and on the pages that he left blank in the Little Notebook allows for new and important conclusions about the sequence of composition in 1619. External evidence from Isaac Beeckman's *Journal* and from Descartes's own *Discourse* helps confirm these conclusions: the notebook included two series of dossiers that correspond to the two known preoccupations from 1619, mathematics and physics from the beginning of the year and personal and philosophical reflections from its end; all other documents in the notebook preceded the *Olympica,* which came at the end of the second series, so that they all form part of the historical background of the dreams.[6]

The cataloger began sensibly enough at the cover inscribed "1 January 1619," after which he found seven discriminable documents, here designated by the first seven letters of the alphabet and ordered as cataloged in the Stockholm Inventory:

    a. *Parnassus;*
    b. *Olympica;*
    c. untitled "considerations on the sciences";
    d. untitled "algebra";
    e. *Democritica;*
    f. *Experimenta;* and
    g. *Praeambula.*

The *Olympica* seems to come second. However, to get from this first, the *Parnassus,* to this second, the *Olympica,* the cataloger had both to turn the "six sheets left blank" (SI 5) and, more curiously, to hold the notebook itself "in another way" (SI 6–7), which can only mean upside down with respect to the "front" cover marked by the New Year's date (SI 1–2, 6–7, and 12; compare 19). The blanks are easily

23

explained as spaces left by an aspiring author and prudent person after he had suspended without necessarily completing work on each of the several dossiers. The flip-flopping is another matter. Henri Gouhier was surely right to identify two separate series of drafts, one written right side up from the perspective of the cataloger, the other, upside down.[7] Let series 1 designate the "right-side-up" documents: the *Parnassus*, the untitled pages, and the *Democritica*. Let series 2 designate the "upside-down" documents: the *Olympica*, the *Experimenta*, and the *Praeambula*.

Gouhier's line of argument reaches further than he saw. Descartes must have written all the documents in both series with the Little Notebook held in what was for him an upright position, which simply means that the "front" cover with its New Year's date was actually the front only for series 1. The "back" cover for the notebook as held by Chanut or his scribe was actually the front for series 2. If we could still begin again at this second front, we would encounter good evidence of the new beginning in the title and the epigraph: the *Praeambula*. "The beginning of wisdom is the fear of the Lord." The first known excerpt, translated below as CP 1–4, also explicitly concerns beginnings. What could be more perfectly Cartesian, more clear and distinct? Series 1: a-c-d-e; series 2: g-f-b. Thus, for Descartes if not for the cataloger, the *Olympica* ended series 2, and in any historical efforts to understand the antecedent circumstances we can look back to materials from the *Praeambula* and the *Experimenta*.

Leibniz's *Cogitationes Privatae*

Gottfried Wilhelm von Leibniz (1646–1716) needs no introduction. The material entitled the *Cogitationes Privatae* does need at least brief explanation, however, even after the work of Adam and Gouhier.[8] In 1676, when he was in Paris, Leibniz took extensive notes from Descartes's Little Notebook.[9] In 1716, after Leibniz's death, his notes were deposited in the Royal Library of Hanover. For the next century and a half they rested undisturbed, although the copies became much more valuable after the loss of Descartes's originals at an unknown date. In 1859, Count Alexandre Foucher de Careil found them and published the Latin texts with his French translations as *Cogitationes Privatae* in his *Oeuvres inédites de Descartes*.[10] In 1894, Charles Adam began preparing his own more scholarly edition, but, much to his dismay, neither he nor his collaborators could find Leibniz's manuscript. Finally, in 1908, Adam published corrected texts based on Foucher de Careil's first edition, and there the matter rests.[11]

The frustrations of having to rely on Foucher de Careil's defective edition of Leibniz's lost notes on Descartes's lost Little Notebook are obvious. The contrary satisfactions possible from the critical use of such materials are less obvious but no less real. What follows is the translation of that portion of the *Cogitationes Privatae* that corresponds to series 2 in the Little Notebook, as known from the Stockholm Inventory. Informed readers will note that I reclassify three cogitations now customarily assigned to the *Experimenta;* CP 64–87 were almost certainly drawn from the *Olympica.*[12]

[Cogitations from the *Praeambula*]

As actors put on masks in order not to show their blush when cued in the theater, so, as I am about to ascend onto the great stage of this world, having been only a spectator until now, I advance masked.

5   When I was young, on being shown ingenious inventions, I used to wonder whether I could not discover as much by myself, even without having read an authoritative guide. From this I gradually realized that I followed fixed rules.

10   Science is like a woman: if she remains modestly with her husband, she is honorable; but, if she gives herself to all, she becomes contemptible.

When we have read [only] a few lines and examined [only] a few figures, we know all about most books.
15   Everything else has been added just to fill up the pages.

Polybius Cosmopolitanus's *Thesaurus Mathematicus* teaches the true ways of resolving all difficulties of this science and demonstrates that the human mind can go no

20   further in this respect. This calls forth hesitation
and rejects the recklessness of those who promise to
perform new miracles in all sciences. It also supports
the agonizing work of many who (F[raternity of the]
Ros[i-] Cruc[ians]), entangled night and day in some
25   Gordian knots of that discipline, exhaust their minds
in vain. This work is offered again to the savants of
all the world, and especially to the most celebrated
F[raternity of the] R[osi-]C[rucians] in G[ermany].

Now the sciences have been masked; they would appear in
30   all their beauty, if their masks were to be removed.
For to anyone who sees clearly the chains linking
the sciences, it will seem no more difficult to keep them
in mind than to remember the series of numbers.

For every mind, there are certain limits that cannot be
35   overstepped. However, even those who cannot themselves
discover principles, because of their limited
intelligence, can know the true worth of the sciences,
which allows them to judge things truly.

[Cogitations from the *Experimenta*]
    I call mental illnesses "faults." They are more
40   difficult to diagnose than physical illnesses, because
we very often experience the health of the body, [but]
never that of the mind.

I notice about myself that when I feel depressed,
whether confronted by danger or preoccupied by
45   melancholy affairs, I sleep deeply and eat ravenously.
But when I feel elated, I neither eat nor sleep.

In a garden we can make shadows that represent various
shapes, like trees and so on. *Item*: construct fences,
so that from certain perspectives they represent
50   certain figures. *Item*: in a room make certain
openings, so that the rays of the sun represent various
numbers or figures. *Item*: in a room arrange various

mirrors in order to reflect the rays of light, so as to
represent tongues of flame, chariots of fire, and other
55   figures in the air. *Item*: in a room one can make it
appear by parabolic mirrors that the sunlight always
comes from the same direction or even that it goes from
west to east. [One can] make the sun, shining above
the roof overhead, cast beams of light in parallel
60   lines into the room below by directing the reflection
from a focusing mirror through a little hole [in the
roof above] onto another focusing mirror [in the room
below] that is aimed at this [same] little hole.

[Cogitations from the *Olympica*]
In the year 1620, I began to understand the foundation
65   of the wonderful discovery.*
Dream 1619, Nov., in which [there was] poem 7, the
beginning of which is this:
    "What way in life shall I follow?"
                            —Auson[ius]
70   *[Foucher de Careil explains in a footnote, "there is
also this in the margin" of Leibniz's manuscript:]
Olympica, 10 Nov., I began to understand the foundation
of the wonderful discovery.[13]

It is as useful to be blamed by friends as it is
75   glorious to be praised by enemies. From strangers, we
long for praise, from friends, the truth.

In everyone's mind there are certain parts that excite
strong passions, however lightly they are touched. So
a boy with a strong spirit will not cry, when he is
80   rebuked; he will get angry. Another will cry. If we
should be told that a great many misfortunes have
happened, we become sad; but if we should also be told
that someone bad caused them, we become angry. The
change from one passion to another happens by
85   proximity. Nevertheless, the change from opposite passions
is often more powerful, as if bad news should
be announced suddenly in the midst of a joyful feast.

27

Just as the imagination uses figures to conceive
physical things, so the intellect uses certain
90   perceptible bodies like wind or light to represent
spiritual things. Philosophizing in a more elevated
way, it follows from this that, by thinking, we can
lift our minds on high. It could seem surprising that
there are more serious sayings in the writings of the
95   poets than in those of the philosophers. The reason is
that the poets have been inspired in their writings by
enthusiasm and the force of imagination. There are in
us the seeds of understanding, as in flintstone [there are
.the sparks of fire]. Philosophers educe them by reason,
100   but poets strike them by imagination, and they shine
forth the more.

The sayings of the sages can be reduced to a certain
very small number of general rules.

Before the end of November [1619?], I shall travel to
105   Venice and from there to Loretto, on foot, if I can
accomplish it easily and in stages. If not, I shall do
it with at least as much devotion as has been customary
for anyone else.[14]

Moreover, I shall finish my treatise entirely before
110   Easter, and, if I can find copyists and I judge the
work to be worthy, I shall publish it, as I have
promised today, 23 February [1620].[15]

There is [only] one active force in [all] things: love,
charity, harmony.

115   Perceptible things permit us to conceive Olympian
things. Wind signifies the spirit; motion in time
signifies life; light signifies understanding; heat
signifies love; instantaneous activity signifies
creation. Every physical phot form acts through harmony.
120   There are more moist parts than dry and more cold parts
than warm, since otherwise the active parts would too

28

quickly have won the day and the world would not have lasted long.

125 Genesis says that God separated the light from the darkness, meaning that he separated the good angels from the bad. Because it is impossible to separate a positive quality from a privation, this cannot be taken literally. God is pure intelligence.

130 The Lord made three miracles: matter, from the void; the will, free; and God, man.

Man understands natural things only by their likeness to those that are subject to the senses. And, indeed, we think that he has philosophized more truly, who has more fittingly related the subject under discussion to 135 things known by the senses.

The extreme perfection that we observe in certain actions of the animals leads us to believe that they do not have free will.

It is certain that these notes derive from Leibniz's reading of the Little Notebook because the complete *Cogitationes Privatae* begins with the same date, 1 January 1619, in the same form that appears in the Stockholm Inventory, Item C, line 2. What follows immediately in Leibniz's notes does not correspond to the "mathematical considerations" of the *Parnassus* known from the inventory, but these lines (CP 1–138) do include several passages (64–73, 93–101, 104–12) that independent evidence from Baillet shows to be material from the *Olympica*. Furthermore, after having completed the previously cited entries, Leibniz or his copyist did turn to "mathematical considerations" that must have come from the *Parnassus*.

What seems to have happened is that the reader in 1676 began with Descartes's New Year's date at the "front" cover. Then, noticing the peculiar combination of "right-side-up" drafts from series 1, beginning with the *Parnassus*, and "upside-down" drafts from series 2, beginning with the *Praeambula*, he decided to invert the Little Notebook so as to begin copying at the "back" cover. This was an alternative beginning, marked by the title, the epigraph (SI 23–24), and the theme of the first recorded fragment (CP 1–4). I agree fully with Gouhier's assignment of the first seven of these cogitations (CP 1–38) to this same dossier, the *Praeambula*.[16] I also agree that the next three cogitations (CP 39–63) must have come from the *Experimenta*.[17] However, I cannot accept the historical argument for his claim that the eleventh, twelfth, and thirteenth cogitations (CP 64–87) are also literal quotations from Descartes's *Experimenta*.[18] They must instead have been his notes on the *Olympica*. This reattribution gives new prominence to the reflections on friends, rebuke, and opposed passions (CP 74–87) and correspondingly subordinates the reflections on figures (CP 88–91, 115–19, 131–35).

2

ADRIEN BAILLET AND HIS
VIE de MONSIEUR DES CARTES

Adrien Baillet's *Vie de Monsieur Des Cartes* (1691) is the only source for Descartes's dream narratives and interpretations. This first important biographer, who had privileged access to the Little Notebook and other materials that have since been lost, saw fit to incorporate a six-page paraphrase of Descartes's own dream record and related reflections.[1] My analysis of the dreams depends absolutely on a much more favorable opinion of this portion of Baillet's work than has become customary.

The best-qualified scholars still look respectfully to the prefatory remarks with which Charles Adam introduces his edition of the crucial pages, but the great editor confuses matters as much as he clarifies them. On the one hand, he had satisfied himself that Baillet's version of Descartes's original preserved something quite like the truth, the whole truth, and nothing but the truth, so he edited it as the philosopher's *Olympica*. On the other hand, his arguments *for* Baillet's truthfulness in this instance are casual, undocumented, and, what is worse, accompanied by a counterargument *against* Baillet in other instances, which he documents with apparent care. Thus, he offers weak arguments for reliability and a strong counterargument against reliability, teaching scholarly readers to distrust Baillet's version of the *Olympica* (I review this unfortunately influential lesson in appendix 1).[2]

Baillet's Version of Descartes's *Olympica*

Here, I approach Adrien Baillet's text directly, without obstructing progress by critical commentary. My retranslation begins with the biographer's attempt to bridge the chasm that separates Descartes's retrospective and rationalistic history in the *Discourse*, part 2, and his contemporaneous and enthusiastic account in the *Olympica*. It should be apparent that the humble author felt more and more uncomfortable as he approached the heated chamber of his proud subject:

> In the new ardor of his resolutions [to reject all
> received opinions and to rebuild on the new foundations
> of his own reason, as known from the *Discourse*, part 2],
> he undertook to execute the first part of his
> 5   plans, which consisted of destruction only. This was
> surely easier than reconstruction. But very soon he
> noticed that even destruction, when it is a matter of a
> man ridding himself of his prejudices, is not as easy
> as burning down one's house. He had already prepared
> 10   himself for this renunciation after leaving school. . . .
> Despite these dispositions, he had nevertheless
> to suffer as if it were a matter of stripping himself of
> himself. He believed that he had come to the end.
> And, in truth, it was enough that his imagination
> 15   presented his mind to himself entirely naked, to make
> him believe that he had really stripped it bare.
> Nothing was left but the love of Truth, the pursuit of
> which was to be his sole occupation for the rest of his
> life. This was to be the only subject of torment that
> 20   his mind would have to endure henceforth.
>
> However, the means of making this happy conquest
> [Truth] caused him as much trouble as that goal itself.
> The search that he wanted to make for these ways
> agitated his mind violently. These disturbances
> 25   augmented more and more, as he found himself caught
> in a continual contention in which he could find diver-
> sion neither in walking nor in human society. This so

30 exhausted him that his brain took fire, and he fell
into a sort of enthusiasm, which so affected his mind,
already over-tired, that it left him in the condition
to receive the impressions of dreams and visions [in
Baillet's margin: "Cart. Olymp. init. Ms."].

He tells us that on 10 November 1619, having gone to
bed *completely filled with his enthusiasm,* and wholly
35 preoccupied with the thought *of having found that very
day the foundation of the wonderful science,* he had
three consecutive dreams in the same night, which he
imagined could have come only from on high.

[Baillet's Version of Descartes's Dream I: The Street Scene]

After he fell asleep, his imagination felt itself
40 struck by the representation of some ghosts who
presented themselves to him and who so frightened him
that, thinking that he was walking down the streets [in
Baillet's margin: "Cart. Olymp."], he had to lean to
his left side in order to be able to reach the place
45 where he wanted to go, because he felt a great weakness
on his right side, so that he could not hold himself
upright. Because he was ashamed to walk in this way,
he tried to straighten up, but he was buffeted by gusts
that carried him off in a sort of whirlwind that spun
50 him around three or four times on his left foot. Even
this was not what alarmed him. His difficulty in
dragging himself along meant that he thought he would
fall at each step until, noticing a school open along
his way,

[Baillet's Version of Descartes's Dream I: The School Scene]

55 he entered in search of a refuge and a remedy for his
trouble. He tried to reach the school church, where
his first thought was to say his prayers. However,
having noticed that he had passed an acquaintance
without greeting him, he wanted to retrace his steps to
60 pay his respects, and he was thrust back by the wind

33

that was blowing against the church. At the same time
he saw another person in the middle of the school
courtyard who addressed him by name in kind and polite
terms and told him that, if he wanted to go to find
65   Monsieur N., he had something to give him. Monsieur
Descartes imagined that it was a melon from a foreign
land. What surprised him more was to see that those
who clustered around that person in order to talk with
him were upright and steady on their feet, although he
70   was still bent over and unsteady on the same ground.
Having almost knocked him down many times, the wind
had greatly abated.

[Baillet's Version of Descartes's Interpretation I]

He woke up imagining this and then felt a real pain,
which made him fear that it had been the work of some
75   Evil Spirit who had wanted to seduce him. Immediately,
he turned over onto his right side, for he had slept
and dreamed on his left side. He prayed that God would
protect him from the evil effects of his dream and
preserve him from all of the miseries that could
80   threaten him as his punishment for his sins, which he
acknowledged to be great enough to call down upon his
head thunderbolts of heaven, although he had led a
more or less blameless life in the eyes of men. In this
situation he fell asleep after an interval of almost
85   two hours of various thoughts on good and evil in this
life.

[Baillet's Version of Descartes's Dream II: The Thunder Dream]

Immediately, a new dream came to him in which he
thought that he heard a sudden, loud noise, which he
took for thunder.

[Baillet's Version of Descartes's Interpretation II]

90   Terrified, he awoke at once. Having opened his eyes,
he noticed many sparks of fire scattered around the

room. He had experienced this phenomenon on many
other occasions, and it did not seem too strange to him,
when he awoke in the middle of the night, that his eyes
95   sparkled enough that he could make out the objects
closest to him. But, on this last occasion, he wanted
to find [scientific] reasons drawn from [natural]
Philosophy, and he was able to reassure himself about his
mind/spirit. After having opened and closed his
100   eyes in turn and observed what was represented to him,
he saw that his terrors faded away, and he fell asleep
again quite calmly.

[Baillet's Version of Descartes's Dream III: The Books Dream]

A moment afterward he had a third dream, unlike the
first two, about which there was nothing frightful. In
105   this last dream, he found a book on his table without
having any idea who had put it there. He opened it and
saw that it was a *Dictionary*, which delighted him, because he hoped that it might be very useful to him. At
the same moment, he noticed that another book came
110   to hand which was no less new to him. He did not know
from whence it had come. He discovered that it was a
collection of poems by different authors, entitled
Corpus Poetarum etc. [In Baillet's margin: "Divided
into five books, printed at Lyon and at Geneva, etc."]

115   He was curious to read some of it, and, opening the book,
he chanced upon this verse:
        What way in life shall I follow? Etc.
Just then he noticed a man whom he did not know. This
unknown man gave him a piece of poetry that began with
120   these words:
        Yes and No.
The man recommended it to him as an excellent piece.
M. Descartes told him that he knew this verse: it was
one of the *Idylls* of Ausonius included in the big
125   anthology of poetry on the table.

130

135

He wanted to show it to this man himself, and he began
to leaf through the book, the order and scheme of which
he boasted of knowing perfectly. While he searched for
the passage, the man asked him where he had gotten this
book, and M. Descartes answered that he could not say
how he happened to have it, but that a moment before
he had leafed through still another book that had just
disappeared, although he did not know either who had
brought it to him or who had taken it away again. He
had not finished [his search for "Yes and No" in the
Corpus], when he saw the [other] book reappear at the
other end of the table. But he saw that this
Dictionary was no longer as complete as the one he had
seen the first time.

140

145

150

Nevertheless, he came to the poems of Ausonius in the
anthology through which he paged, and, although he
could not find the poem beginning with the words "Yes
and No," he told this man that he knew another one by
the same poet that was still finer. It began with the
words "What way in life shall I follow?" The person
begged him to show it to him, and Monsieur Descartes
set himself the task of trying to find it. Then he
happened upon several little portraits engraved by
copperplate, which led him to remark that this was a
very handsome book but that it was not the same edition
as the one that he knew. It was at this point that the
books and the man disappeared. They vanished from
his imagination, although they did not awaken him.

[Baillet's Version of Descartes's Interpretation III, Phase 1]

155

160

It is a most remarkable thing that, wondering whether
what he had seen was a dream or a vision, he not only
decided that it was a dream while he was still asleep
but also interpreted it before he was fully awake. He
judged that the *Dictionary* could only mean all the
Sciences gathered together and that the anthology of
the poets entitled the *Corpus Poetarum* represented in

particular and in a more distinct way the union of
Philosophy and Wisdom.

For he did not believe that we should be too surprised
to see that the poets, even the most mediocre, were
165   full of maxims that were more serious, more sensible,
and better expressed than anything in the writings of
the philosophers. He attributed this marvel to the
divinity of Enthusiasm and the strength of Imagination [in
the poets], which bring out the seeds of wisdom
170   that are found in all men's minds—like the sparks of
fire in [flint] stones—much more easily and much more
brilliantly than can the Reason of the philosophers.
Monsieur Descartes continued to interpret his dream
while asleep, thinking that the piece of verse on the
175   uncertainty of what sort of life one should choose,
beginning "What way in life shall I follow,"
represented the good advice of a wise person or even of
Moral Theology.

[Baillet's Version of Descartes's Interpretation III, Phase 2]

Thereupon, uncertain whether he was dreaming or
180   thinking, he awoke and calmly continued to interpret
the dream in the same sense. By the poets collected in
the anthology, he understood Revelation and Enthusiasm,
for the favors of which he did not despair at all. By
the verse "Yes and No," which is the Yes and the No [in
185   Baillet's margin: "nai kai ou"] of Pythagoras, he
understood Truth and Falsehood in human understanding
and the profane sciences. Seeing that the
interpretation of all of these things succeeded so well
to his liking, he was bold enough to persuade himself
190   that it was the Spirit of Truth [God] that had wanted
to open unto him the treasures of all the sciences by
this dream. There remained to explain only the little
portraits in copperplate that he had found in
the second book. He sought no further explanation for

37

195   them after an Italian painter paid him a visit on the
       next day.

[Baillet's Version of Descartes's Interpretation III, Phase 3]

       This last dream, which had all been very soothing and
       very agreeable, seemed to him to reveal the future, and
       it showed him nothing but what would happen in the
200   rest of his life. Contrarily, he took the two preceding
       dreams for warnings and threats concerning his past
       life, which could not have been as innocent in the eyes
       of God as in those of man. He believed that this was
       the reason that these two dreams had been accompanied
205   by terror and dread.

       The melon offered him as a present in the first dream
       signified, he said, the charms of solitude, but
       presented by purely human solicitations. The wind that
       pushed him toward the school church [in Baillet's
210   margin: "A malo Spiritu ad Templum propellebar"], when
       he had trouble with his right side, was nothing other
       than the Evil Spirit who was trying to throw him by
       force into a place that he intended to enter by his own
       free will. This was why God did not permit him to
215   advance any farther even into a holy place or let him
       be carried away by a Spirit whom He had not sent.
       Nevertheless, he was firmly convinced that it had been
       the Spirit of God that had made him take the first
       steps toward that church.

220   The fear with which he had been struck in the
       second dream marked, in his opinion, his synderesis, that
       is, remorse of conscience concerning the sins that he
       could have committed in the course of his life to date.
       The thunder that he heard was the Spirit of Truth [God]
225   descending to take possession of him.

       This last notion surely smacks of Enthusiasm [Baillet's
       pejorative, echoing Descartes's own known language], and

38

it might well lead us to think that M. Descartes had
been drinking in the evening before going to bed.
230   Indeed, this was Saint Martin's Eve, when the local
inhabitants [Germans] customarily made their debauch,
just as Frenchmen do. But he assures us that he had
been completely sober this evening and the entire day
beforehand; [indeed,] he had not drunk [a drop of] wine
235   for three whole months. He adds that the Spirit who
had aroused in him the enthusiasm with which he had
felt his brain on fire for the past several days had
predicted these dreams before he had gone to bed.
[Furthermore, he states] that his human mind had
240   nothing to do with them.

[Baillet on Descartes's Decision, Prayer, and Vow]

In any case, these agitations so impressed him that he
pondered on the decision he should make. In the
straits in which he found himself, he had recourse in
prayer to God, so that He might make known His will to
245   him, enlighten him, and guide him in the search for
truth. Then he appealed to the Holy Virgin, laying
before her this affair, which he considered the most
important in his life. And in his effort to interest
the Blessed Mother of God in a more pressing way, he
250   took the occasion of a trip to Italy that he was
planning to take in a few days, to vow a pilgrimage to
the Notre Dame of Loretto. [In Baillet's margin:
"Olympic. Cartes. ut supr."] His zeal went even
further and made him promise that, as soon as he
255   reached Venice, he would set out on the land route to
Loretto in order to make his pilgrimage on foot. If
his strength could not sustain these rigors, he would
acquit himself by adopting at least the appearance of
the greatest possible devotion and humility. He said
260   that he would leave for this trip before the end of
November [1619].

But it seems that God disposed otherwise than he had

265 proposed. He had to postpone the accomplishment of this vow to another time, being forced to defer his Italian journey for reasons that remain wholly unknown. Some four years passed after this resolution before he undertook it.

[Descartes's Treatise and Baillet's Epilogue]

270 His enthusiasm left him a few days afterward. Although his mind had returned to its normal state and its prior composure, he remained just as indecisive concerning the resolutions that he had to make. The time of his winter quarters passed slowly in the solitude of his heated chamber, and, to make it less tiresome, he be-

275 gan to compose a treatise that he hoped to finish before Easter, 1620. [In Baillet's margin: "Ibidem. Die 23 Febr."] In February, he began to think of seeking a printer with whom to contract for the publication of this work. But it seems very likely that he then interrupted work on this treatise, and that it was

280 never finally completed. We still do not know what [the subject of] this treatise could have been, nor even whether it ever had a title [the *Regulae*?].

It is certain that the *Olympica* was written at the end of 1619 and the beginning of 1620—and that it has this

285 in common with the treatise in question, that it was never finished. But there is so little order and sequence in the manuscript materials that compose the *Olympica*, that it is easy to see that M. Descartes never thought to make a regularly composed treatise of

290 them, still less to publish them.

Baillet's purposes were very different from Leibniz's, and it is hardly surprising that he used the *Olympica* so differently. His predecessor had been concerned with Descartes's thoughts to the virtual exclusion of the events of November 1619, especially the Olympian dreams. Baillet was concerned with these events to the virtual exclusion of the thoughts of November 1619, which, after Foucher de Careil, I dub the Olympian cogitations. Given both neoclassical impatience with disordered and fragmentary juvenilia and rationalistic suspicions of dreams, visions, and dream visions, it is extraordinary that these two men should have left any such material. I am indebted to both, but, despite the understandable tendency of scholars to overvalue materials from Leibniz and to undervalue those from Baillet, my debt to the lesser man is far greater.

Baillet's Bad History and Our Good Fortune

Adrien Baillet's work is bad history by almost any standards, those of the neoclassical Academy in the seventeenth century as much as those of critical history in the twentieth. Paradoxically, this bad historian's badness is the good fortune of working scholars. Baillet swallowed the *Olympica* whole, but he neither chewed much nor digested at all. There, in the fat belly of his *Vie de Monsieur Des Cartes*, the *Olympica* remains almost intact. I begin this section with that good historian, Charles Adam, then work backward to Antoine Boschet, S.J., and his still-substantial, still-penetrating, and still-amusing contemporary critique. This hostile reviewer fully appreciated Baillet's limitations as Descartes's biographer: he was not a historian, properly speaking; he was only a compiler.

Baillet's first principles as Descartes's biographer were those of an unshakable Christian faith. He was a priest and an abbé whose first historical venture as a sixteen-year-old schoolboy had been to "collect" all that he could from the Latin poets on the pagans' theology, divinities, sacrifices, temples, games, and the like.[3] His last historical accomplishment would be to work his way through the liturgical listings of the saints in the Roman Breviary, the Paris Breviary, and other breviaries and then to write, rewrite, or perhaps as appropriately, "collect" the *Vies des Saints*.[4] There is a complementary unity to the lost juvenilia on the pagans and the mature monument on the Christians, and in the years between the two, Baillet never wavered from his first principles.

Adam was right to emphasize the primacy of Baillet's faith and the apologetic nature of his biographical enterprise, which redeemed Descartes as something of a *dévot* at a time when his philosophy was being damned as Jansenism or worse.[5] Baillet's masterpiece was to be a monumental *Vies des Saints* (1695–1701),

41

in which he opened himself to the criticisms of later secularists. He was willing to accept almost anything on the word of "good authorities," particularly if it had served to reaffirm Christian doctrine, to establish the Faith, or to win converts. "Good authorities" for this historian of saintly miracles or visions included not only "eyewitnesses" but also "pure traditions" and "holy persons," these last recognizable by their own "sincerity" and by the "consideration" that they enjoyed in the Church.[6] However, it would be wrong to suspect Baillet's devotion as a threat to the historical integrity of Descartes's *Olympica*. Even as a hagiographer, he was never simply uncritical, never merely inventive. Indeed, as the century of baroque Catholicism turned to that of skeptical Enlightenment, he raised banners of belief-and-doubt where the scouts of the army of belief-and-belief were surest to look.

Baillet's contemporaries were most exercised by his tendency to question pious traditions, as in these prefatory remarks:

> The attribution of miracles to the saints is the part of their history that seems to demand the most precaution against falsehood and imposture. . . . The reasons that justify my treatment of miracles will have the same effect, if it please my readers, on that of revelations, dreams, and visions. I also include in this category ecstasies, transports, spiritual flights, spiritual delights, and prophecies. We do not deny that there are many [truly] supernatural and miraculous things among all of these. Readers will see from the space allotted that I accept the revelations of Saint Perpetua on the basis of the written records that she herself made [the "eyewitness"] and of testimony from Tertullian and Saint Augustine [the "holy persons"].
>
> I report dreams and visions when nothing in them is contrary to the gravity of history, but I often report them as natural events without denying that they may be marvelous. I do not always stop [to report] the consequences attributed to them; often, we find that they are false.[7]

There is something disturbingly Cartesian about all of this; the hagiographer trusts his individual "reasons" and doubts away the saints' "miracles, revelations, dreams, visions." He seems proud to have found sufficient evidence in one case of notably saintly dream visions, prouder to have doubted away so many others, letting "the gravity of history" decide whether anything of the sort is acceptable even as a "natural event."[8]

The best that could be said—or printed—about Baillet's work was that his morals seemed severe, even if he did "make sport of the devout life, of visions, and of miracles." Or perhaps it was a better defense—or pretense of defense—to say that he had "read a lot and composed hardly anything; all he had done was to copy and to translate, leaving the printer with all of the trouble of composition."[9]

Baillet's distinctive belief and doubt as hagiographer and historian is relevant to the reliability of his version of Descartes's *Olympica*. He was quite unsophisticated historically but also quite open-minded philosophically, probably more open-minded than his most vigorous critics, doctrinaire believers then and doctrinaire rationalists now. He had received from a "pure tradition" what amounted to the report of an "eyewitness." He retold Descartes's story, but he did not commit himself to accepting dream visions as anything more than "natural events" without demonstrable "consequences." This was to remain true to his Christian faith, his rationalistic doubts, and his historical canons: "I have believed that the obligations of my engagement [to 'write' the Descartes book] consist only in saying simply what this philosopher was and showing what he thought, what he said, and what he did. My desire is to lay bare his thoughts, his words, and his actions."[10]

If Baillet's first principles were those of the priest and the abbé, his true vocation combined the several functions of the librarian, the schoolmaster, and the critic. In his productive years, the priest and abbé had no parish and no community. He had a patron. From 1680 to 1706, the year of Baillet's death, this patron was François de Lamoignon, Advocate General in the Parlement of Paris. Lamoignon entrusted the care of his great library and his small son to Baillet, who would have been too bookish for most functions in religion and too unpolished for most positions in the world. Prior to entering this great household, he spent four years teaching Latin at the College of Beauvais, where he had been successful enough that his superiors had wanted to raise him up faster than he was willing to rise, successful enough, too, that Godefroy Hermant, himself a notable Latinist, could recommend him to Lamoignon for what he called "the essentials," which quite explicitly did not mean social graces but implicitly must have meant faith, morals, and Latin.[11]

In Paris, Baillet found his life's work. He cataloged all the books in the Lamoignon library. He conceived and began an impossible project of compiling all criticisms of all books, ancient and modern, profane and sacred, everything. As part of his tutorial responsibilities, he put together for his own pupil an inspirational little book on the youthful accomplishments of other bright little fellows, all of this gathered from others' books. Then, within the twelve months in which he began *and completed* the immense *Vie de Monsieur Des Cartes*,[12] he saw into print a wonderful little book on pseudonyms and authorial masks. The subject intrigued him so much that he left his biography of Godefroy Hermant in manuscript for posthumous publication with a riddling pseudonym masking Baillet the author, a riddling title swirling a veil over Hermant the subject, and, within, a riddling list of twenty-seven nonexistent books by twenty-seven Baillets in twenty-seven anagrammatic disguises.[13]

This is the unusual background that qualified Baillet in his patron's eyes to serve as Descartes's biographer. Along with Baillet himself[14] and his critics,[15] I suppose to the contrary that it did not qualify him. The most important thing about Descartes, after all, was and is his thought. Baillet was quite simply incapable of a critical overview of Cartesian philosophy, mathematics, or physics, let alone of the broader significance of Cartesian ways of thinking. He was informed but not reflective, erudite but not disciplined, at most a hunter-gatherer of thoughts but not a cultivator. His subject may have been the Thinking Thing, but Baillet himself was only the Compiling Thing. Baillet's critics saw in the big book on Descartes not the work of a hagiographer-in-the-making, the future author of the *Vies des Saints,* but that of a compiler-in-the-taking, the past author of the *Jugemens des Savans.* Father Antoine Boschet's now-forgotten *Réflexions d'un académicien sur la Vie de Monsieur Des Cartes* still pertains. According to him, the worst feature of Baillet's bad history was its mindless inclusiveness, although this bad seemed so bad that it was funny, which was, of course, good. Boschet set up an instructive contrast between the work of a hypothetical Good Historian (let us call him Monsieur A) and that of the actual Bad Historian (let us call him Monsieur B). The former would know more than he writes and understand all that he writes. The latter, alas, would attempt to write, if not to understand, all that he knew.[16]

For one example, Boschet's Monsieur A would tell us briefly about Descartes's father and mother, supposing that this would help to introduce the son. In contrast, Monsieur B reaches all the way up to the fifth generation of René Descartes's ancestors, then all the way down to the grandnephew, also René, "who entered the Novitiate of the Jesuits at Paris last year. His superiors have a very good opinion of him."[17] For another example, Boschet's Monsieur A would tell us something about signs of genius in the philosopher's childhood. In contrast, Monsieur B goes on at great length about the foundation of the Collège de la Flèche, where Descartes was to study, and about the ceremonial reception there for the heart of Henri IV, cut out of the slain king and presented to his school. This, B says, is important for our understanding of the philosopher's life, in that Descartes must have attended the ceremonies, classes having been suspended for the occasion, after which he must have gone back to his studies, classes having resumed once again. Finally, for a last example, Boschet's Monsieur A would devote perhaps ten pages to the relatively unknown but apparently unproductive years between Descartes's studies at La Flèche and his retirement to Holland. In contrast, Monsieur B spends over two hundred pages on the entire military and diplomatic history of the period without demonstrating that Descartes had anything to do with it—or that it had anything to do with Descartes.[18]

Above all, the Good Historian would be competent to discuss Cartesian philosophy, to explain its novelties, and to debate its difficulties. The Bad Historian cannot instruct us about Descartes's thoughts. However, he can amuse us with Descartes's dreams, three dreams in one chapter alone, leaving nothing left unsaid and nothing more to be desired on the subject. Much to his surprise and delight, Boschet finds that Cartesian philosophy began in a "sort of transport" or "fit of madness."[19] There is no better reduction to absurdity of Baillet's composition by compilation. His sole grand trait as a historian is his memory, a memory untroubled by others' concerns for method, order, style, thought, eloquence, transitions, and judgment.[20]

For Antoine Boschet, this bad history was so bad that it was good because it gave him and his friends and allies a chance to laugh at Adrien Baillet, who was cordially detested for the acerbity of his *Jugemens des Savans,* for the Jansenism associated with Beauvais and Godefroy Hermant, and last, for the radicalism of the Cartesian philosophy that his book seemed to defend. For me, this bad history is so bad that it is good because, with its uncritical inclusiveness, it preserves so much information more useful than the names of the father (Jean), mother (Élisabeth), and cook (Louise) of Descartes's friend, the Abbé (Claude) Picot,[21] *and* so many texts that we would otherwise have lost, including, of course, the *Olympica.* The "extraordinary" thing about this "incomparable" history—the terms are Boschet's[22]—is that, for whatever reasons, Baillet did incorporate Cartesian materials that he did not deform by his own historical, philosophical, theological, or psychological ideas.

We can watch him at work in his *Vie de Monsieur Des Cartes,* book 2, chapter 1, which starts with the thoughts of the heated chamber and ends with its dreams. Baillet's *Vie,* page 78, lines 1–10, is a loose paraphrase of the beginning of Descartes's *Discourse,* part 2 (AT, 6:11, lines 3–8). Baillet's lines 10–14 echo Descartes's words (AT, 6:11, lines 8–11), which are signaled by an accurate marginal reference but not by any punctuation. Baillet's lines 14–17 show the philosopher's "thoughts" transmuted into "the preludes of the imagination," becoming bolder thought by thought. Baillet's lines 17–28 combine an unpunctuated but exact quotation with well-chosen and well-paraphrased summaries of Descartes's text (AT, 6, from 11, line 12, to 12, line 25). Finally, from his page 78, line 29, to his page 79, line 8, Baillet accurately represents the Cartesian conclusion to this (weak) Cartesian argument by analogy in Cartesian terms, some quoted directly, some paraphrased closely (AT, 6, from 12, line 25, to 13, line 12).

This necessarily tedious line-by-line comparison lets me retrace Baillet's steps from a primary source that we still have, the *Discourse,* into the finished *Vie de Monsieur Des Cartes.* The next two paragraphs (*Vie,* from page 79, line 9, to page 80, line 21) follow very much the same pattern: Baillet contributes very occasional, very brief, and generally "Cartesian" words, phrases, or sentences to his own text in lines that have no close equivalent in his source. In this long block, his own voice emerges only at page 79, lines

9–12, at the beginning, and page 80, lines 17–21, at the end, the latter best read as the beginning of the necessarily awkward transition from the rationalistic *Discourse* to the enthusiastic *Olympica*.

Everything else is demonstrably Cartesian in the strictest senses short of verbatim transcription. Baillet's text includes Descartes's ideas, including the closest paraphrase of the crucial, philosophically radical "resolution"—Baillet's word, but a good one (AT, 6, from 13, line 27, to 14, line 6, corresponding to *Vie*, page 79, lines 22–31). It includes Descartes's favorite images of the house and the road, with roles for himself as the philosopher-architect (and -wrecker) and the philosopher-traveler. Finally, it includes Descartes's words, with some innocuous substitutions, some very minor additions, and more significant subtractions, made either to keep the semblance of a biographical narrative going (AT, 6:12, 15–16) or to avoid even the impression of potential social and political radicalism that may be left when the philosophical radical protests too much (AT, 6:13, lines 6–8, 20–24; AT, 6, from 14, line 27, to 15, line 4; AT, 6:16). The best aspect of this bad history is that, where at all possible, Baillet seems to have remained faithful to the texts in front of him. Such tests of his work as are possible show that he sometimes omitted prudently but did not invent irresponsibly.

The worst aspects are that Baillet himself had to provide the bridgework from one authentically Cartesian island to the next; that he may have had nothing better with which to support these bridges than his own inferences, often sensible but always unsafe; and that he did not indicate clearly where in his text he left the solid ground of his translation-paraphrase for the airy bridge of his transition-inference. This is all very bad, indeed. It means that we cannot trust anything in the paragraph between the point where my deconstruction of the crucial chapter shows that he has taken leave of the *Discourse* (*Vie*, page 80, line 17) and the point where his marginal reference and his text show that he has reached the *Olympica* (*Vie*, page 81, margins and line 10, confirmed by page 51).

This sort of composition by compilation could never impress a critical reader, then or now, with Baillet's genius, but that was hardly the point for Monsieur de Lamoignon's man, who had begun his career as a bookman seeking only to make a "useful" collection, a "rather simple" compilation: "I profess to say nothing of my own, I have no reason to fear that anyone will require me to answer for the solidity and the truth of these *Jugemens*. I hold myself responsible only for the fidelity with which I present them, and to show more clearly that I do not impose on anyone, I have taken care to cite my sources exactly."[23] Of course, nothing is simple, certainly not Baillet or his books. These sentences betray the naive intentions of a man for whom critical nonresponsibility seemed a real possibility, attractive in part because of its apparent conformity to Christian humility.

The sentences may also reflect obscure self-doubts that seem to have recurred whenever Baillet was called on to put himself forward, whether as a Latin teacher, a parish priest, a private librarian, a published metacritic, or Descartes's biographer. This characteristic hesitation on occasions that seem to have called for self-affirmation may have had to do with his consciousness of lowly social origins among the peasantry as well as with who knows what else.[24] Formally, Baillet deferred to others' materials in all of his most important writings, metacritical, biographical, and hagiographical. Informally, he did manage to express an authorial voice even when he was copying, collecting, and compiling. This voice often grates unpleasantly.

Gilles Ménage, the angriest victim of Baillet's *Jugemens des Savans*, demands the last word. His sputtered insults could not be printed in France, where supervision of the book trade protected at least the protégé of the Advocate General Lamoignon. But they do have a point, even if, paradoxically, they favor my historical uses of Baillet's materials: Newcomer to Parnassus! Man who knows no science! No Greek, the language of sciences! *Just a copyist of copyists,* who has never read any originals![25]

After he took over the Descartes project from Legrand, if never before, Baillet read and used originals, but he remained at heart a copyist. Perhaps he is just the man for us, we who no longer have the original *Olympica*. It would have been our misfortune if Baillet *had not* been "just a copyist" of the "originals" that he *had* read. His bad history is our good fortune.

LA VIE
DE
Mʳ DESCARTES.

Contenant ce qui s'eſt paſſé depuis qu'il ſe fût
défait des Préjugez de l'Ecole, juſqu'à ſon
établiſſement en Hollande.

CHAPITRE PREMIER.

Où l'on reprend ſon hiſtoire à la fin de l'an 1619. Il ſe trouve
dans une eſpéce de ſolitude, qui luy fait naître diverſes penſées
contre ce qui avoit été penſé avant luy. Il ſe hazarde à ſe dé-
poüiller de toutes les opinions qu'il avoit reçuës juſqu'alors. Ré-
cit de quelques ſonges qu'il eut, avec leur explication. Il com-
mençe ſon traité des Olympiques, qu'il n'a point achevé depuis.

Pʀᴇ's avoir rapporté de ſuite les affaires qui
ſe ſont paſſées en Allemagne ſous les yeux de
M. Deſcartes, nous nous ſommes fait un plus
grand jour, pour expoſer aux yeux des autres ce qui ſe paſſa dans ſon eſprit, & dont
il fut le ſeul acteur peu de têms aprés s'être
engagé dans les troupes du Duc de Baviére. Nous avons
K iij   remarqué

remarqué qu'àprés avoir quitté fur la fin de Septembre
de l'an 1619 la ville de Francford , où il avoit affifté au
couronnement de l'Empereur , il s'arrêta fur les fron-
tiéres de Baviére au mois d'Octobre , & qu'il commen-
ça la campagne par fe mettre en quartier d'hiver. Il
fe trouva en un lieu fi écarté du commerce , & fi peu fré-
quenté de gens dont la converfation fût capable de le di-
vertir , qu'il s'y procura une folitude telle que fon efprit la

Difc. de la
Méth. part.1.
p. 12.& feqq.

pouvoit avoir dans fon état de vie ambulante. S'étant ainfi
affuré des dehors , & par bonheur n'ayant d'ailleurs aucuns
foins ni aucunes paffions au dedans qui puffent le troubler ,
il demeuroit tout le jour enfermé feul dans un poëfle, où il
avoit tout le loifir de s'entretenir de fes penfées. Ce n'é-
toient d'abord que des préludes d'imagination : & il ne devint hardi que par dégrez en paffant d'une penfée à une
autre , à mefure qu'il fentoit augmenter le plaifir que fon
efprit trouvoit dans leur enchaînement. Une de celles qui
fe préfentérent à lui des prémiéres , fut de confidérer qu'il
ne fe trouve point tant de perfection dans les ouvrages com-
pofez de plufieurs piéces & faits de la main de divers maîtres , que dans ceux aufquels un feul a travaillé. Il lui fut
aifé de trouver dequoi foutenir cette penfée, non feulement
dans ce qui fe void de l'Architecture , de la Peinture, & des

Ibid. p. 13.
& 14.

autres Arts, où l'on remarque la difficulté qu'il y a de faire
quelque chofe d'accompli en ne travaillant que fur l'ouvrage d'autrui , mais même dans la police qui regarde le gou-
vernement des Peuples , & dans l'établiffement de la Religion qui eft l'ouvrage de Dieu feul.

Il appliqua enfuite cette penfée aux Sciences, dont la connoiffance où les préceptes fe trouvent en dépôt dans les livres. Il s'imagina que les Sciences, au moins celles dont les
raifons ne font que probables,& qui n'ont aucunes démonftra-
tions, s'étant groffies peu à peu des opinions de divers Par-
ticuliers , & ne fe trouvant compofées que des réfléxions
de plufieurs Perfonnes d'un caractére d'efprit tout différent,
approchent moins de la vérité , que les fimples raifonne-
mens que peut faire naturellement un homme de bon fens
touchant les chofes qui fe préfentent à lui. Delà il entreprît
de paffer à la Raifon humaine avec la même penfée. Il con-
fidéra

fidéra que pour avoir été enfans avant que d'être hommes,
& pour nous être laiffez gouverner long têms par nos ap-
pétits, & par nos maîtres, qui fe font fouvent trouvez con-
traires les uns aux autres, il eft prefque impoffible que nos
jugemens foient auffi purs, auffi folides qu'ils auroient été, fi
nous avions eu l'ufage entier de nôtre raifon dés le point de
nôtre naiffance, & fi nous n'avions jamais été conduits que
par elle.

La liberté qu'il donnoit à fon génie ne rencontrant point
d'obftacles, le conduifoit infenfiblement au renouvellement
de tous les anciens fyftêmes. Mais il fe retint par la vuë de l'in-
difcrétion qu'il auroit blâmée dans un homme, qui auroit
entrepris de jetter par terre toutes les maifons d'une ville,
dans le feul deffein de les rebâtir d'une autre maniére. Cependant comme on ne trouve point à redire qu'un Particulier faffe abattre la fienne lors qu'elle le menace d'une ruï-
ne inévitable, pour la rétablir fur des fondemens plus folides: il fe perfuada qu'il y auroit en lui de la témérité à vouloir réformer le corps des fciences ou l'ordre établi dans les
Ecoles pour les enfeigner ; mais qu'on ne pourroit le blâmer
avec juftice d'en faire l'épreuve fur lui même fans rien en-
treprendre fur autruy. Ainfi il fe réfolut une bonne fois de
fe défaire de toutes les opinions qu'il avoit reçuës jufqu'à-
lors; de les ôter entiérement de fa créance, afin d'y en fub-
ftituer d'autres enfuite qui fuffent meilleures, ou d'y remettre les mêmes, aprés qu'il les auroit vérifiées, & qu'il les
auroit *ajuftées au niveau de la Raifon.* Il crut trouver en ce Ibid. p. 1
point les moiens de réüffir à conduire fa vie, beaucoup mieux
que s'il ne bâtiffoit que fur de vieux fondemens, ne s'ap-
puyant que fur les principes qu'il s'étoit laiffé donner dans fa
prémiére jeuneffe, fans avoir jamais éxaminé s'ils étoient vrays.

Il prévoioit pourtant qu'un projet fi hardi & fi nouveau
ne feroit pas fans difficultez. Mais il fe flatoit que ces difficultez ne feroient pas auffi fans reméde: outre qu'elles ne mé-
riteroient pas d'entrer en comparaifon avec celles qui fe
trouveroient dans la réformation des moindres chofes qui
touchent le Public. Il mettoit une grande différence entre
ce qu'il entreprenoit de détruire en lui même, & les établif-
femens publics de ce monde, qu'il comparoit à de grands
corps

corps, dont la chute ne peut être que tres-rude, & qui font
encore plus difficiles à relever quand ils font abatus, qu'à re-
tenir quand ils font ébranlez. Il eftimoit que l'ufage avoit
adouci beaucoup de leurs imperfeƈtions, & qu'il en avoit infenfiblement corrigé d'autres, beaucoup mieux que n'auroit
pû faire la prudence du plus fage des Politiques ou des Philo-
fophes. Il convenoit même que ces imperfeƈtions font encore plus fupportables que ne feroit leur changement : de même que les grands chemins qui tournoïent entre des mon-
tagnes, deviennent fi unis & fi commodes à force d'être ba-
tus & fréquentez, qu'on fe rendroit ridicule de vouloir
grimper fur les rochers, ou defcendre dans les précipices,
fous prétexte d'aller plus droit. Son deffein n'étoit pas de
cette nature. Ses vuës ne s'étendoient pas alors jufqu'aux
intérêts du Public. Il ne prétendoit point réformer autre
chofe que fes propres penfées, & il ne fongeoit à bâtir que
dans un fonds qui fût tout à lui. En cas de mauvais fuccés,
il croioit ne pas rifquer beaucoup, puis que le pis qu'il en
arriveroit, ne pourroit être que la perte de fon têms & de fes
peines, qu'il ne jugeoit pas fort néceffaires au bien du genre
humain.

Dans la nouvelle ardeur de fes réfolutions, il entreprit
d'éxécuter la prémiére partie de fes deffeins qui ne confiftoit
qu'à détruire. C'étoit affurément la plus facile des deux.
Mais il s'apperçut bien tôt qu'il n'eft pas auffi aifé à un
homme de fe défaire de fes préjugez, que de brûler fa mai-
fon. Il s'étoit déja préparé à ce renoncement dés le fortir du
collége : il en avoit fait quelques effais prémiérement durant fa retraitte du fauxbourg S. Germain à Paris, & enfuite durant fon féjour de Breda. Avec toutes ces difpofi-
tions, il n'eut pas moins à fouffrir, que s'il eût été queftion
de fe dépoüiller de foi-même. Il crût pourtant en être venu
à bout. Et à dire vrai, ç'étoit affez que fon imagination lui
préfentât fon efprit tout nud, pour lui faire croire qu'il l'a-
voit mis effeƈtivement en cét état. Il ne lui reftoit que l'a-
mour de la Vérité, dont la pourfuitte devoit faire d'orénp-
vant toute l'occupation de fa vie. Ce fut la matiére unique
des tourmens qu'il fit fouffrir à fon efprit pour lors. Mais
les moyens de parvenir à cette heureufe conquête ne lui cau-
férent

férent pas moins d'embarras que la fin même. La recherche qu'il voulut faire de ces moiens, jetta fon efprit dans
de violentes agitations, qui augmentérent de plus en plus
par une contention continuelle où il le tenoit, fans fouffrir
que la promenade ni les compagnies y fiffent diverfion. Il
le fatigua de telle forte que le feu lui prît au cerveau, &
qu'il tomba dans une efpéce d'enthoufiafme, qui difpofa
de telle maniére fon efprit déja abatu, qu'il le mit en état de
reçevoir les impreffions des fonges & des vifions.

Il nous apprend que le dixiéme de Novembre mil fix
cent dix-neuf, s'étant couché *tout rempli de fon enthoufiafme*,
& tout occupé de la penfée *d'avoir trouvé ce jour là les
fondemens de la fcience admirable*, il eut trois fonges confé-
cutifs en une feule nuit, qu'il s'imagina ne pouvoir être ve-
nus que d'enhaut. Aprés s'être endormi, fon imagination fe
fentit frappée de la repréfentation de quelques fantômes
qui fe préfentérent à lui, & qui l'épouvantérent de telle forte, que croyant marcher par les ruës, il étoit obligé de fe
renverfer fur le côté gauche pour pouvoir avancer au lieu
où il vouloit aller, parce qu'il fentoit une grande foibleffe
au côté droit dont il ne pouvoit fe foutenir. Etant honteux
de marcher de la forte, il fit un effort pour fe redreffer:
mais il fentit un vent impétueux qui l'emportant dans une
efpéce de tourbillon lui fit faire trois ou quatre tours fur le
pied gauche. Ce ne fut pas encore ce qui l'épouvanta. La
difficulté qu'il avoit de fe traîner faifoit qu'il croioit tomber
à chaque pas, jufqu'à ce qu'ayant apperçû un collége ouvert fur fon chemin, il entra dedans pour y trouver une re-
traite, & un reméde à fon mal. Il tâcha de gagner l'Eglife
du collége, où fa prémiére penfée étoit d'aller faire fa priére: mais s'étant apperçu qu'il avoit paffé un homme de fa
connoiffance fans le faluër, il voulut retourner fur fes pas
pour lui faire civilité, & il fut repouffé avec violence par le
vent qui foufflloit contre l'Eglife. Dans le même tems il vid
au milieu de la cour du collége une autre perfonne qui l'ap-
pella par fon nom en des termes civils & obligeans: & lui dit
que s'il vouloit aller trouver Monfieur N. il avoit quelque
chofe à lui donner. M. Defc. s'imagina que c'étoit un melon
qu'on avoit apporté de quelque païs étranger. Mais ce qui

L   le

le furprit d'avantage, fut de voir que ceux qui fe raffembloient avec cette perfonne autour de lui pour s'entretenir, étoient droits & fermes fur leurs pieds: quoi qu'il fût toujours courbé & chancelant fur le même terrain, & que le vent qui avoit penfé le renverfer plufieurs fois eût beaucoup diminué. Il fe réveilla fur cette imagination, & il fentit à l'heure même une douleur effective, qui lui fit craindre que ce ne fût l'opé_ration de quelque mauvais génie qui l'auroit voulu fédui_re. Auffi-tôt il fe retourna fur le côté droit, car c'étoit fur le gauche qu'il s'étoit endormi, & qu'il avoit eu le fonge. Il fit une priére à Dieu pour demander d'être garanti du mauvais effet de fon fonge, & d'être préfervé de tous les malheurs qui pourroient le menacer en punition de fes pé_chez, qu'il reconnoiffoit pouvoir être affez griefs pour atti_rer les foudres du ciel fur fa tête : quoiqu'il eût mené juf_ques-là une vie affez irréprochable aux yeux des hommes.

Dans cette fituation il fe rendormit aprés un intervalle de prés de deux heures dans des penfées diverfes fur les biens & les maux de ce monde. Il lui vint auffitôt un nouveau fonge dans lequel il crût entendre un bruit aigu & éclatant qu'il prit pour un coup de tonnére. La frayeur qu'il en eut le ré_veilla fur l'heure même : & ayant ouvert les yeux, il apper_çût beaucoup d'étincelles de feu répanduës par la chambre. La chofe lui étoit déja fouvent arrivée en d'autres têms : & il ne lui étoit pas fort extraordinaire en fe réveillant au mi_lieu de la nuit d'avoir les yeux affez étincellans, pour lui fai_re entrevoir les objets les plus proches de lui. Mais en cette derniére occafion il voulut recourir à des raifons prifes de la Philofophie : & il en tira des conclufions favorables pour fon efprit, aprés avoir obfervé en ouvrant, puis en fermant les yeux alternativement, la qualité des efpéces qui lui étoient repréfentées. Ainfi fa frayeur fe diffipa, & il fe rendormit dans un affez grand calme.

Un moment aprés il eut un troifiéme fonge, qui n'eut rien de terrible comme les deux prémiers. Dans ce dernier il trou_va un livre fur fa table, fans fçavoir qui l'y avoit mis. Il l'ou_vrit, & voyant que c'étoit un *Dictionnaire*, il en fut ravi dans l'efpérance qu'il pourroit lui être fort utile. Dans le même inftant il fe rencontra un autre livre fous fa main, qui ne lui étoit

étoit pas moins nouveau, ne fçachant d'où il lui étoit venu.
Il trouva que c'étoit un recueil des Poëſies de différens Au-
teurs, intitulé *Corpus Poëtarum* &c. Il eut la curioſité d'y
vouloir lire quelque choſe : & à l'ouverture du livre il tomba ſur le vers *Quod vitæ ſectabor iter ?* &c. Au même moment
il apperçût un homme qu'il ne connoiſſoit pas, mais qui
lui préſenta une piéce de Vers, commençant par *Eſt &*
Non, & qui la lui vantoit comme une piéce excellente.
M. Deſcartes lui dit qu'il ſçavoit ce que c'étoit, & que cette piéce étoit parmi les Idylles d'Auſone qui ſe trouvoit dans
le gros Recüeil des Poëtes qui étoit ſur ſa table. Il voulut
la montrer lui même à cét homme : & il ſe mit à feüilleter
le livre dont il ſe vantoit de connoître parfaitement l'ordre
& l'œconomie. Pendant qu'il cherchoit l'endroit, l'homme lui
demanda où il avoit pris ce livre, & M. Deſcartes lui répondit
qu'il ne pouvoit lui dire comment il l'avoit eu : mais qu'un moment auparavant il en avoit manié encore un autre qui venoit
de diſparoître, ſans ſçavoir qui le lui avoit apporté, ni qui le lui
avoit repris. Il n'avoit pas achevé, qu'il revid paroître le livre
a l'autre bout de la table. Mais il trouva que ce *Dictionnai-*
re n'étoit plus entier comme il l'avoit vû la prémiére fois.
Cependant il en vint aux Poëſies d'Auſone dans le Recüeil
des Poëtes qu'il feüilletoit : & ne pouvant trouver la piéce
qui commence par *Eſt & Non*, il dit à cét homme qu'il en
connoiſſoit une du même Poëte encoré plus belle que cel-
le là, & qu'elle commençoit par *Quod vitæ ſectabor iter ?* La
perſonne le pria de la lui montrer, & M. Deſcartes ſe mettoit en devoir de la chercher, lors qu'il tomba ſur divers
petits portraits gravez en taille douce : ce qui lui fit dire
que ce livre étoit fort beau, mais qu'il n'étoit pas de la même impreſſion que celui qu'il connoiſſoit. Il en étoit là, lors
que les livres & l'homme diſparurent, & s'effacérent de ſon
imagination, ſans néantmoins le réveiller. Ce qu'il y a de
ſingulier à remarquer, c'eſt que doutant ſi ce qu'il venoit
de voir étoit ſonge ou viſion, non ſeulement il décida en
dormant que c'étoit un ſonge, mais il en fit encore l'interprétation avant que le ſommeil le quittât. Il jugea que le
Dictionnaire ne vouloit dire autre choſe que toutes les Sciences ramaſſées enſemble : & que le Recueil de Poëſies intitulé

1 6 1 9.

Diviſé en 5.
livres, impri-
mé à Lion &
à Genéve &c.

L ij

lé *Corpus Poëtarum*, marquoit en particulier & d'une maniére plus diſtincte la Philoſophie & la Sageſſe jointes enſemble. Car il ne croioit pas qu'on dût s'étonner ſi fort de voir que les Poëtes, même ceux qui ne font que niaiſer, fuſſent pleins de ſentences plus graves, plus ſenſées, & mieux exprimées que celles qui ſe trouvent dans les écrits des Philoſophes. Il attribuoit cette merveille à la divinité de l'Enthouſiaſme, & à la force de l'Imagination, qui fait ſortir les ſemences de la ſageſſe (qui ſe trouvent dans l'eſprit de tous les hommes comme les étincelles de feu dans les cailloux) avec beaucoup plus de facilité & beaucoup plus de brillant même, que ne peut faire la Raiſon dans les Philoſophes. M. Deſcartes continuant d'interpreter ſon ſonge dans le ſommeil, eſtimoit que la piéce de Vers ſur l'incertitude du genre de vie qu'on doit choiſir, & qui commençe par *Quod vitæ ſectabor iter*, marquoit le bon conſeil d'une perſonne ſage, ou même la Théologie Morale. Là deſſus, doutant s'il révoit ou s'il méditoit, il ſe réveilla ſans émotion: & continua les yeux ouverts, l'interprétation de ſon ſonge ſur la même idée. Par les Poëtes raſſemblez dans le Recueil il entendoit la Révélation & l'Enthouſiaſme, dont il ne deſeſpéroit pas de ſe voir favoriſé. Par la piéce de Vers *Eſt & Non*, qui eſt le Ouy & le Non de Pythagore, il comprenoit la Vérité & la Fauſſeté dans les connoiſſances humaines, & les ſciences profanes. Voyant que l'application de toutes ces choſes réüſſiſſoit ſi bien à ſon gré, il fut aſſez hardy pour ſe perſuader, que c'étoit l'Eſprit de Vérité qui avoit voulu lui ouvrir les tréſors de toutes les ſciences par ce ſonge. Et comme il ne lui reſtoit plus à expliquer que les petits Portraits de taille-douce qu'il avoit trouvez dans le ſecond livre, il n'en chercha plus l'explication aprés la viſite qu'un Peintre Italien lui rendit dés le lendemain.

Ce dernier ſonge qui n'avoit eu rien que de fort doux & de fort agréable, marquoit l'avenir ſelon luy: & il n'étoit que pour ce qui devoit luy arriver dans le reſte de ſa vie. Mais il prit les deux précédens pour des avertiſſemens menaçans touchant ſa vie paſſée, qui pouvoit n'avoir pas été auſſi innocente devant Dieu que devant les hommes. Et il crut que c'étoit la raiſon de la terreur & de l'éfroy dont

ces

ces deux fonges étoient accompagnez. Le melon dont on
vouloit luy faire préfent dans le prémier fonge, fignifioit,
difoit-il, les charmes de la folitude, mais préfentez par des
follicitations purement humaines, Le vent qui le pouffoit
vers l'Eglife du collége, lorfqu'il avoit mal au côté droit,
n'étoit autre chofe que le mauvais Génie qui tâchoit de le
jetter par force dans un lieu, où fon deffein étoit d'aller vo-
lontairement. C'eft pourquoy Dieu ne permit pas qu'il a-
vançât plus loin, & qu'il fe laiffât emporter même en un
lieu faint par un Efprit qu'il n'avoit pas envoyé: quoy qu'il
fût trés-perfuadé que ç'eût été l'Efprit de Dieu qui luy avoit
fait faire les prémiéres démarches vers cette Eglife. L'épou-
vante dont il fut frappé dans le fecond fonge, marquoit,
à fon fens, fa fyndéréfe, c'eft-à-dire, les remords de fa con-
fcience touchant les péchez qu'il pouvoit avoir commis pendant le cours de fa vie jufqu'alors. La foudre dont il en-
tendit l'éclat, étoit le fignal de l'Efprit de vérité qui def-
cendoit fur luy pour le poffeder.

Cette derniére imagination tenoit affurément quelque
chofe de l'Enthoufiafme: & elle nous porteroit volontiers à
croire que M. Defcartes auroit bû le foir avant que de fe
coucher. En effet c'étoit la veille de faint Martin, au foir
de laquelle on avoit coûtume de faire la débauche au lieu
où il étoit, comme en France. Mais il nous affure qu'il a-
voit paffé le foir & toute la journée dans une grande fo-
briété, & qu'il y avoit trois mois entiers qu'il n'avoit bû de
vin. Il ajoûte que le Génie qui excitoit en luy l'enthoufiafme dont il fe fentoit le cerveau échauffé depuis quelques
jours, luy avoit prédit ces fonges avant que de fe mettre au
lit; & que l'efprit humain n'y avoit aucune part.

Quoy qu'il en foit, l'impreffion qui luy refta de ces agitations, luy fit faire le lendemain diverfes réfléxions fur le par-
ti qu'il devoit prendre. L'embarras où il fe trouva, le fit recourir à Dieu pour le prier de luy faire connoître fa vo-
lonté, de vouloir l'éclairer. & le conduire dans la recherche de la vérité. Il s'adreffa enfuite à la fainte Vierge pour
luy recommander cette affaire, qu'il jugeoit la plus impor-
tante de fa vie. Et pour tâcher d'intéreffer cette bien-heu-
reufe Mére de Dieu d'une maniére plus preffante, il prit

L iij   occafion

1619.

*A malo fpiri-
tu ad Tem-
plum propelle-
bar.*

1 6 1 9.

Olympic.
Cartel. ut
fupr.

occafion du voyage qu'il méditoit en Italie dans peu de jours, pour former le vœu d'un pélerinage à Nôtre-Dame de Lorette. Son zéle alloit encore plus loin, & il luy fit promettre que dés qu'il feroit à Venife, il fe mettroit en chemin par terre, pour faire le pélerinage à pied jufqu'à Lorette : que fi fes forces ne pouvoient pas fournir à cette fatigue, il prendroit au moins l'extérieur le plus dévot & le plus humilié qu'il luy feroit poffible pour s'en acquitter. Il prétendoit partir avant la fin de Novembre pour ce voyage. Mais il paroît que Dieu difpofa de fes moyens d'une autre maniére qu'il ne les avoit propofez. Il fallut remettre l'accompliffement de fon vœu à un autre têms, ayant été obligé de différer fon voyage d'Italie pour des raifons que l'on n'a point fçeuës, & ne l'ayant entrepris qu'environ quatre ans depuis cette réfolution.

Son enthoufiafme le quitta peu de jours aprés : & quoique fon efprit eût repris fon affiéte ordinaire, & fût rentré dans fon prémier calme, il n'en devint pas plus décifif fur les réfolutions qu'il avoit à prendre. Le têms de fon quartier d'hyver s'écouloit peu à peu dans la folitude de fon poëfle : & pour la rendre moins ennuyeufe, il fe mit à compofer un traité, qu'il efpéroit achever avant Pâques de l'an Ibidem.

Die 23 Febr. 1620. Dés le mois de Février il fongeoit à chercher des Libraires pour traiter avec eux de l'impreffion de cet ouvrage. Mais il y a beaucoup d'apparence que ce traité fut interrompu pour lors, & qu'il eft toûjours demeuré imparfait depuis ce téms-là. On a ignoré jufqu'icy, ce que pouvoit être ce traité qui n'a peut-être jamais eu de titre. Il eft certain que les *Olympiques* font de la fin de 1619, & du commençement de 1620 ; & qu'ils ont cela de commun avec le traité dont il s'agit, qu'ils ne font pas achevez. Mais il y a fi peu d'ordre & de liaifon dans ce qui compofe ces *Olympiques* parmi fes Manufcrits, qu'il eft aifé de juger que M. Defcartes n'a jamais fongé à en faire un traité régulier & fuivi, moins encore à le rendre public.

CHAP.

PART TWO

THE DREAM DAY,
10 NOVEMBER 1619

hat daytime thoughts inform nighttime dreams has long been a commonplace. Historians and philosophers had already made the point in antiquity, before there was a disciplined psychology of any sort, let alone a scientific dream psychology. Herodotus gave these words to the Persian Artabanus: "Whatever a man has been thinking of during the day is likely to hover round him in the visions of his dreams at night." Cicero and Lucretius also left pronouncements to the same effect, and Scipion du Pleix, the humanistic student of sleep and dreaming who was to become Historiographer Royal to Louis XIII, brought all this up to date for contemporaries of Descartes. For these worthies, however, both ancient and early modern, the significance of this valid observation about dream content lay in a skepticism about the possibilities of dream interpretation. The implication was that dreams are just a confused rehash of fully comprehensible waking experiences, telling us at most what we already know about the past, not what we want to learn about the future.[1]

Sigmund Freud's great distinction in this respect was his paradoxical claim that the interpretation of our dreams *can* teach us new truths about what has been most important to us in our waking experience, which we do *not* already know all about. By endorsing clinical inquiry into the dreamer's recent experience as a perfectly proper way to begin an analysis, he converted an old skeptical commonplace into a new interpretive technique: "One can begin by entirely disregarding the manifest content and instead ask the dreamer what events of the previous day are associated in his mind with the dream he has just described."[2] Freud wrote as if in theory only the previous day and the years of early childhood were truly significant in the formation of dreams.[3] In practice, however, he often traced the historical threads of associated memories further back into the previous days and weeks, even months and years, and he consistently stopped short of early childhood.[4]

In the case of Descartes's Olympian dreams, analysis by inquiry into the experiences of the recent past, which is already quasi-historical, can be extended in an inquiry that is fully historical. The dead man cannot speak, but the living man wrote. However problematic the *Discourse on Method* is as a ready-made "history," its account of the revolutionary thinking "at the beginning of winter [1619]" provides invaluable evidence on the discovery of "the foundation of the wonderful science" reported at the head of the dreams from 10 November 1619. In addition, we have the *Regulae,* parts of which almost certainly go back to the season of the dreams, and relevant bits and pieces from the *Praeambula* and the *Experimenta,* the dossiers preceding the *Olympica* in the Little Notebook. These materials ground my hypothesis, which relates Descartes's apparently well-known intellectual revolution to a previously unknown vocational decision. The interpretation of these dreams offers a wholly new perspective on the most crucial stage of his intellectual development, showing that his personal search for truth was inseparable from a rejection of the law.

3

INTELLECTUAL REVOLUTION AND
VOCATIONAL DECISION

"10 November 1619. When I was full of enthusiasm and I discovered the foundation of the wonderful science. . . ." The date of the dreams and the association with the dreamer's intellectual discovery are the two most certain facts known from the beginning of Descartes's *Olympica*.[1] Before he fell asleep, he was convinced that he was in the process of making a significant intellectual breakthrough, and, as he awakened from his last dream, this conviction was still very much on his mind. The initial reference to the "wonderful science" is notoriously obscure, but it must mean that he somehow related the new discoveries of his daytime thinking to the whole experience of his Olympian dreaming, because the reference comes at the head of the dream record. He must also have associated thoughts and dreams with the specific date, because he echoed this claim for a "wonderful discovery" in a marginal note dated exactly a year after his awakening from the dreams.

The apparent coincidence of the dream day from the *Olympica* with the day of thinking in the heated chamber from the *Discourse* is so important to my argument that I begin this chapter with a preliminary reexamination of pertinent evidence. Then I turn to the old problem of Descartes's discovery on the dream day. A solution to this can help explain the young man's Olympian dreams. A historical analysis of the dreams, in turn, can help explain the mature philosopher's formal thought. Finally, I begin a new argument that Descartes's intellectual discovery was contemporaneous with and inseparable from his vocational decision for his own idiosyncratic "search for truth"—and against the law. This decision was emotionally charged in a way that helps to explain the explosive power of his revolutionary thought, and it is the early *Olympica*, not the late *Discourse*, that gives the best evidence on the interrelationship of discovery and decision.

The celebrated passage on "the entire day" of reflection in the heated chamber has become so familiar that we may have to remind ourselves how extraordinary it is in a life story otherwise so silent on particular events. Part 1 of the *Discourse* ends with "a few years" of travel that culminate in "one day" of resolution. This "one day" is the only possible referent for the "then" at the beginning of part 2:

> [Part 1:] But after I had spent a few years studying in the book of the world in this way and in trying to gain some experience, *one day I resolved to study also in myself and to employ all the powers of my mind in the choice of the ways I ought to follow.* This succeeded much better for me, it seems to me, than if I had never left my country and my books.

> [Part 2:] I was *then* in Germany, where I had been called by the wars that have still not ended. As I was returning from the coronation of the Emperor toward the army, *the beginning of winter* stopped me in a quarter where, finding no conversation to divert me and, fortunately, having neither cares nor passions to trouble me, *I remained the entire day shut up alone in a heated chamber, where I had every opportunity to consider my thoughts* [emphases added].[2]

Descartes later tells us that he was twenty-three years old at the time, which establishes the year as 1619.[3] This was indeed a coronation year, and external evidence shows that the eight weeks of festivities in Frankfurt for Ferdinand II ended on 9 September.[4] That date does not help establish a time for Descartes's retreat into winter quarters "at the frontier of Bavaria" or "in the Duchy of Neuburg on the banks of the Rhine" or wherever,[5] because we do not really know when he left Frankfurt, where he was headed, or how he got however far he got.

When was "the beginning of winter"? Étienne Gilson is still the standard historical authority on the mature *Discourse,* and his commentary gives a brief exposition on the point: "The evidence of the *Olympica*, later confirmed [?] by the *Cogitationes Privatae*, fixes the decisive date of Descartes's reflections; [it was] 10 November 1619:

X novembris 1619, cum plenus forem Enthusiasmo, et mirabilis scientiae fundamenta reperirem, etc.

Therefore, 'the beginning of winter' must mean: 'toward the beginning of the month of November 1619.' "[6] Henri Gouhier inherited Gilson's mantle, and his *Premières pensées* has become the most respected study of the *Olympica*. Commenting on the youthful text, he too concludes that "the beginning of winter" must have meant about the same thing as "10 November 1619."[7]

The evening of 10 November 1619 was Saint Martin's Eve, as Descartes, a son of the Touraine,[8] well knew and explicitly recalls in the *Olympica,* where he protests sobriety in an apparent effort to forestall the objection that his dreams were merely an effect of the drinking bouts with which this pre-Advent carnival was commonly celebrated.[9] Of course, there was much more to this great feast than alcoholic indulgence. All sorts of rents and leases came due then, because the day symbolized the end of warm weather.[10] Folk wisdom, grounded in agricultural practice, made Saint Martin's Day the beginning of winter:

> A la Saint Martin
> L'hiver est en chemin.
>
> A la Saint Martin
> L'été prend sa fin.[11]

Even verses on the year-to-year variations of the weather made Saint Martin's the normal beginning of winter:

> Si l'hiver va son droit chemin,
> Vous l'aurez à la Saint Martin [11 November].
> S'il arrive tant et quand,
> Vous l'aurez à la Saint Clément [23 November].
> Et s'il trouve encombré,
> Vous l'aurez à la Saint André [30 November].
> Mais s'il va, je ne sais au vrai,
> Vous l'aurez en avril ou mai.[12]

The feast had a similar seasonal significance for Germans, and folklorists inform us of a saying to the effect that this was the time to light the fire, a happy truth that the young Descartes may have learned in his heated chamber: "St. Martin lights the hearth-fire."[13] René Descartes surely did not govern his intellectual life by the customary laws of agricultural leases or heating seasons, but no matter how isolated he may have felt in his heated chamber, he was inescapably part of a wider world in which the festival of Saint Martin marked the change from fall to winter, so signaling new beginnings.

Descartes's reference in the *Discourse* to the turn of seasons ("the beginning of winter") and his date from the *Olympica* ("10 November 1619") were two ways of marking the same time, the one apparently as vague as the other is precise. For him, the change from the warm and dry months to the cold and wet months meant a change from a season of foreign travel to a season of settled work on his writing projects. This date relates his first steps toward "the method of rightly conducting reason and seeking truth in the sciences" (*Discourse*) and his discovery of "the foundation of the wonderful science" (*Olympica*).

The Dream Day and Descartes's Intellectual Revolution

What was the Saint Martin's discovery that seemed so exciting at the time and so decisive even in retrospect? The *Olympica* says almost nothing. The *Discourse* says almost too much, insofar as it suggests that the mature method with its four rules was both the sudden inspiration of a single day's creative thought and a more gradual achievement initiated on a memorable day but completed only after "slow" and "circumspect" advances "in the search for the true method."[14] This may not be philosophically clear and distinct, but other historical evidence also suggests both a creative burst at the beginning of winter and gradual refinement in the course of work on a methodological "treatise" in the ensuing months.

Descartes's repeated use of the image of "the foundation(s)" in the *Discourse* and in the *Olympica* provides a verbal clue about the occasion for the discoverer's intellectual excitement. In the first part of his "history," the mature philosopher recalls his schoolboy delight in the wonderful clarity and certainty of mathematics and his contrary frustration at the obscurity and doubtfulness of philosophy. He implies that, before leaving La Flèche as a precocious teenager, he had already recognized mathematical reasoning to be "so firm and so solid" that it could provide the firm and solid "foundations" for nonmathematical subjects of study.[15] Likewise, he implies that he had already condemned traditional philosophy, both in itself and as the "infirm foundation" on which nothing "solid" could ever have been built. Although he probably was not thinking so radically in 1614, when he left La Flèche, his later use of the image is very telling: in Descartes's view, *mathematical foundations could support other sciences.*

The Descartes of the *Discourse* was an intellectual revolutionary, but he was anxious not to seem rebellious.[16] Nevertheless, the mature philosopher does offer evidence of the younger man's boldness, even recklessness. The revolutionary proclamation of his egocentric rationalism begins in the second part with his report on the "first thoughts" from the heated chamber, the awful argument by quintuple analogy to the dubious conclusion that one mind is always better than many.[17] Down with the past and all others! Up with the present and the self!

Then come four instances of Descartes's "foundations"[18] and, as if supported by them, a personal manifesto: "As for the opinions that I had accepted up to then, I couldn't do better than to undertake, for once and for all, to reject them all. I could replace them afterward, either with better ones or with the very same, after I had adjusted them to the level of reason."[19] Destructively, the image of the philosopher-wrecker getting down to foundations represents his radical rejection of older standards of truth: tradition, authority, and consensus. Constructively, the image of the philosopher-builder working up from foundations represents his radical affirmation of that which was *new, mathematical,* and *his very own.*[20]

The early rules in the *Regulae* express the younger man's intellectual excitement. This is particularly true of rule IV, within which Jean-Paul Weber discerns two chronological strata. Weber thinks that the first four paragraphs (rule IVa) were written just after the Olympian dreams, because they are full of the "Olympian" enthusiasms.[21] It is equally likely, however, that they were written just beforehand, because the *Olympica* states that the thinker's enthusiasm preceded the dreams. The last two paragraphs (rule IVb) were almost certainly earlier.

The author of rule IVb was preoccupied with mathematics, even if it was a "universal mathematics." This was not a new idea for Descartes at the beginning of winter, 1619, but it does signal what was to come: the "seeds of truth" in every mind but not in books; simpler disciplines as the "way" to the knowledge of related disciplines; and the necessity for an orderly progression from the simplest and easiest thoughts to the more complex.[22]

Rule IVa sounds the tocsin. Its composition may have followed that of rule I (study all the sciences, which are interconnected) and rule III (test everything by "intuition" and "deduction"). In this context, what sets rule IVa apart are its perfervid tone and its explicit claim of "method" as such. Mortal men have been blind wanderers, but René Descartes will show them the way of his method. Following his rules, *anyone* can be sure of *never* making a mistake, *never* wasting any effort, and, finally, *"arriving at the knowledge of everything."*[23] In comparison, the philosopher of the *Discourse* seems almost prudent.

The young Descartes anxiously wondered whether others had anticipated his discovery, given the wide dispersal of the "seeds of thought" and the evident truthfulness of the "fruits of his thought." Nevertheless, from his hothouse, the author of rule IVa also proudly proclaims his own achievement as the discoverer of the method by which thinkers can extend the clarity and certainty of mathematics to all sciences: "I am not thinking of ordinary mathematics, but am setting forth a certain other discipline. . . . For this [regular method] ought to contain the first rudiments of human reason and to extend far enough to elicit truths from any subject whatsoever. And to speak freely, I am persuaded that it is more powerful than any other [science] handed down to us by men, because it is source of all others [sciences]."[24]

I now turn to the less familiar and less orderly materials that Leibniz and Baillet copied from the dossiers immediately preceding the *Olympica*.[25] The *Praeambula* includes various expressions of new beginnings that recall the "one day" at the beginning of winter, 1619, when Descartes "resolved to study also in myself and to employ all the powers of my mind in the choice of the ways I ought to follow." The intellectual new beginning was physically symbolized by the new orientation of series 2. Having flip-flopped the Little Notebook with its "old" mathematical manuscripts from the previous winter (series 1), Descartes produced a "new" front cover for a new set of dossiers (series 2). In this second series, he started afresh with a beginner's title and a beginner's epigraph: *Praeambula*, "The fear of the Lord is the beginning of wisdom."[26]

What followed may or may not have been wise. The twenty-three-year-old imagined himself ascending onto "the great stage of this world" (CP 1–4); rivaling others' "ingenious inventions" with his own intellectual discoveries (CP 5–8); succeeding, without anyone else's help, by his own "fixed rules" (CP 8–9); courting science or even, like a jealously possessive husband, claiming her for himself alone (CP 10–12); setting aside others' books (CP 13–16) and bettering their pseudo-scientific pansophism with his own *Thesaurus Mathematicus* (CP 17–28); unmasking the truth as he unmasks himself, so as to display the beautiful necklace that links the sciences (CP 29–33, compare 1–4, 10–12); and instructing even limited minds how to "judge things truly" and to "know the true worth of the sciences" (CP 34–38, compare 8–12, 17–20).

Considered by themselves as they appear in Leibniz's certainly disconnected notes from Descartes's probably disorderly *Praeambula,* these cogitations do not add up to much more than youthful rodomontade. Read as a documentary appendix to parts 1 and 2 of the *Discourse,* however, this juvenilia shows a young man anxious to assert a new identity as a great thinker. There is no way of knowing just when was the "one day" on which Descartes began "to study also in himself," but the sequences of the dossiers in the Little Notebook and of the narrative in the *Discourse* suggest that it must have been before the time of enthusiastic discovery, but very little before. It would almost have to have been in November to justify dating it at "the beginning of winter," the terminus post quem, even if it was not 10 November, the terminus ante quo.

What Baillet cites from "Descartes's fragmentary manuscripts" seems to have come from the *Experimenta,* and these four pensées probably come as close as possible to a contemporaneous record of the philosopher's thoughts immediately before his famous dreams. In the first of the four pensées, Baillet repeats Descartes's observation on the relationship between his mood swings and his eating and sleeping (CP 43–46).[27] Then, copying away on the very next page and giving the same marginal attribution to "Descartes's fragmentary manuscripts," Baillet adds a second pensée, otherwise unknown, which is also concerned with the philosopher's health. In it, Descartes's memory of his first bleeding takes him back to the year of his studies of classical rhetoric at La Flèche,[28] a memory of some interest for potential day-residues, given the peculiar malady, the school setting, and the classical bookishness in the Olympian dreams.

In the third pensée, like the fourth also preserved only by Baillet and attributed to "Descartes's fragmentary manuscripts," the young philosopher reflects on ancients and moderns, either reinventing or repeating what Robert Merton calls "Bacon's Paradox." Francis Bacon first published it in *The Advancement of Learning* (1605): "Antiquitas saeculi, juventus mundi." So-called antiquity was actually the youth of the world; the real antiquity is the present day.[29] Descartes's version was more aggressive and more personal: *they* are not worthy of being called "the ancients"; *we* are. Whereas Bacon was advocating a moderate position, respectful of past ages if not submissive to them, Descartes was preparing his own radical rejection of traditional book learning and affirmation of self.[30]

In the fourth pensée, the last of this set from the *Vie de Monsieur Des Cartes,* the would-be discoverer of new truths defends himself against what can only have been his own anxiety that his new books would merely repeat others' old ones:

> Just as we cannot either write a word in which there is anything but the letters of the Alphabet or fill a sentence with anything but words from the Dictionary, so we cannot write a book without some sentences that are found to be in others' works. But if that which I shall say should be so coherent and so inter-connected that each assertion follows from others, I shall have no more borrowed these sentences as an argument from others, than appropriated the words themselves from the Dictionary.[31]

It is not certain that this fourth pensée came from the *Experimenta,* still less so that it followed the third in the Little Notebook (Descartes's version of Bacon's Paradox), but what an appropriate sequence for *Baillet's* work, perfect texts for that "copyist of copyists." Descartes's justifiable claim of an original argument follows his reinvention or repetition of another's thought. At least the association of these materials seems to be Descartes's, and not merely Baillet's.[32]

Descartes's "Dictionary," remembered as a day-residue, seems to have made its way into the beginning of his Dream III. It serves as an intrinsically indifferent tracer that takes us back to a most significant concern in the dream thoughts.[33] In the manifest dream, he pairs the *Dictionary* with the *Corpus poetarum,* that anthology of wisdom from the Latin poets, and this other dream book, too, may be a distorted expression of related themes known from the same set of daytime pensées. I have just reviewed the evidence for a current memory extending back to his schoolboy studies in the Latin classics, for a current image of himself as a modern ancient who could claim a paradoxical precedence over the ancient ancients, and, not least, for the current ambition to write a book, a book of his own.

68

Why not emulate Descartes's youthful boldness? I suggest that the first two of these pensées copied by Baillet were indeed from the *Experimenta;* that the third and fourth were from either the *Experimenta* or the *Praeambula;* that all four reflect the reclusive hero's resolution "to study also in himself" and "to choose the ways he ought to follow"; that they preceded the *Olympica* in time as well as in sequence; that these daytime preoccupations became at least in part the subject of his nighttime dreams; and that the apparent place of these day-residues in the Olympian dreams allows us to date them: very shortly before 10 November 1619, if not on the dream day itself. The young philosopher had thought about thought: the sciences were one; the true method was one; both were fundamentally mathematical. But this "thought" was also emphatically self-assertion: *he* was the one who had discovered this, and *he* could demonstrate it. Henceforth, that was to be *his* calling.

The Dream Day and Descartes's Vocational Decision

In the *Discourse,* the philosopher portrays himself as already having been a mature thinker on the completion of his studies at La Flèche.[34] This brings the "history of his mind" up to 1614, although the philosophical autobiographer does not offer mere particulars like dates. He was then just eighteen years old. What next? The last three paragraphs of part 1 summarily recall uncounted years of unspecified travels, association with unnamed men of "different dispositions and conditions, and "various experiences." This period came to an end in 1619, when he was twenty-three. There is so little other evidence on the years between his departure from La Flèche and his arrival at the heated chamber that Charles Adam, the best-informed scholar ever to have attempted a history of Descartes's whole life, simply announces that he has "no idea just how he spent the seven years that followed [the end of his studies at La Flèche], from 1612 [*sic*] to 1619, years in which he was so fully occupied. On so interesting a part of the philosopher's life, we are reduced to conjectures."[35] As if to make the point of this extreme uncertainty, within the same volume Adam recalculates the years that Descartes spent at La Flèche, postponing his

69

departure from 1612 to 1614 and so slightly shortening the unknown period.[36]

Adam's own documentation shows that this ignorance is not quite complete. A baptismal record places Descartes in Poitiers on 21 May 1616. The twenty-year-old then stood as godfather for an infant son of the tailor with whom he lodged. This relationship implies familiarity over a period of time and so at least some stability for the lodger.[37] A second document explains what he was doing in Poitiers: he was studying the law. University records show that he passed his examinations with distinction, receiving his baccalaureate on 9 November 1616 and his licentiate in both canon and civil law on that Saint Martin's Eve, 10 November 1616.[38]

The fact of Descartes's legal education has never seemed very important. In Adam's 628 pages on Descartes's life and works, the one relevant sentence concerns its apparent insignificance: "Here and there in his works, we find a few legal terms."[39] The learned historian's cavalier dismissal of Descartes's youthful training in the law is possible only because of the mature philosopher's own cavalier dismissal of this part of his past.

After professional training as a lawyer and volunteer service with the troops of Maurice of Nassau, René Descartes settled on another vocation. He determined to become a "searcher for truth."[40] From our great distance, we may suppose that his decision was uncomplicated, affirmative, perhaps even inevitable. The philosopher would simply have had to become a full-time thinker, if only because we cannot now imagine any other sort of life for him. But how could there have been an uncomplicated vocational commitment to anything as indefinite as the solitary search for all truths by new methods, on principle beginning with the rejection of everything old? And how could this young traveler have committed himself affirmatively to such a "search for truth" without deciding against his legal training and the status, wealth, and power of the robe?

The vigor of Descartes's positive commitment to "the search for truth" is readily apparent at the very begining and the very end of the Discourse. Part 1 begins with a rhetorical disclaimer of special intellectual gifts, then advances a claim for the progress possible even for a slow thinker who follows le droit chemin, "the straight path" or "right method." Two paragraphs later, this image for a favored way of thinking becomes also an image for a favored way of life:

I don't hesitate to say that I think that I have been very fortunate in that as a young man I stumbled upon certain paths that have led me to considerations and maxims with which I have constructed a method. It seems to me that this gives me the means of progressively increasing my understanding and raising it little by little to the highest point. . . . [After almost obligatory disclaimers, there comes the voluntary claim not only for his way of thinking but also for his way of life:] *Casting a philosophical eye over the various [other] activities and undertakings of men, I see that there is hardly one that doesn't appear vain and useless.* But I remain so extremely satisfied with the progress that I think I have already made in the search for truth and so hopeful about the future, that [I make this claim:] *If there is any one occupation among all those of men as men that is solidly good and important, I dare to believe that it is the one that I have chosen* [emphases added].[41]

The self-satisfaction of this last claim is so striking that it almost overshadows the equally significant condemnation of all vocational alternatives in the first italicized sentence.

The *Discourse* ends with a prospective complement to the retrospective paragraph just quoted. The philosopher formally renounces the world, its employments, and its honors:[42]

I have resolved to devote the rest of my life to just one thing, the attempt to gain some understanding of nature. This will allow the formulation of medical principles more certain than those that have been adopted until now. *My [vocational] inclinations are so strongly opposed to any other plans, especially to those that could help some only by harming others [apparently, the law or arms], that, if I were ever to be forced by circumstances to employ myself in any such way, I don't think I could do it.* Therefore, I make this declaration. I understand very well that it won't gain me worldly consideration—but that's something for which I have no desire whatsoever. *I will always remain more grateful to those by whose favor I enjoy an untroubled leisure [the civil governments of the United Provinces], than I would ever have been to anyone [whether French king or Dutch prince] who could have offered me the world's most honored employment.*[43]

In the more strictly historical parts of the *Discourse,* only two other passages directly concern the younger Descartes's vocation. The first comes toward the end of part 1; the second, at the end of the "provisional morality" in part 3.[44] These two passages frame the self-portrait of the heroic thinker in part 2, but they are thereby detached from one another. They are also vague, unreliable on the most important fact, and awkward in other respects. It is hardly surprising that they should have been largely ignored.[45] In the first, Descartes repudiates his legal training and justifies his failure to pursue a legal career. In the second, he gives better evidence that there was a particular occasion of decision against the law and other more traditional vocations, medicine included.

In the first of these two passages, Descartes remarks, as if in passing, that "jurisprudence, medicine, and the other branches of learning" taught after philosophy in the schools "bring honors and wealth to those who cultivate them."[46] Gilson supposes a reference to a dictum neatly discriminating between the wealth of doctors and the honors of lawyers: "Dat Galenus opes, dat Justinianus honores."[47] So much by way of apparent concession. But Descartes, who mentions law first, not medicine, goes on to express his contempt for the subject matter and his superiority to its professional rewards:

> As for the other branches of learning [law and medicine] that borrow their principles from philosophy, I judged for that very reason that nothing solid could have been built on such infirm foundations. And *neither the honor nor the gain that they promise were sufficient to induce me to learn them. For, thank God, I did not feel that I was of a condition that obliged me to make a trade of learning [law or medicine] for the sake of my purse. And, although I did not profess to scorn [all] glory in a cynical manner, nevertheless, I had a very low regard for that which I could not hope to acquire except by false titles* [emphasis added].[48]

The combination of gross error and strong emotion is what makes this passage so interesting. Descartes's historical error is certain. The records of the University of Poitiers unequivocally show that he *had* studied the law. Why then did he so emphatically deny this seemingly innocent fact? Nonrational complications related to his youthful refusal to practice what he had learned must have been involved. The emotionality of his repudiation of the law is as certain as such things can be. Evidence in this passage includes the exclamatory thanksgiving and the emphatic negation: Thank God! I was never so base as to cash in ignobly on my learning or to aspire to false titles above my true condition.

The "false titles" that Descartes so scorned are best understood as those of the high robe magistrates, who rose from the moneyed bourgeoisie into the honored nobility by means of venal offices. His lifetime coincided exactly with the first Bourbon kings' equivocal successes as vendors of judgeships, raising revenue by selling status. His father and his two brothers were among the happy purchasers and inheritors.

A parallel passage from the first rule of the *Regulae* is still more telling: "Non de perversis loquor et damnandis, ut sunt inanis gloria vel lucrum turpe...."[49] Here, it is "perverse and damnable" to pursue "vain ambition and filthy lucre." The vigor of this language suggests something quite different from a dispassionate weighing of alternative careers. Weber builds a very strong case for the early composition of this part of the *Regulae*, which he dates within a few days of the dreams. No one could ever hope for perfect certainty on the chronology of this passage, but this does seem likely enough.[50]

There was new philosophy in Descartes's rejection of old "foundations," but there was also more, the nonphilosophical passion with which he embraced prejudices that were vaguely aristocratic and emphatically antirobe. His abandonment of books, his travels in the world, his frequentation of "courts and armies," and his self-testing in various encounters that follow in the *Discourse* are also aristocratic and unlawyerlike, even if this son of the robe and not the sword was in fact only a watcher and not truly a warrior even in 1619–20.[51]

The second passage from the *Discourse* concerns a vocational decision in the winter of 1619–20. It establishes the bare fact of a one-time, systematic, moralistic review of all possible occupations, followed by Descartes's happy reaffirmation of what a Frenchman of more ordinary aspirations might have dismissed as a confessedly idle *non*occupation, "the search for truth":

Finally, to conclude this morality [the provisional maxims of moderation, resolution, and resignation], *I decided to make a review of the various occupations of men in this life, so that I might try to choose the best.* Although I don't [now] want to say anything about [against] those of others, I thought [then] that I couldn't do any better than to continue with the very one in which I found myself. That is, *[I decided] to employ my whole life in the cultivation of my reason and to make what progress I could in the knowledge of truth, following the method that I had prescribed for myself. I had felt such extreme happiness since I had begun to use this method, that I didn't think that there could be anything more delightful or anything more innocent [N.B.] in this life.* In this way, every day I discovered several truths, which seemed to me rather

73

important, and which most other men seemed not to know. The satisfaction that I felt so filled my mind and spirit that *nothing else mattered at all* [emphases added].[52]

Philosophically, this passage occupies an awkward position in the argument, in that Descartes's report of his nongeneralizable but definitive vocational decision makes so odd a "conclusion" to the *three* generalizable but nondefinitive maxims of neostoic moderation, resolution, and resignation.[53]

Descartes's own introductory count of *"three or four* maxims" reflects this awkwardness, as does the continuation of the quoted passage, in which he goes on to say that this "conclusion" to the provisional morality is in fact its *precondition:*

> Moreover, the three preceding maxims were *founded* only on my plan of continuing to study [as a searcher for truth]. . . . I wouldn't for a moment have contented myself with the opinions of others [by the first maxim] if I hadn't planned to judge them myself when the time came. I wouldn't have been able to exempt myself from scruples, following them [by the second maxim], if I hadn't also intended to miss no opportunity to find better, if better there were. And finally, I wouldn't have been able to limit my desires [by the third maxim] or to be happy, if I hadn't followed *a way (or path)* by which I would be assured of acquiring not only all the knowledge within my capacities [the fruits of the intellectual revolution] but also all the true goods that might ever be in my power [the fruits of the contemporaneous vocational decision] [emphases added].[54]

Descartes's *fourth* maxim/nonmaxim, which leads into so radical a declaration of his egocentric rationalism, cannot have been invented in 1637 to placate the Chancellor or any other censorious reader. Nor can it have been conceived in the intervening years as part of a systematic, if provisional, morality. Its very awkwardness as a "conclusion" and its *im*moderate, *un*resigned defiance help reassure the reader that there was in fact a significant moment of vocational decision in the winter of 1619–20.

The twinning of "foundations," vocational decision together with intellectual self-examination, would have seemed utterly unremarkable to other Christian humanists. It appears, for example, in Pierre de Charron's *De la sagesse* (1601). This bulky compendium now rests in peace, dust to dust, but it was once more popular than Montaigne's *Essays,* running to twenty-five editions in the years from 1601 to 1634, not counting the many editions of an abridged *Petit traicté de la sagesse*.[55] Charron's great virtues, his rational orderliness and ethical complacency, suited him ideally as a guide for the young Descartes.[56] In book 2 of the *Sagesse*, he prescribes two "dispositions" and two "foundations" for the wise and the would-be wise:

Première disposition à la sagesse: Exemption et affranchissement des erreurs et vices du monde, et des passions. (*Sagesse*, book 2: chap. 1)	Having sequestered himself in the *poêle*, Descartes "exempts and frees himself" from all "errors and vices of the world" and from "cares and passions." (*Discourse*, part 2)
Seconde disposition à la sagesse: Universelle et pleine liberté de l'esprit, tant en jugement qu'en volonté. (*Sagesse*, 2:2)	Formally and repeatedly, Descartes declares perfect independence for his rational judgment and his moral will. (*Discourse*, pts. 2 and 3)
Première et fondamentale partie de la sagesse: vraie et essentielle preud'hommie [i.e. "une droite et ferme dispositon de la volonté à suivre le conseil de la raison"]. (*Sagesse*, 2:3)	Descartes establishes "firm foundations" and goes the "right way" when he decides "for once and for all" to "reject all mere "opinion" and to rely only on his methodical "reason." (*Discourse*, pt. 2)
Second fondement de la sagesse: avoir un but et un train de vie certain [i.e. "prendre une vocation à laquele on soit propre," which requires rational choice made after careful reconsideration of one's own nature, first, and the proposed occupation, second]. (*Sagesse*, 2:4)	Descartes resolves "one day to study also in himself." He reviews other occupations before deciding as the "fundamental" basis of right action and right thinking that his "search for truth" is the best course for the rest of his life. (*Discourse*, pts. 1 and 3)

The texts are not exactly parallel, and Descartes's argument is quite different from Charron's. Nevertheless, the much more powerful mind seems to have adopted as its own the formulations of an influential precursor. These ideas encouraged not only a philosophical study of self but also a particularly deliberate exercise of vocational decision making.[57] Charron's twinning of the "foundations" of wisdom brings together ideas that recur in Descartes's account of epochal winter as intellectual revolution (Cartesian mathematical "foundations" that Charron could hardly have imagined) and vocational decision (more personal "foundations" on which Charron did teach useful lessons).

It might seem tempting to dismiss such a similar conjunction of ideas and terms as merely fortuitous, because, as Charron had said in 1601, "the seeds of all sciences and virtues are naturally scattered . . . in [all] our minds."[58] Naturally, the seed having been sown, Descartes repeated this, too, and he did so in his reflections on the Olympian dreams of 10 November 1619 *and* in the parts of the *Regulae* that apparently came before *and* just after the dreams.[59] As Charron had also said in 1601, anticipating criticisms that he had drawn all his best material from the works of the ancients: "The form and the order are my own."[60] Descartes repeated this idea, too, doing so just before the dreams of 10 November 1619.[61]

Descartes's echoes of Charron's "foundations of wisdom" are most impressive because of additional Cartesian counterparts to the humanist's twin "dispositions" *and* to his subsequent chapters on piety (book 2: chap. 5), on the regulation of desire (2:6), on the moderation of conduct (2:7), *and* on obedience to the law and customs of the land (2:8). This means that, for all the acknowledged differences between the two works, there are notable similarities between the thought of the *Discourse on Method,* parts 2 and 3, and eight consecutive chapters from *De la sagesse,* book 2. The mature Descartes was no plagiarist, but the younger man does seem to have used materials from the respected handbook when he laid his own foundations at the beginning of the decisive winter.

Although Descartes's *Discourse* does not give a more precise date for the youthful vocational decision, Baillet's version of the *Olympica* does provide perfectly satisfactory evidence on the matter. The first tag from Ausonius in Dream III, "Quod vitae sectabor iter," has always been recognized as the most prominent single dream element.[62] The dreamer chances on this verse as an aleatory reader of the *Corpus poetarum* (VDC 107–13). Then he recommends it to the other character in his dream and sets out to find it intentionally (VDC 136–41). Finally, while at least nominally still asleep, he interprets its *question* as if it had been a morally or even theologically sanctioned *answer* to the problem of "what sort of life one should choose" (VDC 166–71).

The question seems clear enough, coming from a twenty-three-year-old who had not yet settled down, but what was the answer? Descartes's final, fully awakened generalization on the dream is this: "This last dream, which had all been very soothing and agreeable, seemed to him to reveal the future, and it showed him nothing but what would happen in the rest of his life" (VDC 189–92). What was this? Baillet's version of Descartes's text does not say, leaving us in the dark on this matter. But on the morning after his Olympian dreaming, he awoke with the conviction that he had at last seen the light.

The best explanation for this most emphatic but also most obscure theme in a dream also supposed by the dreamer to have promised "Philosophy and Wisdom," "Revelation and Enthusiasm," and "the treasures of all the sciences" (VDC 167–68, 189, 198) is that Descartes confronted a vocational decision that was contemporaneous with and inseparable from his intellectual revolution. The documentary record of legal studies at the University of Poitiers and the two historical parts from the *Discourse* allow me to begin a definition of its terms, but it is material from the *Olympica* that documents its date and its force.

4

SAINT MARTIN'S EVE AND SAINT MARTIN'S DAY-AFTER

Gustave Cohen first observed that the dream day, 10 November 1619, was an anniversary date for Descartes, who had made his first appearance in Beeckman's *Journal* on 10 November 1618.[1] This line of argument can go further than Cohen realized, and in a different direction than he supposed. There had also been a still-earlier Saint-Martin's-Eve date in Descartes's intellectual life: he had completed his legal education on this date in 1616, receiving his baccalaureate in civil and canon law on 9 November and his licentiate on the following day.[2] Furthermore, *every* Saint Martin's was also the feast that marked the ceremonial beginning of the judicial year in the French courts.

Saint Martin's Eve as an Anniversary Date for René Descartes

Henri Gouhier waved aside Cohen's vague suggestion that Descartes believed in an incremental revelation, occurring year after year on the same blessed date. This does smack of small-minded "superstition,"[3] not great-souled reason, but Cohen is certainly not to blame for the historical pattern of anniversary dates that he first tried to retrace, however unsuccessfully. There is exceptionally good evidence that the Saint Martin's date marked the most significant events in the young Descartes's intellectual life in 1616,

1618, and 1619. He commemorated the last in 1620. Furthermore, other evidence not considered by Cohen or Gouhier suggests still another significant Saint Martin's event in 1628:

1. 1616, 10 November: Descartes successfully completes his professional training in the law(s) at Poitiers and receives his licentiate with honors.

2. 1618, 10 November: Descartes first impresses Beeckman, self-consciously displaying his mathematical prowess to the man who would later inspire his ambitions.

3. 1619, 10 November: Descartes experiences his dream day enthusiasm, ongoing discovery of "the foundations of the wonderful science," and heaven-sent dreams.

4. 1620, 11 November: Descartes enters an anniversary annotation in the *Olympica* on "the foundations of the wonderful discovery" as an accomplished fact.

5(?). 1628: "A few days after" having arrived at Paris "for Saint Martin's," Descartes first proclaims his new "rule or Method" and promises to publish it.

Event 1 is absolutely certain; its significance is not. There can be no question of either the fact of Descartes's licentiate or the accuracy of the Saint Martin's Eve date.[4] However, there is no direct evidence that the lawyer-nonlawyer himself later associated this date with his legal training, and without some explanation of why he should have remembered it two, three, four, or twelve years later, its apparent place at the beginning of a list of Saint Martin's anniversaries or pseudo-anniversaries may seem merely coincidental. But there is a perfectly good explanation for any Frenchman's association of every Saint Martin's with legal vocations. Saint Martin's Day-after was the ceremonial beginning of the judicial year, as Descartes would certainly have known. I consider the impressive annual ceremonies in the second part of this chapter.

Event 2 was already a Saint-Martin's anniversary in Descartes's life, whether or not he thought of it as such. Isaac Beeckman's *Journal* records what seems to have been the initial encounter between the two men on 10 November 1618.[5] At that time, Beeckman referred to the young foreigner only as "a Frenchman from Poitou," but within a week he would write "René, the Poitevin," and within several weeks' time he would know "René Descartes" or "M. Du Peron," his young friend's pseudogenteel affectation. After 10 November 1618, the nameless "Frenchman" quickly acquired an identity.[6] Because Beeckman used the new-style Gregorian calendar, his 10 November date was the same as Descartes'.[7]

The meeting of minds came on a point of mathematics that seemed to Beeckman to merit a serious response, but we may well wonder in what spirit of mathematical gamesmanship Descartes, who was too clever by a half, said his lines:

> Yesterday, which was 10 November [1618, new style], at Breda a Frenchman from Poitou tried to prove this proposition: "In truth, there is no such thing as an angle." This was his argument: "An angle is the meeting of two lines at one point, so that line *ab* and line *cb* meet at point *b*. But if you intersect angle *abc* by the line *de*, you divide point *b* into two parts, so that half of it is added to line *ab*, the other half, to line *bc*. But this contradicts the definition of a point, which has no part. [Therefore, there is no such thing as an angle.]"[8]

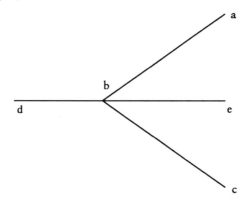

Beeckman rehearsed Descartes's argument, then refuted it. If this was a game, Beeckman won and Descartes lost.

Descartes's seventeenth-century biographers told a very different story of the first meeting. Baillet gives the full-blown version, but Adam questions much of it, including all parts here italicized:[9] An *unknown glory seeker* placards a mathematical problem as a challenge for all comers; Descartes asks for a translation from the Flemish into Latin or French, so that he can take up the challenge; it *happens to be* Beeckman, *then in the city of Breda,* who obliges him *in Latin,* setting the condition that the stranger return the favor by communicating the solution *to what he himself considered a very difficult problem;* Descartes accepts *with an air so resolute* that Beeckman writes down for him the name and address, *so that he can bring the solution.* The young soldier-mathematician (b. 1596), who is already armed with "the rules of his Method," surprises the older savant (b. 1588) with the full solution *on the next day,* then *astonishes him in a long conversation on the sciences.* Beeckman promptly asks for Descartes's friendship and for an entire life *of research and writing together. Descartes responds with a sincere friendship.* Here, Descartes wins; Beeckman, who could never have hoped to beat him, joins him.[10]

Any critical historian will prefer Beeckman's journal entry on the initial encounter to Baillet's later and more elaborate version, but there is an intriguing possibility that this late story may go back in some form to Descartes himself. Baillet formally cites Daniel Lipstorp as his authority, and Lipstorp's *Specimina philosophiae cartesianae* (1653) does indeed include almost all of it, with allowances made for the sort of relatively insignificant changes that improved Baillet's story at some cost to verifiable history.[11]

But where did Lipstorp get this tale of Descartes's youthful genius? There had been no prior biographical publication other than Descartes's own *Discourse,* and Lipstorp cites no oral source. We know that he drew on written materials derived indirectly from one Dutch Cartesian, Jean de Raey, but this anecdote seems much more likely to have been based on an oral tradition from another Dutch Cartesian, Franz Schooten (d. 1660), who is considered on good authority to have been Lipstorp's other principal source. Schooten had been close enough to Descartes to have drawn the figures for the *Principles* (1644) and the Latin *Dioptrics* and *Meteors* (1644), to have translated into Latin the *Geometry,* and to have added both the copperplate engraving of the philosopher and the mathematical commentary to this Latin *Geometry* (1659).[12]

The following filiation would account for what is primarily an oral tradition beyond any critical control: Descartes himself told the story to Schooten, who retold it to Lipstorp, who retold it in print for Baillet, who finally retold it yet again with the small "improvements" that have been so criticized. The worst problems are probably further back than Baillet, however, before the first

81

published version. Working backward, it is easy to identify two possible sources for exaggeration, if not outright invention: first, Schooten's understandable admiration for Descartes and, second, Descartes's own understandable admiration for himself.[13] It would be naive to underestimate the effects of either one.

Event 2, the first meeting of Descartes and Beeckman in Breda on 10 November 1618, is significant because it led to a brief but exceptionally intense relationship and because that relationship in turn inspired the more systematic thought of the more famous mathematician, physicist, and philosopher. Descartes was to credit Beeckman for having awakened him from his slumbers and to embrace him as "the promoter and first author of his [scientific and mathematical] studies."[14] It is the hero's version of the event that counts, not the historical fact of the matter. Apparently, in Descartes's memory of Descartes's perception of Descartes's display, the young thinker had played a heroic role. That dramatic fact was enough to attract Schooten, Lipstorp, and Baillet—but there were almost certainly other attractions for Descartes.

The Descartes-Beeckman relationship is the subject of chapter 6. Here, however, without further argument, necessary qualification, or specific documentation, I remark that Descartes loved Beeckman and that Beeckman left Descartes. The younger man sought the approval and assistance of the older; Beeckman inspired him as a thinker and encouraged him as an author on subjects of mutual interest, especially mechanics; Descartes promised to remember his mentor and to return to his writing table when he stopped in his travels; Beeckman then scolded him for his travel plans and his lack of steady productivity, offering what must have seemed a grudging and almost insulting assistance.[15] Therefore, if Descartes recalled their initial encounter in 1618 on the first Saint-Martin's-Eve anniversary, he would have recalled an intense and complex relationship, not merely a momentary display. And how could he not have recalled this meeting on the anniversary date when, having finally settled down for the sort of work promised to Beeckman, he began to discover something grander and more portentous than the *Mechanics* or the *Geometry*, ambitious projects respectively appropriated from Beeckman and discussed with Beeckman?

Event 3, the dream day, 10 November 1619, was a *double* anniversary, both of the well-trodden legal way not taken after 1616 and of the less-trodden mathematical way that he had begun to pursue in 1618. This fact already begins to define the terms of my hypothesis. Descartes's intellectual revolution was inseparable from his vocational decision: no to the law; yes to the "search for truth." This seems to be the principal meaning looking backward *from* the dream day to 10 November 1616 and 1618. Later, Descartes was also to look backward *to* the dream day.

Event 4, or, more properly, the anniversary commemoration of Event 3, is the marginal annotation made on 11 November 1620. The best understanding of the corresponding passage from the text of 1619 on the discovery of "the foundation of the wonderful science" is that the quoted words refer to the method-in-the-making. Therefore, Descartes's verbs for his enthusiasm and his discovery had been imperfects in 1619. He could use the perfect tense in 1620, because he had in hand a manuscript comparable to the *Regulae,* rules I-VIII. This was a real accomplishment, if not quite the published "treatise" that he had promised himself on 23 February 1620. Most of the parts of *the* Method, if not the whole, are present in the bits and pieces of the *Praeambula* (the Cartesian cogitations from Leibniz and perhaps also the third and fourth of the Cartesian pensées from Baillet, previously discussed), the early entries of the *Regulae* (as Weber argues, rules I-III and IVb), and the first five paragraphs of the second part of the *Discourse*.[16]

When Descartes looked back from 11 November 1620 to his Olympian record from the beginning of the previous winter, he could more calmly confirm its enthusiastic claims. He had produced a relatively comprehensive and coherent code of rules, *a* method if not quite *the* Method given in the much later *Discourse*. A process of discovery had become the fact of something discovered, and he could refer retrospectively to "the foundation of the wonderful discovery" in the perfect tense. That he chose to do so on the anniversary demonstrates that he was mindful about the date(s), if not superstitious.[17]

Event 5, philosophizing at the Nuncio's in 1628, is most uncertain. I depend on Baillet, who in turn depended in part on a letter from Descartes to Étienne de Ville-Bressieu, which is very good, and in part on the narrative of Pierre Borel in his *Vitae*

Renati Cartesii compendium, which may be very bad. Baillet offers some gold in his formal quotation from the letter, which is otherwise unknown, setting the quotation apart from the rest of his narrative by punctuation marks,[18] but what is the rest worth? If any part is Baillet's paraphrase of Descartes's letter, it is at least silver, but if it is only his paraphrase of Borel's little biography, supplemented by other tradition written into the mysterious "Mém. Mss. de Claude Clerselier,"[19] it is probably only copper. And if the part is only his own bridgework from insular source to insular source, it is base metal, worthless counterfeit.

Here is Descartes's own gold. This undated account is of exceptional interest as recording Descartes's first known display of his "beautiful rule or natural Method":

> You have seen these two fruits of my beautiful rule or natural Method.[20] I was obliged [N.B.] to present them in the conversation that I had with the Papal Nuncio [Guidi di Bagno], the Cardinal [Pierre] de Bérulle, Père [Marin] Mersenne, and all that exalted and learned company that had assembled at the residence of the Nuncio to hear the presentation of his new philosophy by M. de Chandoux. It was there that I confessed to the whole troop of them what the art of reasoning well can do for those who are moderately learned and by how much my principles are better established, more true, and more natural than others that the learned have received. You were convinced of this, as they all were, making a point of entreating me to write them and to teach them to the public.[21]

The golden truth was Descartes's truth, which others, Chandoux first among them, might have remembered differently. Then again, this very Chandoux was a counterfeiter who was to be hanged for having used his science "to alter and to falsify metals"![22]

For Descartes, there had been a shining occasion when he had dazzled the greatest luminaries with the "wonderful science" that had been his alone since the beginning of winter, 1619. On this later occasion, as he remembered it, he had incurred something like a spiritual obligation to write for the larger public. What Charles Adam calls a "perhaps decisive" event is still a part of "the philosopher's" story.[23]

But when did the event occur? Saint Martin's, 1628? That seems to be the implication of the existing evidence, lacking Descartes's full letter, Clerselier's mysterious memorial, and the living memories of the distinguished company. Borel does not date the event, but he does place it at the Siege of La Rochelle. Baillet accepts this assertion of Descartes's presence at the siege, but then sends him back to Paris after the last act at La Rochelle, the procession on 3 November 1628: "There being nothing further to see in the pays d'Aunis, . . . Descartes took the post back to Paris, where he spent Saint Martin's. A few days after he had arrived at Paris, there occurred the meeting of learned and curious persons at the Papal Nuncio's."[24]

If Baillet's only evidence on the date of the conference was his uncritical inference from Borel's account[25] and whatever else he could learn about the siege, then this vague "Saint Martin's" chronology is worthless. On the other hand, if he had good evidence from the Descartes letter, the Clerselier memorial, or other oral tradition, the chronology may be quite accurate.[26]

Bits from later correspondence concerning relevant writing projects also fall into place at Saint Martin's. In 1633, it was on Saint Martin's Day that Mersenne wrote to remind Descartes of debts incurred by past promises to publish.[27] In 1640, it was on Saint Martin's Day that Descartes wrote to Mersenne to say that he had finally sent the *Meditations* on its way, having posted the work to Constantin Huygens on the day before. On this same occasion, Descartes also first announced his plan to publish the *Principles,* an ordered course of philosophy.[28] 11 November 1640 was twenty-one long years after the Olympian enthusiasms and the three dreams. Had he forgotten all about them? *That* would be the reckless guess.[29]

Saint Martin's Day-after
as the Annual *Entrée* for *Robins*

It was a fact of French jurisprudence since the fourteenth century that 12 November, Saint Martin's Day-*after,* was the ceremonial opening of the judicial year, with the Mass of the Holy Spirit, solemn exhortations, the reading of the laws, and the taking of oaths.[30] These practices of the Parlement of Paris became the law for all French courts in Charles VIII's *Ordonnance sur l'adminis-*

tration de la justice, 1493. Henri III added further legislation on the subject in 1579.[31]

Without having to school himself in the literature on the subject, Descartes already knew what we shall have to learn from Bernard de La Roche Flavin's *Treize livres des Parlements de France* (1617). This is the lesson from his book 5: "We can call the day of these *entrées* ["at Saint Martin's"] the solemn day of the Parlements [the highest courts in the French judicial system] and the happy day of our embarkation on the sea of justice, *diem natalem navigationis nostrae*."[32] This same authority offers Louis d'Orléans's summation on the meaning of Saint Martin's Day-after as the great public occasion of the year in the French courts: "The day that this oath is taken, Saint Martin's Day-after, is the festival of the law courts, the grand festival, the high solemnization of justice. On this day, justice holds its plenary session, its chambers decorated and courtroom doors thrown open. Its oracles are displayed before all, and it is legitimate for anyone to consult its tripods."[33] This last humanistic effusion seems to represent the venal officers themselves as the "oracles" of justice and the laws as the "tripods" of justice.

Brevity was hardly a virtue for a seventeenth-century *officier* writing on the dignities of his *office,* and it took La Roche Flavin fifteen "chapters" to rehearse the annual ceremonies in the courts on Saint Martin's:

1. On the *entrées* and the opening of the Parlements at Saint Martin's.

2. Rank and order observed at the *entrées* of Saint Martin's.

3. On the solemnity of the *entrées* and the oath of Saint Martin's.

4. The origin of the remonstrances that are made at Saint Martin's.

5. The cause of the *entrées* and harangues of Saint Martin's . . .

6. Of the harangues at the *entrées* of Saint Martin's.

7. That the *Présidents* delivering the harangues of Saint Martin's and pronouncing the *arrêts généraux* ought to learn them . . .

8. The cause of the reading of the ordinances at the *entrées* of Saint Martin's.

9. On the solemn Mass of the Holy Spirit said on the day after Saint Martin's at the opening of Parlement.

10. On the form, solemnity, and authority of the oath of Saint Martin's.

11. On the observation of the oath that is made at the *entrées* of Saint Martin's.

12. Why the frequent oath taking that is forbidden to all other estates is permitted and required of the officers of the Parlements.

13. Of the oath on the Crucifix and the Holy Gospels.

14. Of the oath[s] that the Roman magistrates and the Greeks were accustomed to take.

15. Ordinances sworn by the Presidents, Councilors, King's Attorneys, Clerks, and Ushers of the Court on the day of the *entrées*, the day after Saint-Martin's.[34]

In short, for a *parlementaire* like La Roche Flavin (or for the *son* of a *parlementaire*, like René Descartes), the *entrées* of Saint Martin's were more than memorable as the annual occasion for the taking of oaths, the reading of the ordinances, and the display of the majesty of the courts. They were unforgettable.

Lest anyone outside the judicial establishment should forget the beginning of the new judicial year, bell ringing at the Palais—"as loud as possible"—began on Saint Martin's Eve, continued throughout Saint Martin's Day, and lasted until the solemn Mass of the Holy Spirit on the morning of Saint Martin's Day-after.[35] Then came a short harangue or remonstrance to the magistrates in closed chambers, the reading of the ordinances, the formal oaths of the officers, a longer harangue open to the public, the formal oaths of all lawyers qualified as advocates or procurers, a break for dinner, and, at long last, the customary exchange of salutations.[36]

René Descartes had something else in mind for himself on Saint Martin's Eve in 1619. Having reviewed the various occupations of men in the world at the foundational stage of his provisional morality, he determined that he would not become a practicing lawyer or an office-holding judge. He would be a "searcher for truth."[37] In the solitude of his heated chamber, with the door firmly closed, he formulated a "first maxim" or rule of conduct for himself, an otherwise unexceptional principle of "moderation" that justifies his refusal of all oaths:

Particularly, I included among excesses all promises by which we surrender any of our liberty. Not that I disapproved of the laws . . . of vows or contracts. But, because I saw nothing in the world that always remained in the same estate, and because, for my own part, I had promised myself to perfect myself more and more in my judgments, and *not* to make them worse, I thought that I would have committed a great offense against common sense, if, because I had once approved of something, I considered myself ever afterward obligated to consider it good.[38]

Then what? How about a "second maxim," a rule of resolution? Once he has made up his mind, even on matters acknowledged as uncertain, he will not change it, and he will not admit any regrets.[39]

PART THREE

THE FATHER AND THE FRIEND, ATTRACTION AND REPULSION

o understand the situation of the solitary dreamer in his heated chamber, we have to reconsider the Descartes family. In the hierarchical society of the seventeenth century, its head was Joachim Descartes, *conseiller* in the Parlement of Brittany. René Descartes was a brilliant but rather wayward cadet son, no less but also no more. And for Joachim and the other Descartes, the law was far more than a profession freely chosen by this or that equal individual. It was instead the dominant fact of social life for the lineage and the household.

The purpose of chapter 5 is to establish this point and to show how Joachim in particular used judicial offices to raise himself and his descendants socially. He seems to have used every means at his disposal to induce René to follow him into the magistracy along with his *two* favored sons, René's older full brother, Pierre, and younger half brother, the second Joachim. He failed. René chose against a career in the law. The one precious if tattered scrap of testimony on the father-son relationship documents what might otherwise be inferred more tentatively, that the father was displeased by his son's deviance from the familial norm. Joachim's displeasure lasted, and René was still fighting old battles in 1637 when he proclaimed emphatically and repeatedly that he had made the *right* choice in 1619–20. *His* occupation was the one most "solidly good and important." *His* vocational choice had been "the best," in that "the search for truth" had brought him "such extreme happiness," the "sweetest and most innocent possible here below."[1] Against whose criticisms, if not Joachim's, was René defending the solid goodness and perfect innocence of his idiosyncratic way of life?

The purpose of chapter 6 is to reconsider Descartes's brief but passionate friendship with Isaac Beeckman, the somewhat older savant whom he had first tried to impress on Saint Martin's Eve 1618 and whom he grew to love in the following months. Beeckman sanctioned a way of life very different from the law. Descartes was to follow him as a searcher for truth. It is the most serious shortcoming of the *Discourse* as an intellectual autobiography that it effectively obliterates this formative friendship, for it was Beeckman who first inspired his more gifted friend with a new way of mathematical-physical thinking and who first exhorted him to write books.

So far, so good? But Descartes was restive under even the gentlest tutelage and restless enough to prefer touring to writing in the spring, summer, and fall of 1619. This much is certain, and there seem also to have been other, more personal tensions between the two men. So, at the beginning of winter, Descartes's relationship with this one intimate friend, Beeckman, was almost as problematic as his relationship with his father, Joachim. All this greatly complicated his life at the time of intellectual discovery and vocational choice.

5

JOACHIM DESCARTES'S FAMILY
AND THE LAW

This chapter concerns the forgotten father of a famous son. I am apt to sympathize with the admiring friend who wrote to the latter in May 1637 that he had higher esteem for the historical royal privilege to print the *Discourse* than he would have had for a hypothetical royal patent of nobility.[1] In November 1619, however, *the* Descartes had not yet established his intellectual aristocracy. Indeed, as he turned decisively away from the law and toward the "search for truth," he was defying the values of the world that was not only his father's but also his own, like it or not. His truth searching was to be an idiosyncratic departure from the established norms. It was the judicial offices of his father, his two brothers, and his three nephews that would bring them and the rest of the family from what had been merely local prominence in Poitou to transmissible nobility, great wealth, and substantial power in Brittany.

Judicial Office and the
Making of the Descartes Dynasty

Joachim Descartes had two marriages and, loosely speaking, two families, the first in Poitou, the second in Brittany. René was born on 31 March 1596, the second son of the first bed (see table 1). This was a Poitevin family, established at Châtellerault, although

Table 1.
Joachim Descartes's First Marriage and Children

Joachim Descartes (1563–1640) = Jeanne Brochard (?–13 May 1597)				
Pierre	Pierre	Jeanne	**René**	Infant
b. 1589	b. 1591	b. unknown	b. 1596	b. May 1597
d. infancy	d. 1660	d. 1640	d. 1650	d. May 1597

Joachim had purchased his office as a *conseiller non-originaire* in the Parlement of Brittany at Rennes in 1585,[2] and Jeanne had borne him their five children in the Touraine at La Haye in an unknown year and in 1589, 1591, 1596, and 1597.[3] The last lying-in was fatal to the mother and newborn child alike.

Jeanne Sain, the maternal grandmother of the three surviving children, seems to have accepted responsibility for the maternally orphaned children. Jeanne Descartes stood, however tall, as a god-mother to newborns at La Haye in 1598, 1599, 1603, 1604, 1605, 1606, and 1609. Pierre, too, appears there as a very young god-father in records from 1598 and 1599.[4] Finally, sometime between 1606 and 1610, either Pierre or his younger brother René addressed grandmother Jeanne Sain as "Mademoiselle ma mère" in a juvenile thank-you letter from La Flèche signed "Votre très humble et obéissant fils."[5]

During these years, father Joachim Descartes was establishing himself ever more firmly in Brittany. The crucial domestic events were his remarriage to a Breton and the birth of four more children, of whom a son and a daughter survived infancy (see table 2). The second Joachim was to displace his older half brother René.[6]

As for René himself, he was placed as a boarder in the *collège* of La Flèche in Anjou (1606–14). The Jesuit Fathers there were quite determined to break the ties that bound their young students to their several households, as shown by an academic calendar that allowed the boys in the grammar classes, the first three years, just one week as the annual "long vacation."[7] In the context of a request for familial support made after Joachim's death, René was to say

Table 2.
Joachim Descartes's Second Marriage and Children

Joachim Descartes = Anne Morin (1579–1634)			
Joachim	Claude	François	Anne
b. ca. 1601	b. 1604	b. 1609	b. 1611
d. ca. 1680	d. infancy	d. infancy	d. date unknown

that he had regarded his blood relative, Étienne Charlet, S.J., the rector at La Flèche, as his true father: "I am very much indebted to the members of your Society and more particularly to you, because, for my whole childhood, your place was that of my father. . . . Because I think of you as my father, I trust that you won't mind if I address you just as I would him, were he still living. And I am [yours] passionately . . ."[8]

Very few particulars are known about René Descartes's social situation in childhood and none about his affective life or his father's place in it. The available information about his mother's early death, his father's Breton affiliations, and his own schooling at La Flèche could suggest that he was an almost-orphan who could not have had much experience of anything like normal parenting by father or mother. Nevertheless, René was raised in a family closely identified with the law and judicial offices: his father was a judge; his mother came from a judicial family; his surrogate father was closely related to judges; and his surrogate mother was the widow of a judge.[9] I can best show this fact by a systematic review of the entire family.

Whatever the vicissitudes of his upbringing as an almost-orphan, René Descartes could not easily have escaped the ties that bound him and his father's family to the law. One need only consider the following four genealogical tables, the four quarters of René Descartes, to appreciate just how pervasive was the law in the family even before Joachim.

The surviving documentation on Pierre Descartes,[10] doctor of Châtellerault, begins only in 1543, and none of it mentions any father, mother, or brother (see table 3).[11] Furthermore, both the

Table 3.
The Paternal Antecedents of Joachim Descartes

Pierre Desquartes or Descartes (d. 1566)
   medicine
   acquired nonnoble lands
   doctor of medicine, Châtellerault
= Claude Ferrand (1531–1610 or later)

Joachim Descartes
   law
   seigneur de Chavagne
   conseiller, Parlement of Brittany
= Jeanne Brochard

---

aristocratic pretensions of the later Descartes and the provincial loyalties of still later *érudits* have complicated discussions of the family line.[12] Given the Saint Martin's dreams as the subject matter of this book and the Saint Martin's anniversaries as a fact in Descartes's intellectual life, it is at least a curiosity that Joachim's family may have come from Tours, where two Gilles Desquartes, possibly Joachim's grandfather and uncle, had been mayor of the city and treasurer of the Cathedral Chapter. This would establish the family at the very tomb of Saint Martin.

More certainly, table 3 shows that, other than René's siblings, father Joachim, the *conseiller,* was the one Descartes whom René could have known. Grandfather Pierre, the physician, had died when Joachim was a very young child, fully thirty years before René's birth. There were no uncles or aunts on this side of the family.

The maternal ascendants of Joachim Descartes are quite certain, and his collateral relatives on this side were both much more numerous and much more important in his and his son's world. Although Joachim's father was far removed from René's experience, Joachim's mother, Claude Ferrand, was still living in Châtellerault as late as 1610. It was she who had brought the Descartes house into the Descartes family, and it was she who presided there after Pierre's death and Joachim's departure.[13] I shall consider first the ascending line, then the instructive cases of Claude's four brothers and four sisters, Joachim's uncles and aunts (see tables 4,[14] 5, and 6[15]).

The two Jean Ferrands were both distinguished physicians, but they were both dead before René Descartes was born. In 1597, the family was headed by Michel Ferrand, René's godfather and a magistrate. Michel and his cadet, Antoine, another magistrate, represent the norms of Joachim's world, in which an honorable man should strive to achieve three things: the ownership of landed estates; a judicial office or, failing that, a legal career; and an honorable marriage. Claude Ferrand's sisters married within the

Table 4.
The Maternal Antecedents of Joachim Descartes

Jean Ferrand (d. by 1576)
   medicine
   sieur de la Coindrie
   médecin ordinaire de la Reine
   rector of the University, Poitiers
   = Louise Rasseteau

Jean   Michel   Antoine   Louis   Claude   Martine   Catherine   Jeanne   Louise
   = Pierre Descartes (d. 1566)
      medicine
      small properties
      doctor of medicine
      Châtellerault

Table 5.
Joachim Descartes's Uncles: Estates, Careers, Marriages

Jean II	Michel	Antoine	Louis
sieur de	sieur de	sieur de	sieur de la
Soudun	Beaufort	la Coindrie	Fouchardier
médecin	*lieutenant gén'l.*	*lieutenant*	*avocat*
ordinaire	Présidial,	Châtelet,	Présidial,
du Roi	Châtellerault	Paris	Poitiers
	= Marie Catherine	= Madeleine	= Marguerite
no marriage	Puy	Vallée	Cotherau

Table 6.
Joachim Descartes's Aunts: Marriages, Estates, Careers

Martine	Catherine	Jeanne	Louise
= Barthélemy	= René	= Pierre	= Antoine
de la Vau	Repin	Bruneau	Desmons, *écuyer*
sieur du	sieur de la	sieur de la	sieur de la
Tureau	Ronde	Roussière	Salle
président in	*avocat* at	*avocat* at	*exempt des armes*
the Élection,	the Présidial,	the Présidial,	*du Roi*
Poitiers;	Poitiers	Poitiers	
mayor			

world of *bourgeois gentilshommes*. If the elder Jean Ferrand were to have had either more money for dowries or fewer children to establish, he would have been able to negotiate more brilliant alliances, but the dominant pattern of marital affiliations with families of officers and lawyers would surely have been the same.

The paternal antecedents of Jeanne Brochard were also notable magistrates, originally from Châtellerault, who achieved great prominence at Poitiers and Paris. I consider only the Brochards de la Cossaye, descending from Aymé, although the Brochards de la Clielle, descending from Aymé's younger brother Pierre, achieved even greater distinction in the early seventeenth century.[16] René Brochard, sieur des Fontaines, was René's uncle and godfather, and he lived to be *doyen* of the *échevins* at Poitiers and of the *conseillers* in its Présidial (see table 7).[17]

Jeanne Sain, René's maternal grandmother, whom he or his brother addressed as "Mademoiselle ma mère" after the death of their own mother, was *Mademoiselle la lieutenante de Poitou* to the rest of the world long after the death of her husband, the *lieutenant général* at Poitiers.[18] This is an identity worth remembering because of René Brochard de la Coussaye's frustrated attempts to pass on this office to his elder son, Claude, and others' frustrated attempts to persuade young René Descartes to purchase the lieutenant generalcy at Châtellerault in 1625.[19] Jeanne Sain's own family completes the four quarters (see table 8).[20]

Looking backward from Joachim Descartes and his first wife, we see an honorable Poitevin family in which the law and, in earlier

96

Table 7.
The Paternal Antecedents of Jeanne Brochard

Aymé Borchard (d. 1533)
law
conservateur des privilèges
at the University, Poitiers
one of the codifiers of the
customary law of Poitou
= Anne de Sauzay

René Brochard (d. 1586) Jeanne Brochard
law   = Jean de Moulins
sieur de la Coussaye law
lieutenant général at the sieur d'Archange
 Présidial, Poiters   *conseiller* at the
= Jeanne Sain (d. 1610)   Présidial, Poitiers

Claude Brochard	René Brochard	Jeanne Brochard
law (d. 1586)	law (d. 1648)	(d. 1597)
sieur de la	sieur des	**= Joachim Descartes**
Coussaye	Fontaines	law
conseiller at the	*conseiller* at	seigneur de
Présidial, then	the Présidial,	Chavagne
Parlement, Paris	Poitiers; mayor	*conseiller* at the
= Charlotte de Moulins	= Jeanne d'Elbène	Parlement, Rennes

generations, medicine were the preferred vocations. But this is only half the story. Looking forward from Joachim, we see a noble Breton family in which the ownership of parlementary office was the means by which the patriarch elevated himself and his heirs. For them, the law was the firm foundation of a great house, not just one vocational possibility among others.

For Joachim Descartes and his family, a secular change came around 1600, the approximate date of his Breton remarriage and the conception of his third son. This was also the time when the Parlement in Rennes began to sit in longer and more regular semesters, necessitating Breton residence even for a *conseiller non-*

Table 8.
The Maternal Antecedents of Jeanne Brochard

Claude Sain (d. ca. 1585)
commerce
sieur de Bellecroix
merchant at Orléans
= Étiennette Cathelin

Claude Sain	Jeanne Sain (d. 1610)	Renée Sain
?	= René Brochard	= Jacques Amenion
sieur de Luyières	law	commerce
?	sieur de la Coussaye	*marchand-*
= Charlotte Hurault	*lieutenant général,*	*bourgeois,*
(Orléans?)	Présidial, Poitiers	Orléans

Claude Brochard	René Brochard	Jeanne Brochard
law	law	**= Joachim Descartes**
sieur de la	sieur des	law
Coussaye	Fontaines	seigneur de
conseiller at the	*conseiller* at	Chavagne
Présidial, then	the Présidial,	*conseiller* at the
Parlement of Paris	Poitiers, Mayor	Parlement, Rennes
= Charlotte de Moulins	= Jeanne d'Elbène	

originaire like Joachim.[21] Finally, it was the year when King Henri IV presented the sovereign courts with the edict on the *Tailles* that they interpreted as a patent of nobility.

In March 1600, the hopeful springtime of the new century, the paternal ruler of long-suffering subjects promised them tax relief. There had been too many exemptions based on too many usurpations of noble privileges, so that the common people had been forced to carry inequitable burdens. Article 25 promised to lighten the burden by reducing exemptions, which it proposed to accomplish by regulating privileges and punishing usurpations:

> We forbid all persons from taking the quality of *écuyer* and insinuating themselves into the body of the nobility, *unless they are descended from a grandfather and father who have followed the profession*

of arms or served the public in certain honorable charges [high offices],
namely, those which by the laws and customs of the kingdom can give the
beginning of nobility to posterity, without ever having performed any
vile act that would derogate from that quality, *[and unless] they,*
too, [sons and grandsons] emulate the virtue that they [grandfathers and
fathers] have shown in this praiseworthy manner of living, under penalty
of being degraded dishonorably from the title [nobility] that they
have dared to usurp [emphases added].[22]

As the old saying goes, "kings propose; lawyers dispose." The
edict of King Henri IV that was meant to end abusive exemptions
for false nobles became the principal legal basis for the ennoblement of the higher judicial officers, who now had royal sanction
for a generational *cursus honorum* that could transform any roturier
into nobleman. This was the rule of *patre et avo consilibus*. Three
successive generations of service in "certain honorable charges"
would give "the beginning of nobility to posterity." The king had
said so. It was left to the lawyers to explain what he had meant.
Their interpretation was that, as judges in the sovereign courts,
conseillers in the Parlements were *personally* ennobled as soon as
they were received into the body of officers, although they and
their descendants would not be *transmissibly* ennobled until after
the third generation of twenty years' service (or death in office).
Thus, Joachim's sons and grandsons had to complete the advance
that he had begun.[23] René retreated.

Pierre, Joachim II, and their sons did not retreat, however. By
the time that Louis XIV and Colbert attempted their great ref-
ormation of the nobility in 1668, the family of the *bourgeois gen-*
tilshommes from Châtellerault had been transformed. A century
earlier, Pierre Descartes had qualified himself as *honorable homme*
or *honorable homme et sage maître*.[24] That may have been good
enough at the time of Joachim's birth (1563) in the Renaissance,
but then came something better, a true rebirth. By 1668, solely
on the basis of three generations of office holding in the Parlement,
the Descartes were judged to be fully noble *écuyers* (the cadets)
and even *chevaliers* (the office-holding eldest sons).[25] They had left
the "beginning of nobility" far behind; thanks to their offices, they
had reached the end. Indeed, Joachim Descartes de Chavagne, the
last surviving son of Joachim the patriarch, who also held onto
office tenaciously enough to become *doyen* of the *conseillers* in the

Parlement of Brittany, was one of the judges specially commissioned by the king to determine the validity of all others' claims to nobility!²⁶

Roland Mousnier maps the wonderful world in which such things were possible. In *La vénalité des offices sous Henri IV et Louis XIII*, he describes the more elaborate structures that the proud officers and greedy kings of the seventeenth century built on the social, economic, and political foundations left by their ancestors. Officers were able to purchase their way into the sovereign courts, to purchase the right to bequeath their office like any other piece of property, and so to purchase for themselves and, in time, their heirs the useful and honorable privileges of nobility.²⁷ In Brittany, having first bought their titles and then, in 1668, having verified their own credentials, such officers firmly closed the doors of their chambers to other aspiring commoners, leaving the Parlement of Rennes a bastion of newly pure nobility.

As is shown in table 9, Joachim Descartes founded a veritable dynasty of judges. Joachim himself and five of his heirs in two direct lines of fathers and eldest sons held offices in the court continuously from 1586 to 1734. From his first marriage came Pierre and the Descartes de Kerleau, and from his second marriage came Joachim II and the Descartes de Chavagne.²⁸

Joachim's descendants by his daughter (Jeanne), granddaughter (Anne-Louise), and great-granddaughter (Louise-Prudence) included four more *conseillers* (Rogier, the Ferrés, and de Rosnyvinen, respectively), further adding to the distinction of the family. The last named was a marquis, as was Le Prestre, the one marital affliation I deign to list.²⁹ This was Joachim's family, not René's, a family of the law, not of "the search for truth." The family had once included both notable and not-so-notable physicians (the Jean Ferrands and Pierre Descartes, respectively), but it was above all else a family of magistrates.

Of course, in 1619 neither Joachim the patriarch-to-be nor René the philosopher-to-be could have known the further reaches of this remarkable dynasty, but that the former intended just such an outcome is perfectly clear from his management of offices and marriage alliances for himself and his other children. Joachim's eldest son, Pierre, completed his legal training and passed his examinations in 1613, his father's fiftieth year and his twenty-first.

Table 9.
The Parlementary Dynasty of Joachim Descartes

Jeanne Brochard
dr. of René,
s. de la Coussaye
lieutenant général,
Présidial, Poitiers

= (1)

Joachim Descartes
sgr. de Chavagne
conseiller (1586–1628),
Parlement, Rennes

(2) =

Anne Morin
dr. of Jean,
sgr. de Chavagne
premier président,
Chambre des Comptes

Pierre (1591–1660)
sgr. de Kerleau
conseiller 1618–
47 & 1650–54
= Mgte. Chohan

Jeanne
= Pierre Rogier
chevalier
sgr. du Crévy
(Parl. family)

Joachim (1601?–1680?)
sgr. de Chavagne
conseiller
(1628–78)
= Mgte. du Pont

Anne
= Louis d'Avagour
écuyer
sgr. du Bois
de Kergrois

Joachim (1627–1700)
sgr. de Kerleau
conseiller
(1648–1700)
= Marie Porée du Parc

François Rogier
sgr. du Crévy
conseiller
(1649–62)
= Renée Foucault

Anne-Louise
= Rene Ferré
chevalier
sgr. de la Ville-es-blancs

Joachim (1635–1718)
sgr. de Chavagne
conseiller
(1659–1718)
= Prudence Sanguin

François-Joachim (1664–1736)
sgr. de Kerleau
conseiller
(1691–1734)
(1) = Françoise Goret
(2) = A.-M.-L. de Quifistre

Louise-Prudence
= Chr. de Rosnyvinen
chevalier
marquis de Pire
capt. de la noblesse
(Parl. family)

Anne-Louis Ferré
sgr. de la Ville-es-blancs
conseiller
(1689–1722)
= Louise d'Espinoze

Marguerite-Sylvie
= **R.-J.-L. Le Prestre**
marquis de Châteaugiron
conseiller (1742–60)
président à mortier (1760–75)

J.-B. De Rosnyvinen
marquis de Pire
conseiller
(1707–19)
= G.-L. Picquet

F.-L.-J. Ferré
sgr. de la Ville-es-blancs
conseiller
(1723–30)
= J.-H. des Rondiers

After a couple of years of experience as an *avocat,* he could have been "provided" with his father's office, then "received" by his father's colleagues in the Parlement, where his relative youth would have been little problem. Instead, Joachim chose to retain his own office at the cost of purchasing a second familial seat in the same tribunal for his eldest son (1618). This must have been a considerable expense, at least double the dowry that had been provided for Jeanne (15,000 *livres* in 1613), and some land had to be sold.[30] Who benefited from the acquisition of this second parlementary office? Not René, the second son. *Joachim the elder* could now continue his active life in the court, where *Pierre,* the first son, could join him. And *Joachim the younger* could now look forward to an eventual succession to his father's seat (*pourvu* in 1625). That left the brilliant René, who seems never to have been at home in alien Brittany. He had reason to feel disadvantaged in comparison not only with his elder full brother but also with his much younger half brother. No matter? The patriarch had founded his dynasty. In 1625, having transferred formal ownership of his office to the second Joachim, he promptly returned to the court where he had been *doyen* to request approval to sit for yet another four years. He finally gave up only in 1628.[31]

The five Breton marriage alliances negotiated by Joachim the patriarch, starting with his own second marriage, document the extent to which he shaped the family by the social world of his office. They first allied him with a daughter of Jean Morin, *premier président* at the Chambre des Comptes in Nantes, a far more prestigious office at a somewhat less prestigious court. On her mother's side, she was the first cousin of two *conseillers* in the Parlement at Rennes and of two other magistrates' wives. In short, she was very well connected and, particularly after her brothers died without heirs, she was rich. It was from the Morin family that Joachim and the Descartes de Chavagne acquired the chateau and seigneurie at Sucé, near Nantes.[32]

Joachim the patriarch's two parlementary sons, Pierre and Joachim II, were provided with marriages appropriate to their offices. Endogamy within the families of the sovereign courts was the norm, and these alliances provide further circumstantial evidence of Joachim's determination to redefine the Descartes by the Parlement and its social world. Marguerite Chohan was Pierre's bride. Her family had been represented in the Parlement by an uncle, Jérome, a *conseiller* whose fate it was to be "inhumanly assassinated and murdered while leaving church." It was from Pierre's marriage in 1624 that the Descartes de Kerleau acquired the manor house and seigneurie at Elven, near Vannes.[33]

Joachim II de Chavagne was married to Marguerite du Pont. The du Ponts d'Eschuilly were to be represented in the Parlement by two seventeenth-century *conseillers,* Marguerite's brother and nephew. This affiliation allied Joachim the patriarch with Louis du Pont, *conseiller d'État* and another *président* in the Chambre des Comptes. The bride brought a dowry of 50,000 *livres.* A generation later, Joachim III de Chavagne would receive from another daughter of a *conseiller d'État* a dowry of 100,000 *livres.* Toward the end of his life, despite a collapse in the value of his office, this grandson would estimate his fortune at 373,083 *livres,* 11 *sous,* and 1 *denier* (let's not forget the last *denier*).[34] For the Descartes, it had been the Splendid Century.

Joachim the patriarch's two daughters, Jeanne and Anne, were given sons of the robe and, exceptionally, the sword. Pierre Rogier represented the cadet branch of an ennobled family that could boast a *président* and two *conseillers* sitting in the Parlement of Brittany at the time of the marriage in 1611. Pierre's son, François, would become a *conseiller* in his turn. The son of one of these other Rogiers would become not just another *conseiller* but also the "Comte de Villeneuve," a new thing on earth, and *maître des cérémonies* in the Order of the Holy Spirit, for which charge he offered a genealogy testifying to fifteen generations of Rogier *chevaliers,* going all the way back to 1226.[35] Who knows why he stopped there? Perhaps there were limits even to baroque invention, if not to familial vanity.

Joachim the patriarch's younger daughter, Anne, was given a very distinguished name among the Breton swords, but perhaps not too much more, when she was married to Louis d'Avagour du Bois de Kergrois in 1628. Very little is known about this alliance. Baillet does say that the brother of this Louis was "long employed in the embassies to and other negotiations for the King in Sweden, Poland, and Germany" before dying at Lübeck in 1657.[36] Who knows? The hypergamous alliance negotiated by Joachim Descartes with the d'Avagour may have advantaged René in the end, when the cadet who had so distanced himself from the rest of his family was pensioned by Louis XIV and brought to court by Christina. Of course, the philosopher's personal and intellectual friendship with Chanut is better known, but the familial connection could also have served him.

"Of All My Children,
Only One Is a Disappointment."

That brings me to René, my Descartes if not the only Descartes or the head of the Descartes. It is now easier to understand how he deviated from familial norms. What was wanted by the *bourgeois gentilshommes* of the sixteenth century was landed estates, judicial offices, and honorable marriages. What was wanted by the patriarchal *parlementaires* in the seventeenth century was rather more: legal nobility, grander estates, higher judicial offices, and more distinguished and richer marriages. In either scheme, the office was the key.[37] It is possible but not very likely that Joachim did want René to become a soldier,[38] but even if a military instead of a legal career was the paternal intention, René failed on every count.

No surviving evidence documents particular paternal pressures on René as early as 1619, but this silence means absolutely nothing, certainly not that there were no such pressures. As the young man headed into his middle twenties, it was time for him, with his father's direction and assistance, to establish himself. That much was clear, but how and where the cadet was to do so was less clear. There is indirect and incomplete but probably sufficient evidence of familial pressure in four letters from René to his father and elder brother, the first two written in 1622, the third in 1623, and the fourth in 1625. Even this little is very suggestive.[39]

In 1622, the family authorized René to sell his share of the inheritance from his mother. This included the little *métairie* from which he took the name "du Perron," which he used in Holland and no doubt elsewhere as a young man. Descartes termed the property a "fief," although notarial records do not support the distinction.[40] Under conditions dictated by his elders, René sold a house in Poitiers and rural properties, including le Perron, raising some 24,000–25,000 *livres*. He reported the successful sales to his father, but then he failed to use this money to purchase an office, his father's evident intention.[41]

In the following year, 1623, he set off for Italy, where a Sain relative had died in service.[42] An eighteenth-century genealogy does list a René Sain, *intendant de l'armée* in Italy, who died at Turin in 1623. This must be the man, a nephew of Descartes's grandmother Jeanne Sain.[43] After this relative's death, the family must have designated young Descartes for the intendancy. Baillet remarks that they had provided him with all the necessary papers. Nevertheless, they could not make good the deficient will betrayed in his letter of farewell, in which he conceded failure before setting out on the adventure. Financial offices were very lucrative, and that should have been lure enough, but it was not. The young man wrote home apprehensively on what was to have been the eve of his departure at the beginning of spring, saying that even "if he didn't return any richer, he'd at least return more capable."[44] Return? He did not *depart* for another five or six months, that is, until after the campaigning season. Then, according to Baillet, he toured.[45] It is hardly surprising that he acquired neither this office nor the money for another.

Finally, on 24 June 1625, René reported to his father more or less dutifully on the last and probably most serious attempt to get himself established. This, too, was to fail. Once again, we are wholly dependent on Baillet's paraphrasing, which begins with what may very well be the misleading suggestion of happenstance:

> Being at Châtellerault, he [René] was solicited to negotiate for the charge of the *lieutenant général* of the place [by the officer himself], who found himself forced to liquidate this asset in order to buy another office for his son. He [René] was given to understand that he could have it for 16,000 *écus* [the silver equivalent of 48,000 *livres* in account money] or 50,000 *livres*.

> At first, he rejected these overtures on the pretext [Baillet's judgment?] that he couldn't put up more than 10,000 *écus* of his own money, cash down [N.B.], on a judicial office. However, he couldn't resist the importunities [N.B.] of a few friends [family?] who offered [to lend him] money at no interest [N.B.], and he promised [N.B.] to write to his father as soon as he got to Poitiers. That is just

what he did on 24 June, begging him to assist him with his counsel and to decide the matter for him.

He [René] had reason to fear that his father, who was then at Paris, would judge him incapable of filling a charge of this sort, because, having had no experience up to that point other than bearing the sword, he seemed to have come too late [when he was too old] to enter the profession of the robe. That is why he wanted to forewarn him of his own inclination to place himself with a *procureur* at the Châtelet until he had learned enough about the practice [of the law] to be able to fulfill the responsibilities of the office.

His [René's] plan was to go to see his father at Paris, as soon as he had received word from him. However, he was apprehensive about not finding him still there [if he awaited the summons], and so he left [Poitiers] by post [for Paris, where] he arrived at the beginning of July, without having awaited his [father's] response. Nevertheless, he didn't have the satisfaction of seeing his father there, because he had left a few days earlier. This, together with the [contrary] solicitations of friends who wanted him to settle in Paris, contributed not a little to ensure the failure of the Châtel-lerault affair [the judicial office] and to turn him against provincial life.[46]

This letter from René Descartes to Joachim repays the closest study. It shows what was at best ambivalence about office holding and at worst stubborn resistance or even filial disobedience. The first point is that René himself took no initiative. The officer made the first approach, apparently counting on the social substance and judicial traditions of the Ferrands, the Brochards, and now the Descartes. More interestingly, "a few friends" *importuned* René, pressing money on him without expecting interest in return. They even made him *promise* to write to his father with a request for assistance. This is hardly the behavior that we would expect from George Huppert's *rentier* "crocodiles,"[47] and it may well be that behind the importunate offers and extorted promises lurked the hidden hand of the family as defined by Mousnier: "The family is a unit for the defense of social situation and for the conquest of social advantage." Even crocodiles care for their young.[48]

A second set of related points concerns the office in question. From the perspective of others in the family, this would have been an ideal seat for the cadet son. Joachim Descartes had moved himself and the two "elder sons" of his two families, one of them younger than René, from Châtellerault to the grander world of the Parlement at Rennes. At the time, he himself was the *doyen* of the Parlement, and his son Pierre was a *conseiller* in a different chamber of the same court. He had not yet established Joachim II de Chavagne by providing him with his own charge, but that must already have been the plan.

Legal and financial obstacles make it hard to imagine that Joachim could ever have planned to place all three of his sons as *conseillers* in the Parlement; these considerations required that something else be found for René. The legal obstacle was raised by ordinances against *parenté,* or nepotism. Neither fathers and sons nor brothers could sit together on the same court.[49] Kings had said so. In practice, however, robe families managed well enough. For a hundred years after 1618, there were always two Descartes in the Parlement of Brittany. There were three in 1650–54, 1659–78, and 1691–1700.

However, it would have been very reckless indeed for Joachim Descartes to have tried to establish all three of his sons in the Parlement. Cases of two brothers sitting together are easy enough to find.[50] Three brothers would have been another matter. Success with Pierre in 1618 and then, hypothetically, with René sometime in the early 1620s would have jeopardized the chances of his son from the second bed, Joachim II de Chavagne, in the mid- or later 1620s. It was to be very difficult for Pierre Descartes to (re-)join both his brother and his son as the third *conseiller* Descartes on the court in 1650, despite the family's influential relationships.[51]

The financial obstacles were no less real. The size of Joachim's fortune in the years around 1620 is unknown,[52] but it is known that he had just purchased the estate of Jaille in 1617, that he had just provided his eldest son Pierre with an office in 1618, that he still had to arrange a suitable marriage for him, and that his own fortunate marriage to Anne Morin had obligated him to secure an establishment for a second "elder son" as well as a second daughter. Furthermore, the first twenty years or so of the century had seen a remarkable inflation in the price of higher, ennobling offices. The charge that Joachim must have purchased for nine or ten thousand *livres* in 1585 had appreciated by a factor of at least four by the 1620s.[53] This had made the acquisition of his own office a very good investment, but it also made the additional investment in any other charge that much more difficult. There was this much, at least, to be said against an office for René in the Parlement at Rennes.

There was also much to be said for the proffered office in the Présidial at Châtellerault. The *lieutenant général* in the Présidial was the single most prominent judicial officer in the town where Joachim still maintained his childhood home.[54] Michel Ferrand, René's granduncle and godfather, had held this very office there, and René Brochard, his grandfather and Jeanne Sain's husband, had been *lieutenant général* at Poitiers. For a cadet son of the judicial family who had not participated as fully as his siblings in the move to Brittany, this would have been a very responsible and honorable position in itself, and it might well have been a way station to higher office.[55]

A third set of related points concerns the terms of sale that René refused. I cannot hope to set an absolute value on this office at Châtellerault in 1625, although the *asking* price of 50,000 *livres*— with a four percent discount for cash—may have been more or less reasonable in the inflationary market.[56] René raised no objection to the price, even in a letter filled with almost every other imaginable objection. It was certainly unreasonable for René to conclude that a purchase was out of the question because he did not have the 16,000 *écus* ready in hand to commit to the office. Even supposing that the eager seller would not have settled for any less, it is the mark of a most reluctant buyer that he should ever have considered his inability to pay the full amount at the time of purchase as a decisive argument against pursuing the matter.

Mousnier's studies of completed contracts are conclusive: the buyer "almost always" spread out payments over time, with a down payment in silver, perhaps, and an agreement to meet the balance by an annual *rente* with no specified term. In the economy of the seventeenth century, with its chronic shortage of hard money and of more lucrative opportunities for honorable investment, it was "very rare" for the seller to demand anything else. "Everything transpired as if the buyer believed that he would never be able to procure the necessary capital and as if the seller was never intent on recovering this capital, which he would never have known how to reinvest."[57]

In the case at hand, the seller needed resources for the purchase of his own son's office, but this would not have changed the equations. Silver received down and *rentes* contracted for the balance *from* Descartes could simply be turned over to silver to be paid out and *rentes* for the balance offered *to* some other officeholder on the market. The great virtue of René Descartes as a potential purchaser, given such terms, was the bedrock solidity of his family's social standing in Châtellerault and the almost perfect security of *rentes* constituted by them.

Why, then, did René Descartes make such a point of the money in the letter to his father? His own 10,000 *écus* would have been more than enough, even without the interest-free loans pressed on him by the "few friends." The only explanations seem to be either that he was rather desperately looking for reasons *not* to commit himself to the office or that he was rather awkwardly requesting more money from his father, who, like the *lieutenant général*, should provide for his son. This either/or need not have been fully rational or rigorously exclusive; imperatives of personal autonomy could have mixed with the bribery of filial dependence.

The rest of the letter also suggests ambivalence at best, evasiveness at worst: his *father would judge against him;* his own *inexperience would disqualify him;* he was *a man of the sword, not the robe;* he was *already too old;* he would have to *defer still longer until after he had served a legal internship;* he would *wait for word from the father, the conseiller, at Poitiers;* he would *leave without that word to seek him out at Paris.* . . . In the event, he did not have the "satisfaction" of finding him there, and he did not pursue him back to Brittany. As Baillet explains it, it was René's friends, not his father, who had the last word, advising him against the provincial office.[58]

Am I making too much of this letter? Joachim Descartes would not have thought so. He certainly received it and kept it, because his descendants, the Breton Descartes, had it to give to Baillet. This was the right office in the right place at the right time, or a little past it. The *lieutenant général* was the principal magistrate in the lower court, and for the cadet son to have acquired this legal office would have been for him to have continued familial traditions honorably. There is, however, no record of any answer to a son who must have seemed to be drifting toward his thirties without lands, office, or marriage, because that was his own (wrongheaded) way. His father had done his best for him, in keeping with his other responsibilities. The 10,000 *ecus* that René acknowledged as ready money in 1625 was exactly twice Jeanne's dowry in 1613, and it can only have come from the family.

Now to return to 1619, the year of the Olympian dreams. This was before René's majority and his acquisition of familial capital, but he was already twenty-three years old, headed for twenty-four, and it was time for him to give serious thought to his future. Twenty-five was then the minimum age according to the ordinances, not twenty-seven as assumed by Sigismond Ropartz in 1875, and we have it on the very good authority of La Roche Flavin, writing in 1617, that the good judges lent one another's sons three or four years more readily than they would have lent them three or four hundred *ecus*.[59] Mousnier's calculations show the ineffectiveness of royal attempts to require greater maturity and experience: in the Châtelet at Paris from 1660 to 1700, which was the level of the Présidials elsewhere, entering judicial officers *averaged* 22 years and 10 months; in the Parlement of Paris from 1690 to 1791, which was the most elevated court in all of France, they averaged just 22 years and 7 months.[60] Table 10 shows that Joachim the patriarch and four or five of the other ten judges on my charts of the Descartes dynasty were established in office before they were twenty-five years old.

What was René's *qualité* in 1619? Was he a nobleman of the robe? Not exactly. A nobleman of the sword? Even less. He was a cadet son of a first-generation nobleman of the robe, one who had lost his natural place even as second son of the first bed when his father had sired the second Joachim in the second bed. He may already have resented the relatively privileged positions of his two brothers, the elder full brother and the younger half brother. In the provisional morality that he purports to have drafted for himself in this winter, he makes stoic resignation one of only three maxims, and he uses the unjust deprivation of birthrights as his most prominent example of a situation demanding this philosophical response. Furthermore, in later correspondence, writing after his father's death about the unjust division of the estate, he bitterly

Table 10.
Ages of Parlementary Officers at the Time of Provision

20	21	22	23	24	25	26	27	28	29
4		1,10,11	6	3(?)		9	2,5,8		7

1. Joachim I de Chavagne, the patriarch: age 22 when *pourvu* and *réçu*.
2. Pierre de Kerleau: age 26 when *pourvu* and *réçu*.
3. Joachim II de Chavagne: ca. 24 when *pourvu;* ca. 26 when *réçu*.
4. Joachim de Kerleau: age 20 when *pourvu* and *réçu*.
5. François Rogier: age 26 when *pourvu* and *réçu*.
6. Joachim III de Chavagne: age 23 when *pourvu;* 23 or 24 when *réçu*.
7. Anne-Louis Ferré: age 29 when *pourvu* and *réçu*.
8. François-Joachim de Kerleau: age 26 when *pourvu*.
9. Jean-Baptiste de Rosnyvinen: age 25 when *pourvu;* 26 when *réçu*.
10. François-Louis-Joachim Ferré: age 22 when *pourvu* and *réçu*.
11. René-Jacques-Louis Le Prestre: age 22 when *pourvu*.

compared his elder brother to a "wolf," reserving for himself the role of a "lamb" smart enough to retreat from wolfish attacks. Such resentment may have been cultivated over long time.[61]

We must wonder about bitterness against even the patriarch himself. Remarkably, René the autobiographer omitted father and mother from his story in the *Discourse*. More remarkably, René the philosopher committed a worse crime of *lèse-parenté* when he reasoned away his still-living father as well his too-early dead mother in the *Meditations*. *His* lineage began and ended with God:

> I ask, from whom could I have had my existence [if not from God]? Could it have been from myself or from my parents? [No.] . . .
>
> . . . Perhaps that being upon whom I am dependent is not that which I call God, and I have been produced either by my parents or by some other less perfect cause? Not at all, that cannot be. For . . . there must be at least as much reality in the cause as in the effect. And, since I am a thinking thing with an idea of God . . .
>
> . . . With respect to my parents, to whom it seems that I owe my birth, even if everything that I have ever believed were true, nevertheless, that would not mean that it is they who conserve me, nor who have made and produced me insofar as I am a thinking thing. They have only put a few dispositions in this matter [my

111

body], in which I judge that I, that is, my mind, which I now regard as my only true self, finds itself embodied.[62]

Descartes defied the moral wisdom of his culture when he effectively denied origin from, dependence on, or obligation to his "parents," for which we may read "father." Joachim was alive when these lines were written, although, mercifully, he would die before they were published. René had been summoned home from Holland to visit the old man in Brittany, but he never made the trip intended for the summer of 1640. His last letter to his father, expressing "every assurance of the respect and obedience that he owed him" and "his intense desire to see him again [after over a decade of voluntary exile] to ask for his orders and his blessings," was dated at Leiden on 28 October 1640, eight days after Joachim's burial at Nantes.[63]

What had René owed Joachim? To answer that question in a way that is true to the early seventeenth century, let me take up once again Pierre Charron's *De la sagesse* from René's own table. Children's obligations to their parents were once so obvious, so absolute, and so all-encompassing that this wordiest teacher of Christian humanism could settle the matter in a few sentences:

> We come now to the duty of children to parents, which is so natural and so religious, and which ought not to be performed as if to [mere] men, pure and simple, but as if to demigods, to terrestrial divinities, mortal and visible. According to Philo the Jew, that is why the Commandment on the duty of children was written half on the first table, which holds the Commandments that concern obligations to God, and half on the second table, where are listed the Commandments that concern our obligations to our neighbors. [Thus, the parent] is half divine, half human. This [filial] duty is so certain, so strict, and so absolute that nothing else, however great, whether duty or love, can ever dispense us from it or supersede it.[64]

The "natural" and "religious" imperatives that governed every child's relationship with his or her parents seemed so certain, in fact, that Charron could gloss the Fourth Commandment quickly. A son owes his parents reverence, obedience, and support. He should never do anything at all of any importance without their advice, consent, and approval, and he should put up with any parental bitterness, vexation, severity, or rigor.[65]

112

We are very poorly informed about this father-son relationship, but what little we are told does suggest that Joachim Descartes was bitter, vexed, severe, and rigorous in the judgment that he passed on the son who would become most famous and on the life and works that would earn him that fame. The father lived to see this son's first publication, but he was not pleased. Indeed, his reaction was quite the contrary. He objected to his son's whole way of life as a searcher for truth and maker of books rather than to any particular sin of commission or omission in the *Discourse*. His descendants reported that he had been "very angry to see that his son was devoting himself to the study of philosophy, to the point of writing books." They attributed to him these memorable words: "Of all my children, only one is a disappointment. To think that *I* should have given to the world a son so ridiculous as to have himself bound in *calfskin!*"[66]

6

Isaac Beeckman and the Search for Truth

In February 1618, Joachim Descartes resumed his seat in the Parlement at Rennes, where his eldest son, Pierre, joined him for the first time.[1] René, who had been with the family at Chavagne in the fall and early winter, chose this inclement season to travel to Breda, a garrison town occupied by Dutch troops under Maurice of Nassau. He would spend fifteen months there in arms as an unpaid, unenrolled volunteer.[2] How father and son together settled on this plan is not recorded, but there is no need to consider it a definitive choice of arms over the law.

Within the calendar year, Descartes was already eager to distinguish himself from the ignorant soldiers around him,[3] and, at the beginning of the next campaigning season, he was to set off on independent travels that lacked any apparent military rationale.[4] His closest known approach to the great events of the Thirty Years' War was to observe the coronation ceremonies for Ferdinand II.[5] Much later, when threatened by intolerant Protestants, he would claim to have carried arms to deliver the Dutch from the Spanish Inquisition.[6] However, this self-serving reference to his brief and amateurish association with Protestant forces during an interval of peace is as exceptional as it is misleading. When he considered the vocation "as a philosopher," he denied that the "warrior's trade" was the noblest of all occupations or even that it should be allowed a place among the "honorable professions."[7]

It was during the period of Descartes's nominal soldiering at

Breda in 1618–19, from before his twenty-second birthday until after his twenty-third, that he began to consider himself a philosopher. This tentative identity was formed in the course of an intense relationship with Isaac Beeckman, an obscure chandler from Middelburg who had never published, never shown anyone his manuscripts, and never even spoken with anyone about his own "philosophical" interests. But if anyone would have asked, Beeckman would have had something to say. In 1613–14, it was he who first made the leap from antique notions to a modern law of inertia: "Everything, once in motion, [continues in motion], never coming to rest unless on account of an external impediment."[8] In 1615, it was he who first demonstrated experimentally that the quantity of water passing through a hole in the bottom of a vessel varies as the square root of the height of the water in the vessel.[9] And in 1616–18, it was he who first gave an accurate explanation of the action and limitation of pumps based on atomistic conceptions of water and air pressure.[10]

Beeckman's formal studies had included both theology and medicine. In the last months of 1618, he passed his thirtieth birthday. He had arrived at Breda on 16 October with two definite objectives: to lend his hand to the now-forgotten work of a now-forgotten uncle, Peter, and to pursue an unnamed love interest, perhaps Cateline de Cerf.[11] It was soon after his arrival there that he first encountered the "Frenchman from Poitou" on 10 November, and he remained there only until 2 January 1619. Within the new year he would secure an appointment as a teacher in the Latin school at Utrecht, and in a year and a half he would marry Cateline at Middelburg. All this is recorded in his *Journal,* the edited version of notebooks that he himself called *tafelboeckje,* or "Table Books."[12]

Between 11 November 1618 and 2 January 1619, the Dutch savant devoted fourteen entries in his notebooks to Descartes and his thought.[13] He also included transcriptions of three papers in which the twenty-two-year-old Frenchman had responded to his questions on music, mechanics, and hydrostatics.[14] Finally, and most importantly for my purposes, he kept copies of six letters from the winter and spring of 1619, a correspondence occasioned by his own departure from Breda for his return to Middelburg at the beginning of January and Descartes's departure for travels into Germany at the end of April.[15]

Intellectual Inspiration and Personal Devotion

I begin with Beeckman's fourteen journal entries, which I number by the marginal indications of content that the author added after the fact. In the earliest entries, young Descartes makes his appearance as an intellectual gamesman overeager to win attention and approval by asserting and defending the most outrageous propositions. It is hard to know how else to regard a geometer who tries to prove that angles do not exist. Beeckman recorded both the paradoxical argument of the "Frenchman from Poitou" and his own critical response, nothing more.[16]

Second, sometime between 17 November and 23 November, Beeckman noted in Flemish his own speculations on the physical principles that could explain why spinning tops remain upright. Then he continued in Latin with the related flight of "René, the Poitevin." This foreigner, now named, had said that, given the right sort of spinning hollow vessel, he could hold himself upright and unsupported, hovering if not quite soaring:

> Hence René the Poitevin gave me occasion to ponder that a man might be able to hold himself suspended in air. If he were to sit in a round vessel, this could be turned on its axis very quickly by a specially made machine or by a man sitting on it, who could move [rotate] it with his hands alone, an easy task on account of the small resistance. The [spinning] vessel would then [incline and] fall slowly, so that, by means of another instrument [?], having been moved by only a little force, the air could raise the whole vessel [?]. But the man may sit under the vessel [that is, within it?] or under the center of gravity, so that he himself might hang from the center point in the middle from one straight line [the axis] and not himself be turned in circles with the vessel.[17]

A dizzying thought, if true. Wonderful, even if not!

The other twelve entries, written between 23 November 1618 and 2 January 1619, provide better if less spectacular evidence of a more substantial relationship. The more mature Beeckman had varied scientific interests, and he could challenge the greater genius with questions more fruitful than whether a giant top could serve as a primitive hovercraft. He also offered the example of his own mechanistic physics, served as the attentive and appreciative reader of his friend's drafts, and perhaps most importantly, encouraged him to continue his work and exhorted him to publish his writings.[18]

Within a few weeks of their first meeting, the two men paid exceptional tribute to one another. Sometime after 23 November, Beeckman made this entry on "the very few *Physico-mathematici*": "This Poitevin is familiar with many Jesuits and with other learned men. Nevertheless, he says that he has never met anyone else, other than me, who accurately joins physics and mathematics in his studies in the way that pleases me. And as for me, I, too, [can say that I] have never spoken to anyone other than him about this sort of study."[19] Beeckman's willingness even to discuss his interests with Descartes was thus a unique gesture of intellectual respect. He went further when he opened his notebooks to the young foreigner, something else that he had never done before and would do again only for Marin Mersenne in 1630 and Martinus Hortensius in 1634.[20]

Descartes followed the example of his older friend when, on Beeckman's departure, he, too, began keeping a scientific journal of sorts, his little notebook bound in parchment. It is Geneviéve Rodis-Lewis's very attractive speculation that Descartes's Little Notebook, which was to hold the *Olympica,* was the gift of Isaac Beeckman when the friends parted at New Year's, 1619.[21] It is certain that Descartes presented his *Compendium musicae* to Beeckman as a parting gift, dating it 31 December 1618; he *or Beeckman* dated the Little Notebook 1 January 1619.[22] Leibniz's notes show that the first dossier in the Little Notebook, series 1, the *Parnassus,* began with a thinly veiled tribute to Beeckman as "a man of the greatest genius," followed by an attempt to answer a question concerning free-fall posed by the mathematical physicist. Then came other drafts on other topics also of particular concern to the same mentor.[23]

Descartes was never to be a slavish imitator, of course, but even after he ceased to correspond with his friend, he seems to have followed Beeckman's ways in small matters as well as great. Consider the apparent idiosyncrasies of the more personal series 2 from his Little Notebook in the light of the very similar aspects of Beeckman's Table Books. Descartes's series 2 began with a grand title, the *Praeambula,* and a Biblical maxim on the beginning of wisdom; Beeckman, too, dignified his manuscripts with titles and began with moralistic commonplaces.[24] Descartes left blank pages after he completed or suspended work on a dossier, and he intrigued and confused readers of the *Olympica* with his year-after marginal notation on "the foundation of the wonderful discovery" at the head of the document; Beeckman, too, left blanks, and he more frequently returned to earlier work to add marginal summations.[25] Descartes added the self-analytical cogitations in the *Praeambula* and the *Experimenta* and the historical record of his dreams in the *Olympica* to his Little Notebook of physical-mathematical drafts; Beeckman, too, included personalia lacking any strictly scientific rationale in his Table Books, not just factual information on family matters or employment but also, more rarely, introspective entries.[26]

The first surviving letter from Descartes, which may well have been the first sent, is dated 24 January 1619. It is the best evidence on the quality of the relationship. The two men shared scientific interests, but their relationship went beyond the intellect to the heart. Descartes himself professes love:

> I have received the letter from you that I was awaiting. At first glance I had the pleasure of seeing musical notation. You couldn't offer any better evidence that you haven't forgotten me. But I was also expecting something else, something still more important. Tell me, what have you been doing, what are you doing, and how are you? For, believe me, I am interested not just in your sciences, but in you yourself, and not just in your mind, although that's the main thing, but in the whole man.
>
> As for me, ever idle as is my wont, I have scarcely entitled the books that you tell me I should write. [Then come brief references to his lesser occupations: the study of painting, fortification, and Flemish. He promises a visit to Beeckman at Middelburg. The body of the letter responds to a musical question posed by Beeckman.] But enough of that. Some other time, I'll say more. Meanwhile, love me and rest assured that I could no more forget you than I could forget the Muses themselves. For by them, I have been united with you in the everlasting bond of love.[27]

Beeckman must have written a relatively impersonal letter of thanks for the *Compendium musicae,* adding discussion of some technical points. Descartes wanted something different and something more.

He wanted to be remembered and to be loved—and to express his own love and to hear news of his dear friend. He writes as if the sciences were of special importance to him because of Beeckman, not Beeckman because of the sciences.

The second letter from Descartes, dated 26 March 1619, serves as particularly good evidence of Beeckman's continued power to inspire Descartes's thought, but it also displays aspects of the latter's personality that would almost inevitably have doomed the relationship even without any other complications. Beeckman was apparently the first to arouse Descartes's ambitions as a philosopher and scientist, to discipline his pointless and free-floating imagination, and to sanction his vocation as an aspiring author of innovative books. Cardinal Bérulle and Pére Mersenne played this very important role in much later years, but it appears that Beeckman alone offered appreciation and encouragement in the crucial formative period. On 20 March 1619, Descartes returned from a visit to Beeckman at Middelburg; just six days later, this confessed idler could report back that his renewed zeal had brought him to the verge of a new and universal mathematics, this being the first glimmer of what would become, when he sat down again for steady work the following November, the illumination of a universal method. This much seems clear enough from the recent work of John Schuster.[28]

But there is more. Descartes's letter of 26 March 1619 must have offended the very man who had so recently inspired him. First, Descartes seems almost casually to have set aside the joint work on mechanics, although the letter may not fairly represent the state of the project and the discussions at Middelburg.[29] Second, and more certainly, he proclaims that his new geometry can be accomplished only by one man working alone, thus declaring his absolute independence of and superiority to Beeckman, who was no geometer.[30] Third, with "incredible" arrogance, not mere ambition, he claims for himself Beeckman's prior work on navigation and the determination of longitude; vaguely boasts of his own sudden insight concerning the possible use of stellar observations; pointedly wonders why others should not have reached the same easy conclusions; ignorantly supposes that sailors at sea could make exact measurements of degrees, minutes, seconds, and less; and then, to top it all, presumptuously asks *Beeckman* to reassure him that *he,* Descartes, was the first to have considered this not-so-happy idea.[31]

The third letter, dated 20 April 1619, is the briefest, but it suggests several points of the greatest interest: "I didn't want to send this messenger [whose main function, he hoped, would be to collect a letter from Beeckman] without a letter, although I don't have time enough now to write any more. Please answer me by the bearer, my servant. How are you? What are you doing? Are you still planning to get married? To the same girl? I'm going to be leaving next Wednesday, as soon as my messenger returns. I wrote a longer letter three weeks ago. Farewell and love me."[32] First, Descartes seems to have been more passionately devoted to Beeckman than was Beeckman to Descartes. The younger man had presented the best gifts he had to offer; he had eagerly awaited a response in kind; he had answered a disappointingly impersonal first letter with his own pledge of undying love; he had gone to visit Beeckman on the island of Walcheren, although he had never before ventured "to sea," a matter of evident concern;[33] and now he asked after his friend and bid the first of what would be three successive epistolary farewells before setting off on his own more distant travels. Second, Beeckman was very actively pursuing his courtship in his native Middelburg, which was also the home of his future bride, Cateline de Cerf.[34] This letter clearly implies that, when Descartes visited him if not before, Beekman had informed him of his intentions to marry. In fact, he did marry a year later, whereas Descartes would never marry. Third, Beeckman had not yet answered Descartes's most enthusiastic but, to say the least, insensitive letter of mathematical discovery, dated 26 March.

Taken together, these two letters, Descartes's second and third, document the intensity of his attachment and suggest strains that would doom the relationship. Descartes's genius raced ahead alone, conscious of his own "incredible ambition" but apparently oblivious of his slights to his less-gifted mentor, Beeckman. No less importantly, Beeckman advanced if not raced toward marriage, a settled household, and increasing commitment to steady employment as, not incidentally, a schoolteacher, all of which drew him away from Descartes.[35]

In the fourth letter, written just three days after the third, 23

April 1619, a somewhat dispirited Descartes does acknowledge a response from Beeckman. On the eve of his final departure, he sent new assurances of a "lasting friendship"—if not of an undying love. He says that he has not accomplished anything "for a month" and warns that "our Muse" will have to fall silent for the sake of his forthcoming travels. He does not really know where he is going, and he fears to encounter lots of troops but no battles, a dangerous combination for the lone traveler. If he stops somewhere, he will try to put in order one of two books, either "my *Mechanics*," which had been "our *Mechanics*" a month earlier, or "my *Geometry*," in which Beeckman could never have shared fully. He retreats somewhat from claims on behalf of his work on navigation, but he defends the worth of his new work on geometry, having admitted that he has in hand only bits and pieces too fragmentary to send. Some day, he will achieve "a whole work," something "new and not to be despised."[36]

In this context René Descartes offers *his* most gracious tribute to Isaac Beeckman. Someone else might have managed the gesture without the arrogance that threatens to spoil even this offering. Nevertheless, such as it is, here it is:

> If, as I hope, I stop somewhere, I promise you that I shall undertake to put my *Mechanics* or my *Geometry* in order, and *I shall honor you as the first mover of my studies and their first author.* For, truly, you alone have roused me from my idleness and recalled to me what I had learned and already almost forgotten. When my mind had strayed so far from serious occupations, you led it back to better things. Therefore, *if by chance I produce anything of merit, you can rightfully claim all of it as yours.* As for me, I shall not forget to send it to you, not only so that you can use it, but also so that you can correct it.[37]

For Beeckman, there must have been almost as much to regret as to savor in this letter, even given its "most gracious tribute." First, Descartes's initial "promise" of work on the books is conditional and so not a promise at all, but an awkward reminder that, for him, wandering came before working. Second, the younger man's seemingly innocent reference to "my *Mechanics*," with the possessive pronoun a first-person singular, actually appropriates for himself alone the subject that had first been *Beeckman's*, then a common concern of the two friends together. Beeckman would surely have preferred to read that his friend had been working productively on projects of mutual interest and would continue to do so, but Descartes could neither please him in this respect nor refrain from displeasing him in others.

Third, immediately after his deepest bow to the older man as the "first mover" and "first author" of his studies, Descartes straightens abruptly to make a potentially offensive counterclaim for what, *without* Beeckman and *before* Beeckman, he had *already* "learned and *already almost* forgotten." Fourth, quite similarly, immediately after the next italicized tribute, Descartes's generous offer that Beeckman could rightfully claim as his own any meritorious work from his correspondent, he also says that Beeckman's could "use" it and should "correct" it. The suggestion of use risks condescension in the implication that the junior author will surely teach his senior mentor just what the latter has wanted to know. In addition, the seemingly contrary expectation of correction may actually be as much imposition on a presumed inferior — "fix it up" — as it is submission to an equal or a superior — "tell me what is wrong." Nothing is simple.

Descartes's letter ends with a melancholy paragraph on his month-long "exhaustion" and his lack of the energy even to attempt further discoveries: "But I shall always remember you."[38] Descartes did remember Beeckman, but he betrayed his own arrogance even in his parting acknowledgment of indebtedness as a thinker, and his pride may not have been the only problem. It is common to focus on Descartes and the intellectual itinerary that would lead him to the heated chamber, barely noticing that the "peripheral" friend had already left Breda at the beginning of the year. Descartes's own perspective must have been quite different, wherever he thought he was going. Socially and emotionally, it was *Beeckman* who had left him.

The Mentor's Rebuke and an Unphilosophical Passion

Respect for the two men and the friendship that they shared makes me almost reluctant to continue. The fifth letter, from Descartes to Beeckman on 29 April 1619, is an embarrassment, but together with the sixth, from Beeckman to Descartes one week later, it is an essential part of the story. This exchange seems to have ended the relationship for almost a decade. Apparently, neither man wrote again or visited the other until 8 October 1628. Then, Descartes tried to find Beeckman in Middelburg, which probably means that, "rolling here and there" in the interim, he had not known even about Beeckman's successive teaching appointments at Utrecht (27 November 1619), Rotterdam (26 November 1620), and Dordrecht (20 February 1627).[39] It is not easy to terminate such attachments, however; perhaps it is not possible. Descartes must have thought of Beeckman when he finally stopped in the heated chamber and—as he had promised to his friend—turned his mind back toward the sciences that he had begun to pursue seriously a year earlier, as the follower and companion of his friend.

The embarrassment of Descartes's letter is double. First, he dignifies with his philosophical attention what can only have been barroom braggadocio. On the first stage of his travels, before embarking at Dordrecht, he met "a learned man" at an inn. This "old man" boasted that his knowledge of Ramón Llull's *Ars brevis* enabled him "to talk on any subject at all for a whole hour." On demand, he said, he could talk for another hour without repeating himself, then still another, and so on, up to "twenty hours in a row." Descartes expressed doubts, but he was curious, especially after the old man added that he also knew "certain keys" that had not been revealed by Llull or his commentator, Cornelius Agrippa. Descartes himself probably never read the *Ars brevis,* which he calls the *Ars parva,* but he had already declared to Beeckman his own intention of surpassing Llull, and here was someone else who professed to have done so, adding the "keys" to the "art."[40] The old man might be only another learned fool, but the young man was not quite sure.[41] Had he been beaten? He did not know. It was most disconcerting.

The second embarrassment is that Descartes's solution to his problem was to continue on his travels, assigning the reading to Beeckman. If the travels were so important, it would have been better for him to have shelved the research project until he had the occasion to do the reading himself. Alternatively, if the reading was so important, it would have been better for him to have postponed his departure or to have planned a layover in a major city so that he could find the book and read it himself. Instead, abusing a friendship, he asked his mentor to serve as his research assistant. Beeckman need not rush his report, Descartes wrote, but he would be meeting every ship as it arrived at Copenhagen, looking for his letter. . . . After all, Beeckman was so intelligent that it would be easy for him to find out what was in the "art" and, please remember, what was not, the "keys." Why, Beeckman himself had told him to keep in touch on his researches into learned subjects. Well, then. "I have nothing more to add, except this: Love me, and be happy."[42]

The most charitable explanation of this pathetic letter is that Descartes was still reluctant to leave Beeckman far behind and that he was really demanding a last sign of love to take with him, without caring very much about whatever his more bookish friend might be able to discover by the scholarly labor that he himself so consistently disdained or affected to disdain. In any case, Beeckman did respond promptly, and his letter does include explicit as well as implicit testimonials of affection for Descartes, whom he calls "my friend in more than the ordinary sense."[43]

Nevertheless, his letter also betrays his impatience. He grumbles a bit about the old man, the task imposed, the lack of time, and the uncertainty of posting a letter to Copenhagen without knowing whether the vessel carrying it will arrive before the addressee has departed. Then, he does his best to oblige his friend, even offering to try again, if what he has sent is not sufficient. He does better. Beeckman utters a pious hope for a union of minds in terms that also suggest bodies: "May God grant us to live together long enough to penetrate to the very navel in the field of studies." He adds the sort of things that any older man would say to any younger traveler: Keep well; be careful. And he reminds *this* traveler of his commitments: Remember the book, the *Mechanics!* You have promised! Then, attempting a sort of humor, he laments: If only you had set a deadline![44]

Perhaps Beeckman should have stopped here or added only some chatty nonsense about whatever he was doing. He did not restrain himself, however. Instead, he kept on preaching, contrasting his notion of what Descartes should have been doing, settling down to write his book on Beeckman's subject, mechanics, with his notion of what Descartes was in fact doing, "wandering about," or "turning around and around," or "turning hither and thither," or perhaps even "spinning in circles in the capital city of that kingdom." While he is there, Beeckman says, and wherever else he goes, he should improve his mind in every way possible. Beeckman explains the ways, then signs off.[45] Even this much from the preacher-teacher may have been too much for an unproductive and hypersensitive reader.

But then Beeckman added a postscript in the form of a modern-day parable. If Descartes did receive it, he may never have forgiven its author:

> There came here from your homeland a certain Frenchman, who professed in public the finest arts, [how to make] fountains from which the water runs perpetually, [secrets] of war and of medicine, [and] ways to multiply the supply of daily bread—although he himself was utterly destitute. I went to see him, and, when I examined him, he turned out to be completely ignorant of everything, even those things that he was professing publicly. So he won't stand the test [here], and we must send him farther north, where the numbskulls welcome illusionists and charlatans.[46]

Descartes had three choices: (1) he could suppose that the story of the "certain Frenchman" was literally true; (2) he could suppose that it was a parable based loosely on his true story of the old Llullist; or (3) he could suppose that it was a fictionalized version of the true impression first made by the "Frenchman from Poitou" himself. Any choice meant a sharp rebuke.

The origin and destination of the charlatan in the parable suggest that the third choice and sharpest rebuke is the the one most likely intended. Recall Beeckman's first encounters, forgetting for the moment that Descartes was later to vindicate himself as a thinker. The young Frenchman had presented himself as a mere trickster, attempting to demonstrate that angles do not exist and suggesting that he could levitate in a giant top.[47] What other wonders had Beeckman heard but not taken seriously enough to record at the time or to copy out later? In what little survives from the *Experimenta*, Descartes entertains us with his love of "natural magic," flashing through a light show full of illusions and mirror tricks (CP 47–63).[48] In the *Recherche de la vérité*, the gentleman-savant who represents him boasts: "Having made you admire the most powerful machines, the most rare automata, the most convincing visions, and the most subtle impostures that artifice can invent, I shall reveal to you the secrets. They are so simple and natural that you will find them in the most wonderful works of our hands."[49]

Did Descartes receive this letter, preserved only as a copy in Beeckman's *Journal*? Again, there is no good choice. Either Descartes did receive the obliging but also preaching and censuring letter from the man whose approval and affection he courted, or he did not receive the help that he had requested and the love that he had sought and so was left to wander about, turn around, or spin in circles on his own.

This brings me to Descartes's next known letters to Beeckman, written in 1630. They must be related to the story of the earlier friendship because there is no possible way of accounting for their passionate fury without looking further back than 1628, when, with work in hand, Descartes again sought out his old friend after a decade of separation. Given Descartes's great stature and Beeckman's lesser place in history, perhaps I should repeat that the latter was no fool. In the previous year, Pierre Gassendi, then traveling in Holland, had praised him as "the finest philosopher I have met."[50] In the very year of Descartes's terrible letters, "he established the first meteorological station in Europe, recording wind velocity and direction, rainfall, and temperature." The relationship between air pressure and weather had not been discovered, but Beeckman deserves a place in the history of this science, too.[51]

Descartes was in no mood to list credits when he sent what amounted to letter bombs. His anger was never more explosive. The occasion for his first outburst was the rumor that Beeckman, then the rector of the Latin school at Dordrecht, had spoken publicly as if he had once taught something about music to Descartes, who had not established himself by any institutional affiliation or by any learned publication. But can such slight provocation account for the great rage of this letter?

> Let me give you a bit of advice. If you boast of having taught anything to anyone, even if what you say is true, that's odious. But when what you say is not true, that's still more odious. And, finally, if you have learned from him the very thing that you claim to have taught him, that is the most odious of all. But the civility of my

French manners must have deceived you [as a Dutch boor]. Because I have often told you, both orally and in writing, that I had learned a great deal from you and even that I hoped to profit still more from your observations [on my written work], you probably didn't think that you were wronging me by confirming in your conversations what I myself had already admitted publicly.

As for me, I care very little about all of that, but, out of deference to our former friendship, I want to warn you that when *you* boast of something like this in the presence of those who know *me*, you do great harm to your own reputation. For don't imagine that they will believe anything at all of what you are saying. Instead, believe me, they will mock you for your vanity. And it won't do you any good to show them the testimonials that I have given you in my letters. For there is no one who doesn't know that I habitually draw instruction even from the ants and the worms, and they will never believe that I could ever have learned anything from you in any other way.[52]

This first explosive letter, written in September or October 1630, was followed by a second on 17 October. Beeckman's letters to Descartes, affecting or seeming to affect a master-pupil tone, were now the intolerable provocation. Now, the angry philosopher would not rest content with wounding comparisons to ants and worms, although the ants and the worms are back again, this time with reinforcements: "If you reflect carefully on this [what Descartes teaches about what Beeckman cannot have taught], you will easily see that you couldn't have taught me any more by the dreams of your Mathematical Physics than by the *Batrachomyomachia*."[53] The former, or course, was Beeckman's innovative "discipline," by which he had in fact inspired Descartes. The latter was the Homeric mock-epic taught to Dutch schoolchildren in their first year, "The Battle of the Frogs and the Mice."[54]

Wounding was not enough. Descartes tried to plunge his pen into his former friend's heart. Teacher-Beeckman could not have been so stupid as to think that *he* could ever have taught *Descartes* anything at all. The only possible explanation was that the doctor-Beeckman who thought so must have been sick, crazy, demented. Therefore, Descartes adopted a doctor-patient tone. Hearing only the one man raving on and on, we turn away.

The importance of these letters from 1630 is that they stand as monuments to the force of the attachment and the pains of the separation in 1618–19. Next to Joachim Descartes, Isaac Beeckman was the most important person in René's life. The philosopher had rejected the judicial offices of his father's world in favor of the search for truth that defined his friend's world. But then, spurned and scolded even by this dearest friend and mentor, he turned again, as he was to say about the years between 1620 and 1628, "to roll here and there in the world."[55]

PART FOUR

PARTICULAR DREAM ELEMENTS AND A PARTICULAR'S ASSOCIATIONS

y hypothesis is that Descartes's Olympian dreams concerned his rejection of the law in favor of a life to be spent in "the search for truth" using the new method of his egocentric rationalism. His crisis was as much vocational as philosophical, and what he narrated in the *Discourse* as if it had been a simple, solitary decision was in fact complicated by uneasy relationships with other persons: his father, the *conseiller* Joachim Descartes, and his friend, the savant Isaac Beeckman. The formulation of this hypothesis, as such, rests on ordinary historical inquiry into particular dates, past experiences, social situations, and personal relationships. The verification of the hypothesis, however, requires a psychohistorical analysis of the particular meanings of particular dream elements for the particular dreamer.

Various sources from the seventeenth century provide evidence on these associative meanings. First, there are what I call Descartes's Olympian interpretations. Taken at face value, they have seemed either regrettable or risible, depending on the reader's general sympathy with or antipathy to Cartesian thought. Nevertheless, they provide partially spontaneous, partially reflective commentary by the awakened dreamer on the several elements of his dreams. Descartes's answers provide necessary if not sufficient documentation, true associations if not the free associations of psychoanalytical theory.

The principal limitations of Descartes's interpretive remarks as preserved are that they are doubly or triply selective. They omit most dream elements.[1] Even when they do include an association for an element, they omit the further links from what might have been, hypothetically, more instructive chains of associations (dream element 1 → association 1a → association 1b → association 1c, etc.).[2] More generally, they omit the details of personal experience that could have brought his soaring spirit down to earth, had he known to analyze his dreams as the products of his own mind.

Second, there are scattered clues in the manuscripts and published texts most directly concerned with the young Descartes and his thinking. Beeckman's *Journal* contains very suggestive materials, although they have never been exploited by anyone with even minimal competence in dream psychology. Leibniz's *Cogitationes Privatae,* particularly excerpts from the *Praeambula* and the *Experimenta,* provide a highly selective but also highly reliable record of matters of particular interest and importance to Descartes in the period just before the dreams. The *Regulae* includes some texts that seem to come from just about this time and to pertain to the themes of the dreams as understood by Descartes himself. Finally, the *Discourse,* that most familiar little tract, has much more to teach students of the *Olympica.*

The principal limitation of these materials is that they all tend to simplify complex experience by reducing the young man to his formal thought, as if René Descartes really had been that disembodied phantom of his philosophical imagination, "a thinking thing." This is especially true of Descartes's own writings, the *Regulae* and the *Discourse,* but Leibniz also shared this reductive tendency, and even Beeckman was so impressed by the thinker that he says disappointingly little about the man of flesh and blood.

Third, there are various materials from the culture and the society that Descartes shared with other similarly educated persons of his place and time. Dictionaries are great repositories of past denotations and connotations, of formal culture and folk-wisdom, too. Additionally, all Christian humanists shared canonical texts, which are still accessible, some of them particularly relevant to prominent dream elements, especially the two poems of Ausonius (DE III.5, 13; DE III.6, 8, 10, 12). Finally, students of the law, for all its diversity, shared a common *Corpus* and were trained in similar ways, which can instruct us in the arts and sciences of the dream book encountered at DE III.4 and opened at DE III.5.

The principal limitation of such materials, of course, is that they are common, not particular. Therefore, I must accept the entire burden of relating them to Descartes and to his dream thoughts. That I present an argument despite these several sorts of limitation does imply confidence in its strength when tested by non-Cartesian standards. I do not presume to advance rationally from the starting point of hyperbolical doubt, step by measured step, to a perfectly certain conclusion. I do suppose that I can progress empirically from a historical hypothesis about the dreamer, by way of a series of disconnected inquiries into the particular associations of the particular dream elements, to a final point from which I can venture probabilistic judgments on the meaning of the dreams and the foundations of the Cartesian enterprise itself.

Descartes really does seem to have supposed that his rule of *évidence* represented a human possibility, that he could doubt away all others' opinions *and* all of his own prior opinions. He does seem to have supposed that he could treat all questions as if they were geometrical propositions, to be divided abstractly into little parts and reordered into a stepwise progression from the simple to the complex. He even seems to have supposed that he himself could accomplish the requisite critical review of his own thinking.[3] The great mathematician was wrong on every count. The initial irony of his egocentric rationalism is that so much of his presumption at the crucial moment of his decisive break seems to have rested on the infirm foundation of irrational dreams. The further irony is that these dreams can now be shown to have made sense, a sense unknown to the dreamer-thinker, a sense that explodes the pretensions of his scientist philosophy. Descartes supposed that he could reason away his own historical past, his social relationships, and any psychological complications. He was wrong.

7

DREAM I AND
DREAM II

Descartes's last word was that Dreams I and II had conveyed disturbing "warnings and threats concerning his past life" (VDC 200–205). Interpretation I, and perhaps also Interpretation II in its initial terror, takes a similarly dark view of the first two dreams, but neither interpretation says anything definite about any dream element or about any wrongdoing in that past life (VDC 73–82, 90). Interpretation III.3 does add remarks on the gift melon, the contrary wind, and the thunderclap, but these remarks come down to arbitrary afterthoughts that fail to explain the "warnings and threats" (VDC 213–35). No wonder readers of the *Olympica* as a whole have thrown up their hands! What they have not done is to reconsider particular dream elements in the light of particular associations derived from other sources.

Dream I: The Street Scene and the School Scene

Dream I has two easily discriminable scenes, each of which can be divided into dream elements:

The Street Scene
DE I.1: RD encounters frightening ghosts as he walks the streets.
DE I.2: RD's weakness on his right makes him lean to his left.
DE I.3: RD feels shame at his inability to straighten up.

133

DE I.4: RD is spun around three or four times by a whirlwind.

DE I.5: RD is alarmingly unable to advance and fears falling.

The School Scene

DE I.6: RD enters a school's grounds seeking refuge and remedy.

DE I.7: RD voluntarily approaches a church for prayer.

DE I.8: RD unwittingly snubs an Acquaintance and tries to return.

DE I.9: RD is involuntarily driven back by a contrary wind.

DE I.10: RD is greeted by the Other Person and promised a present from N.

DE I.11: RD interprets the present as a melon from a foreign land.

DE I.12: RD sees others, upright and steady, around the Other Person.

DE I.13: RD is still leaning and unsteady, despite the abated wind.

On the dream day in 1619, Descartes felt that he had discovered or was in the process of discovering "the foundation of the wonderful science." These first words from the *Olympica* orient my interpretation of the first scene of the first dream. Sixteen years later, when he wrote the *Discourse,* the thoughts of this day or, more cautiously, these days, still seemed to him to have been the decisive stage on his way toward the right method. The street scene is almost by definition a "method scene." Etymologically, the term "method" and its cognates in French and Latin go back to the Greek *meta* ("according to") and *hodos* ("the way, path, or road").

The "way" or "road," in French *voie* or *chemin* and in Latin *via* or *iter,* was to be one of Descartes's most characteristic and insistent images in his later writing, where *le droit chemin* suggests "the right method." This favored image recurs some fifteen times in the *Discourse* alone, where it is most familiar, but its first appearance in Descartes's writings on method came much earlier, showing up in the earliest entries of the *Regulae:* IVb, I, II, III, and IVa.[1] In rule IVa, which seems to reflect Olympian excitement, the very first paragraph contains a remarkable set of related images, with men's minds being led down "unknown paths," wandering "through the streets," blundering along "so fortunately," and walking "in the dark." Then comes the annunciation of "the method," the right way to the knowledge of everything.[2] This recalls the street scene of Dream I and the waking interpretation after Dream III with its promise of a universal science.

The most perplexing feature of this dream history is that the brilliant prospects opened up by a new method somehow darken in Dream I. In the street scene, terrifying impediments threaten to overwhelm the dream walker (DE I.1–5). He is fearful, weak, and ashamed (VDC 41, 46, 47). In the school scene, he is similarly impotent (VDC 55–72). After his nighttime awakening, Descartes spent two hours in self-reproachful thinking, and even on the brighter morning of 11 November, this sense of guilt persisted (VDC 73–86, 200–205). But why? Why should this wonderful Discoverer, who was not an unenlightened Everyman, have suffered all this unpleasant affect at just this time? What could have been so wrong about having found "the right way"?

The image of the way, road, or path was vocational as well as methodological.[3] The street scene of uncertain and irregular progress, followed by the school scene with all its backing-and-forthing, represents a dreamer searching for his "way in life," as we can tell most clearly by juxtaposing the action in Dream I with the question from Ausonius reiterated in Dream III (VDC 117, 145) and with the sense of resolution best expressed in Interpretation III (VDC 173–78, 196–200). That sequential dreams on a given night tend to concern the same problems is a common presumption of clinicians and laboratory researchers.[4] After the dreams, if not before, Descartes had an answer to his question on the right way of life, an answer that satisfied him. In the dreams, we have the best evidence that this answer did not satisfy everyone.

The lineage of Joachim Descartes and the other lawyers of the family still gripped the somewhat wayward cadet, even after he had determined in his heated chamber to break its hold and to search for his own truth, as we can *see* in the street scene. Dreaming is a form of thinking in pictures. We cannot identify the specters or the urban setting (DE I.1), but we can *see* the dream Descartes trying to go his own way. Other heroes have had an easier time of it.

In the successive elements (DE I.2–5) that describe this dream-

135

er's uncertain progress down the streets, he limps, bends, and spins, unable to place any weight on his right side, to stand up straight, or to walk in a straight line. His commentary on this scene is limited to Interpretation I: the dreamer awakens, feeling a "real pain," presumably on his right side. He fears the work of an "Evil Spirit," and, having dreamed while sleeping on his "left side," he turns over in bed onto "his right side." Then he prays to the good God for protection against the evil effects of the dream and begins a long meditation on his sins and on good and evil (VDC 73–86).

This mind-boggling, body-bending exercise of mind and body, too, rests on fundamental confusions. However limited our knowledge of modern dream psychology, we *know* that dreaming is neither a manifestation of "spirits," good or evil, nor a mere mental representation of physical position and movement. It is a form of thinking. Descartes, however, *the* Cartesian on *the* night of nights, adopts both these wrong sorts of explanations, seemingly oblivious to their contradictory presuppositions (VDC 73–78), then goes on to pronounce against the only right sort of explanation (VDC 238–40). It is not just that this Descartes has the great misfortune not to think as we do; he does not think like a geometrical, straight-line Thinking Thing.

Instead, he thinks associatively. From physical right and left to spiritual good and evil is associatively only a short hop. It hardly matters that it is metaphysically a great leap. The French language facilitates the jump, and French was Descartes's native tongue, sleeping as well as waking, even if Latin was to be the language of record in the *Olympica*. The late seventeenth-century lexicographer Antoine Furetière explains that the adjective *droit* denotes "the side [of the body] on which is the stronger hand, naturally used to do anything done with one hand. In this sense it is opposed to the left." But then come the connotations (*droit* here is always "right"): "The *right* side is the more honorable. . . . *Right*, in the language of horsemanship, is used for a horse that does not limp. . . . *Right* is used figuratively in spiritual matters. 'This man has a *right* soul, the *right* intention.' This means that he is good and equitable. 'He has a *right* mind or spirit.' This means that he is just and that he doesn't stray to one side or the other."[5]

Of course, *droit* had still other meanings, as we can *see* in the street scene. DE I.2 already represents visually two such meanings,

136

lateral *right* and perpendicular *right:* dream Descartes is weak on his *right*-hand side, and so he cannot stand up*right.* DE I.3 represents the perpendicular *right* along with honorific or moralistic *right:* dream Descartes is ashamed that he cannot stand up*right.* DE I.4 and 5 also represent lateral *right* and perpendicular *right,* while they introduce rectilinear *right,* the geometer's *straight* line: spinning in circles on his *left* foot, he fears falling, unable to stand *straight* and up*right* or to walk in a *straight* line. In successive frames, the dreamer visualizes lateral, perpendicular, and rectilinear *rights* and suggests moralistic *right* (VDC 42–54).

The distinguishing feature of this dictionary of rights in pictures is that Descartes dreams visual antonyms, not-rights. He limps along with his weight on his left side, bent over, spinning around, and getting nowhere on a straight-line route. His own interpretation then moralizes and, in psychoanalytical language, projects. He is anxious about punishment for his sins, evils, and wrongdoing, but he wants to attribute his dream troubles to an alien agency of his own invention, "the Evil Spirit who had wanted to seduce him." This waking sense of evil "seduction" in Interpretation I may recur as questionable "solicitation" in Interpretation III.3 (VDC 75, 206–8).

What moral/spiritual wrong(s) weighed so heavily on the young man's mind on the night of 10 November 1619? The straightest line for historical analysis leads from Descartes's vague verbalizations in Interpretation I back through the visualizations of the street scene to the language and waking experience of the particular young man. As an adjective, *droit* had the general meanings just reviewed and all sorts of special meanings in architecture, astronomy, genealogy, medicine, and venery.[6] As a noun, however, *le droit* had only one great set of meanings generally familiar to everyone and more particularly the vocational concern of a few. Pierre Richelet defined the term thus: "*DROIT, s.m.* Laws, customs. (Written law. Customary law. 'To study the law' is to learn it on one's own. 'To study at law' or 'in law' means to learn it from some teacher.)"[7]

Furetière is wordier. His definitions make it clear that *le droit* as a jurisprudential term could mean "the law" itself in a collective sense, as in "the civil law" or "the canon law," the two great bodies of written laws. By extension, it could mean "jurisprudence," as

137

in "the schools of law" or "the rules of law." By a further extension, it could also mean "that which is just, reasonable, established by law."[8] Thus, the term *droit* happened to give the French a noun for "the law" in all these general senses, with countless particular applications,[9] a noun that was identical in appearance to the adjective for the right side, an upright posture, a straight line, or anything "*honnête* in the eyes of God and man."[10]

Thinking in pictures, a French dreamer could represent "the law" by corporeal images of *le droit:* the right side of the body, standing up straight, following a shortest-distance path. Of course, a *thinker*-dreamer can explain away any disability. It is because he is weak on the right side that he leans to the left side; it is because he has to limp along in this manner that he cannot stand up straight; and it is because he gets caught up by a whirlwind that he turns around and around in circles before deviating from his line of march. But in every respect, he is *non-droit*. When he awakens, he himself makes the hop and skip to moralistic and spiritualistic interpretations, but there is no reason for a modern-day investigator to stop there, given the additional information available. It is just another step further forward, hardly so much as a jump and certainly not a leap, to claim to *see* the younger son of the *conseiller* Joachim Descartes, himself a lawyer-nonlawyer, saying no to the law on the anniversary of his licentiate.

Does this mean that René Descartes was ready to embrace Isaac Beeckman's way of life? Yes and no. He does leave the dream streets for a dream school, but in the school scene the place is an imperfect "refuge," and he finds no "remedy." This scene can be broken down into the eight sequential dream elements listed above (DE I.6–13). Social encounters and failed encounters dominate the scene. Interpreted verbally, they can help explain even that most obscure element, the gift melon, but what will provide the words to identify characters who lack distinguishing traits in the narrative and who simply disappear from the interpretation?

Attributing the following two cogitations to Descartes's *Olympica* points in a promising direction, although the trails of associations do not typically follow direct routes:

CP 74–76: It is as useful to be blamed by one's friends as it is glorious to be praised by one's enemies. From strangers, we long for praise, from friends, for the truth.

CP 77–87: In everyone's mind there are certain parts that excite strong passions, however lightly they are touched. So a boy with a strong spirit will not cry when he is rebuked; he will get angry. Another will cry. If we should be told that a great many misfortunes have happened, we become sad; but if we should also be told that someone bad caused them, we become angry. The change from one passion to another happens by proximity. Nevertheless, the change from opposite passions is often more powerful, as if bad news should be announced suddenly in the midst of a joyous feast.

The material that Leibniz copied out from the Little Notebook just before and just after these two cogitations came from the *Olympica* (CP 64–73, 88–101). That must be the source for these reflections, too. They must have been part of the two hours of self-examination and moral reflection after Dream I (VDC 77–86). Descartes was concerned with friendship and rebuke.

Identification of the dream day as the anniversary of Descartes's first meeting with Isaac Beeckman advances the inquiry along the way, and a new appreciation of the emotional as well as intellectual force of this friendship helps establish the destination. This one source of both affection and inspiration had scolded him in the letter of 6 May 1619, if on no other occasion, and Descartes had apparently responded by getting very angry, breaking off the relationship at the time and exploding long afterward. Can the troubled image of the dreamer spun around in circles on the streets by a whirlwind (DE I.4) have been based on painful memories of Beeckman's criticism that Descartes was "spinning in circles," wasting his time touring the streets of Copenhagen? Possibly. There may also have been reminiscences of their shared interest in tops, which spin upright, lean over, and then fall down. In any case, the waking afterthoughts (CP 74–87 and VDC 77–86) offer good evidence for an analytical emphasis on the friend and his rebuke.

The spirit of Isaac Beeckman haunts these dreams along with Descartes's aspirations for a new science. Beeckman's proper place is the school scene. Isaac's older brother Jacob, whose lead he tended to follow, was already a teacher, and his own first appointment came in November 1619.[11] Descartes must have known about the vocational interest. This could help explain the dream school, which I might otherwise have called "the *collège*" out of deference to Descartes's own education. Nothing specific about this school allows its identification, and the dream Descartes does not seem to be a schoolboy acting out the routines of *collége* or university life. Sufficient information is simply not available, and it is quite possible that the living dreamer's associations might have been to La Flèche, Poitiers, or another school with which he was familiar.

It is certain that Beeckman had exhorted Descartes to settle down for serious study and writing, and it is very likely that the restless genius could no longer accept with equanimity even the memory of such prodding by the preacher-teacher, despite his professed willingness to accept friendly criticism (CP 74–76). The beloved Beeckman may already have become the hated Beeckman by the logic of antithetical passions (CP 77–87). After winter had finally put an end to the traveler's summertime wanderings, he seems to have been anxious to emphasize that the retreat for renewed work was *his* choice, no one else's (VDC 206–19).

The search for a Beeckman figure in the dream requires consideration of the Acquaintance, the Other Person, and the mysterious Mr. N. However, because these dream characters are neither detailed in the narrative nor mentioned in the interpretation, no one can be identified with any certainty. Furthermore, because dreams typically defy the law of the excluded middle and ignore the logic of a one-to-one equivalence of dream characters with real-life persons, even the identification of any one as a Beeckman figure would not rule out the same identification for one or both of the others.

The Acquaintance "enters" the dream in DE I.8 and "exits" in DE I.9, insofar as he ever appears on stage. This shadowy dream figure is most interesting because of the dream Descartes's dramatic reactions to his presence. The dreamer approaches the Acquaintance, then moves away from, back toward, and again away from him (VDC 56–61). The initial approach is unwitting and apparently unimportant to the narrative. What matters in the story as told is that he discovers after the fact that he has bypassed the Acquaintance, snubbing him "unintentionally." Voluntarily, he retraces his steps to make good the slight, but then, "involuntarily," he is blown back again by a contrary wind.

The dream Descartes's failed encounter with the Acquaintance represents visually an approach-avoidance, or, in deference to the emphases of the dream, an avoidance-approach. His contrary motions act out his contrary inclinations. Even without his waking afterthoughts, these vacillations would constitute very good evidence of strongly ambivalent feelings. There are afterthoughts, however, the two cogitations on friendship, rebuke, and strong but opposed passions (CP 74–87). The known anniversary of the first meeting with Beeckman, the known contemporary association of Beeckman with schools, the known friendship with Beeckman and rebuke by Beeckman, and the known ambivalence with which Descartes first loved Beeckman and eventually hated him all help identify the shadowy Acquaintance as very probably a Beeckman figure.

The Other Person and Mr. N. then preoccupy the dreamer in DE I.10–11. The Other Person stands at the center of the school courtyard when we first see him, and others cluster about him as the dream ends. He hails the dream Descartes, calling him by name and greeting him politely, but what he has to say is so mysterious that it would have puzzled a lesser mind. The Other Person tells him that, *if* he cares to seek out a *Monsieur N.*, a "Mr. X,"[12] he can expect to be given "something." The dream Descartes does not offer an opinion on the identity of this Mr. N., but he somehow knows that the gift must be a melon, and not just any melon, but a melon from a foreign land.

The one really distinctive aspect of this part of the dream is the gift melon. It would not seem so important in itself if it had not seemed so important to Descartes himself. It was one of only two elements from Dream I to merit the awakened dreamer's day-after commentary, and that commentary is so peculiar that it further arouses curiosity instead of satisfying it: "The melon offered him as a present in the first dream signified, he said, the charms of solitude, but presented by purely human solicitations" (VDC 206–8). How can a dream *melon* ever have signified "solitude"? And how can "charming" *isolation* ever have been the subject of someone else's "solicitations"? Descartes does not answer these questions, but one of the few rules of dream interpretation is that the awakened dreamer's associations are always right.

The dream melon can be interpreted either as a desired piece of fantasy fruit or as the symbol or recollection of something else. Was the flesh-and-blood Descartes, like Montaigne, really a melon fancier?[13] His school, La Flèche, was in Anjou, a province especially celebrated by contemporaries for the quality of its melons,[14] but it is not clear that the school scene was set at La Flèche or anywhere else in Anjou, the Touraine, or Poitou. In any case, the dreamer's sleeping conviction that Mr. N.'s melon was an import from "some foreign land" mitigates against any overly realistic interpretation, such as a wintertime wish for summertime fruits associated with La Fléche and Anjou. His waking notion that the dream melon meant "the charms of solitude" *is* peculiar, but it also points away from "realism" and toward symbolism.

Jean-Baptiste La Curne de Sainte-Palaye's *Dictionnaire historique de l'ancien langage françoise* reports three figurative usages of melons known from seventeenth-century sources.[15] The first, chronologically, is a proverb reported by Randle Cotgrave (1611): "A peine connoist-on la femme et le melon."[16] This savory piece of sexist wisdom expresses a man's awful predicament when confronted with the necessity of choosing his woman without being able to know by tasting who would be the ripest, sweetest, and juiciest. The second old usage, recorded by Antoine Oudin (1640), might also offend modern taste: "Mourir comme les melons, la semence dans le corps."[17] This means to die a virgin, seeds unsown. Only the third of the figurative usages is wholly innocent. Paul Pellisson-Fontanier (d. 1693) mentions in his account of the campaigns of 1668 that French couriers charged with bundles of letters called these fat bundles "melons."[18]

It is a poetic variant on the old proverb from Cotgrave that opens up this most uncertain dream element. In his slim book of verse entitled *Le temps passé* (1585 and later editions), Claude Mermet includes two successive quatrains on friendship, true and false. He seems to have felt that it was getting as hard to find a good friend as a good woman—or a good melon:

> De L'Amy de parolle
>
> Tu es tout entier mon amy,
> Quand tu as affaire de moy;
> *Mais lors que i'ay besoin de toy,*
> *Tu n'es mon amy qu' à demy.*
> [Your friendship knows no limit
> When you need my help.
> But when I need yours
> It stops halfway.]

142

Des amis encores

Les amis de l'heure *présente*
Ont le naturel du *melon*,
Il en faut essayer cinquante,
Avant qu'en rencountrer un bon.[19]
[Friends in the present day
Have this in common with the melon,
You've got to try fifty
Before you get a good one.]

I suggest a line of associations extending back from the *présent melon* in the dream through Descartes's memory of this proverbial maxim in poetic form to the painful infidelity of Isaac Beeckman, who had written so as to hurt, when his friend had needed help.

Descartes need not have read Mermet to have encountered this proverbial wisdom. The same idea appeared in virtually the same form in a collection of adages published in Frankfurt several years before Descartes's arrival in that city for the coronation of 1619, Philippe Garnier's *Thesaurus Adagiorum Gallico-Latinorum* (1612):

Les amis, pour l'heure présente
sont du naturel du melon.
Il en faut esprouver cinquante,
avant que d'en trouver un bon.[20]

A Dutch collection of proverbs in verse form, Jacob Cats's *Spiegel van den Ouden ende Nieuwen Tijdt* (1632), shows that the saying was known in Holland, too. Along with a handsome plate of a buxom melon vendor and her perplexed customer, who is trying to select a good piece of fruit by its aroma, Cats printed a longer Dutch poem and two short French versions:

Amys sont comme le melon;
De dix souvent pas un est bon.
[Friends are like melons.
In ten, you might not find a good one.]

Les amys sont comme le melon;
Il faut essayer plusieurs pour rancontrer un bon.[21]
[Friends are like melons;
You've got to try many to get a good one.]

Folk wisdom in the form of doggerel comparing friends to melons and a bad pun on "the present" may seem beneath the dignity proper for a great philosopher, even in youthful dreams, but Descartes valued *poèmes sententieux* like these and praised them as such in the *Olympica* (CP 93–101; VDC 163–78). The circumstantial evidence for Descartes's memory of this proverbial wisdom on friendship is compelling. Both Mermet and Garnier were quite concerned to offer poetic counsel on false friendship and true in verses not cited above. All this proverbial wisdom came down to warnings against mere verbal professions of friendship and advice that the real test is a demonstrated willingness to help in time of need, a test that few so-called friends will pass.[22]

Historically, the significant context for Descartes's dream memories and dream expression seems to have been this. Beeckman was the dear friend who turned out to have been the false friend. We see the older man *profess* his friendship just once, in the words of the one letter from Beeckman to Descartes that has survived: my friend for a long life of inquiry together, "my friend in more than the ordinary sense . . ." Surely he had often professed this friendship in Descartes's presence. We also see him seem to *betray* that friendship in the same letter, where he responds to Descartes's most specific request for assistance with what he admits are only faded memories of Llull's *Ars brevis* and Agrippa's commentary— and, from Descartes's perspective, with gratuitous counsel and an insulting parable.[23] Now, because it is Beeckman's copy of the letter that survives and because the movements of Descartes himself and of the mails are uncertain, it is possible that the traveler never received the message, however important it had seemed in prospect. In this case, too, he would have felt betrayed, because the professed friend would have seemed to have refused help that he could easily have offered at a time of Descartes's expressed need.

The mere fact that these letters were preserved does not establish their importance for Descartes. Nevertheless, it is significant that Beeckman kept copies. Furthermore, after the separation at the beginning of 1619, the burdens of the relationship had to be carried by the mails, and, as words can wound, the wounds of written words can fester. The problems were almost certainly greater than the documents show them to have been, even attending only to intellectual matters and the tensions of shared interests independently pursued. Beeckman was older and wiser, which probably did not endear him to the young genius; Descartes was the superior socially and intellectually, which contributed to cavalier attitudes that were probably offensive to his mentor.

What of the *Navigation*, for instance? Descartes's arrogation must have been a sore point for Beeckman. And the *Mechanics?* Descartes had offered something to Beeckman, but historians of science have tended to fault the Cartesian draft on free-fall and to credit Beeckman's alternative version. Did Isaac presume to correct René in his (now lost) response to the enthusiastic letter of 26 March 1619, or, as bad, did he seem to undervalue the offering by ignoring it?[24] And the *Geometry?* Just how much skepticism of Descartes's enthusiasm did Beeckman express to provoke the gracious but also defensive and melancholy letter of 23 April 1619? In all fairness to the older man, I suppose that he could not easily have met his friend's insistent demands for unqualified personal affection and intellectual support.

Psychologically, dream interpretation would be a simpler matter if there were only neat, one-to-one correspondences of dream characters and real-life persons. This is not the case. One character can represent several persons, or, as confusingly, several characters can represent one person.[25] In Descartes's Dream I, Mr. N., the man of the gift melon from a foreign land, does seem to be Isaac Beeckman. Two pieces of evidence support this identification: first, the Olympian cogitations concerning rebuke by friends and rebuke by elders (CP 74–87), read with Beeckman's letter of 6 May 1619 in mind and (re-)placed in Interpretation I; second, the otherwise-puzzling explanation of the melon in Interpretation III.3, human solicitations for charming solitude (VDC 206–8), which would make sense if read as a reference to Beeckman's exhortations that Descartes settle down for the quiet satisfactions of intellectual accomplishment.

Historical inquiry into Leibniz's *Cogitationes*, Beeckman's *Journal*, and the proverbial wisdom versified by Mermet, Garnier, and Cats leads to such coherent and relevant material that I can claim to have gained at least partial insight into the living Descartes's memory on the night of 10 November 1619. Practically speaking, I have recovered some associations from the dead dreamer's dead world.

Dream I ends with DE I.12–13: the dream Descartes looks on

from a distance, as *others* cluster around the unnamed Person, upright and steady; despite the abatement of the winds, the dreamer himself is still leaning and unsteady. His decision against his father's way, the law, seems not to have integrated him with others in his friend's way, the search for truth. Moreover, despite the more cheerful afterthoughts following Dream III (VDC 181–92), here his relative isolation has no apparent "charm."

Dream II: The Thunder Dream

For "almost two hours" spent awake after Dream I, Descartes pondered good and evil. Baillet reports this summarily as an anxious, prayerful self-examination, not a calm, philosophical meditation. The little that Baillet (or Descartes) records (VDC 73–86) is not enough, but even this little yields a glimpse of the young man's apprehensions of divine "punishment for his sins, *which he acknowledged to have been great enough to call down upon his head the thunderbolts of heaven. . . .*" The verbal emphasis is mine, of course, but the moral and spiritual emphasis must have been Descartes's own, perhaps softened a bit in 1619 by the words of self-reassurance that follow immediately, but perhaps so graced only in 1691 by a biographical apologist rightly concerned to reassure his readers: ". . . although he had always led a more or less blameless life in the eyes of men." *More or less* blameless?

Dream II immediately gives the lie to any such happy idea. This terrifying Thunder Dream is linked associatively with the themes of the previous period of wakefulness: waking thoughts of sinful wrongdoing → waking thoughts of divine judgment and retribution metaphorically expressed as "thunderbolts of heaven" → the dream of "a sudden, loud noise that he took for thunder" → terror on first awakening (VDC 79–90). In Dream II, Descartes judges against himself, whether or not he echoes others' judgments and whatever are the complacent rationalizations he records as his anti-interpretation (VDC 90–102).

It is hard not to be impressed by the experimentation that so thoroughly distracted the philosopher-dreamer from the awful moral and spiritual implications of the Thunder Dream. The impromptu pseudoscience fails on critical review, but it is much more important that this exercise succeeded in restoring the dreamer's shaken self-confidence. In modern opthalmological terminology, Descartes stumbled in his darkened chamber onto the entoptic phenomenon of phosphenes, which may be induced simply by pressure on the eye or by such sudden movements of the dark-accommodated eye as those he reported (VDC 99–101).[26] Of course, he was not content with an inner pseudolight. *His* thinking lit up the night.

This is one of the most bizarre moments in an extraordinary episode. The terrified dreamer of Dream II becomes the experimental scientist of Interpretation II: he strikes sparks of fire by blinking his eyes; so, he lights up the nearby objects in his room; so, he explains to his own satisfaction the Thunder Dream; so, he banishes to some dark corner of the heated chamber the guilt and fear that had haunted him; and so, he convinces himself that his "wonderful science" really is pretty wonderful after all. The alert reader blinks in disbelief, then blinks again: in Interpretation III, phase 3, Descartes decides that Dream II was a warning and a threat concerning a sinful past and that his guilty conscience had troubled him (VDC 200–205, 220–23). Even this is not the end of it: last heard from, he has again turned the Thunder Dream into something good, a noise heralding the descent of the "Spirit of Truth," that is, God, with the Good News for René Descartes (VDC 223–25, CP 187–92).

The zigzags of these interpretations themselves demand interpretation; the most plausible is that Descartes was troubled by a profound sense of guilt that he tried to ward off by his waking rationalizations. What had he done wrong? First of all, I suggest, he had chosen to defy his father and to devote his life to the search for all truths by a new method, which, he supposed, would preclude his active pursuit of an official career. There are all sorts of other possibilities for additional guilt arising out of his intimate friendship with Isaac Beeckman, including his failure to satisfy the latter's high expectations for written work and his feelings of anger against the very friend who had meant so much to him and who had apparently turned away from or even against him.

No one else will ever know all that was on René Descartes's conscience, and his own self-awareness cannot have been perfect. His conscience rumbles audibly in the Thunder Dream, but he seems to have been able to stop his ears in Interpretation II and III.3. Any nonspeculative attempt to explain what particularly troubled him on 10 November 1619 must focus on the concomitant events known from the beginning of that winter: the intellectual discovery of "the foundation of the wonderful science" and the vocational decision to spend his life in "the search for truth."

It is almost inconceivable that this young thinker should have suffered pangs of conscience related to his bold attempt to reconstruct philosophy on mathematical foundations. Others might eventually suppose that the rule of *évidence*, read as a prescription for universal doubt, could be corrosive of faith, morals, and perhaps even social and political order, but in the first flush of discovery, the young Descartes himself would hardly have had such self-critical second thoughts about the potentially destructive implications of his own ideas.

His vocational decision would have been another matter. It was then exactly three years after the formal completion of his legal training and just one year after his meeting his scientific mentor. It was the Saint Martin's season of the *rentrées* and the oath taking at the courts, when his father Joachim and now his brother Pierre would display their corporate pride. René Descartes chose against the law and, if I am right, against his father, but in his awkward gropings as a searcher for truths, he had not yet satisfied his friend. It was the beginning of winter. Where were the books that he had promised at the beginning of spring?

8

DREAM III AND THE OLYMPIAN
INTERPRETATIONS

Dream III, the Books Dream, is the last, the longest, and by far the most important. It is also the one Olympian dream in which anxiety over vocational choices is prominent in the manifest narrative itself, the one for which the awakened dreamer makes the most particular as well as the most grandiose claims (notably, the revelation of "the treasures of all the sciences"), and the one for which there are the most associations from other sources. This chapter begins with an analysis of the several dream elements, subordinating the sweeping claims of Descartes's interpretations to my discussion of the several dream elements. It ends with a reconsideration of the Olympian interpretations as such.

Dream III: The Books Dream

Dream III is rather complex, but all its elements relate in one way or another to two books and their contents:

DE III.1: RD discovers a book on his table, its origin unknown.
DE III.2: RD happily identifies this book as the useful *Dictionary*.
DE III.3: RD discovers a second book, its origin also unknown.
DE III.4: RD identifies the second book as the *Corpus poetarum*.
DE III.5: RD opens the *Corpus*, by chance, at "Quod . . . iter?"
DE III.6: RD notices Unknown, who recommends "Est et non."

DE III.7: RD boasts knowledge of this poem and its place in the volume.

DE III.8: RD searches for "Est et non" in the *Corpus poetarum.*

DE III.9: Unknown asks, "Whence these books?" RD cannot explain.

DE III.10: RD loses the *Dictionary* and fails to find "Est et non."

DE III.11: The *Dictionary* reappears, now somehow incomplete.

DE III.12: RD finds Ausonius but not "Est et non" in the *Corpus.*

DE III.13: RD recommends "Quod . . . iter?" as a finer poem.

DE III.14: RD searches for this poem and finds engravings.

DE III.15: RD admires this edition and contrasts it with another.

DE III.16: Books and Unknown disappear without awakening RD.

DE III.1, (3,) 11: The first fact about the dream books is that the dreamer finds them on his *table.* The narrator specifies this placement for the *Dictionary* on the occasions of its initial discovery and subsequent recovery (VDC 105, 137), and, despite Descartes's (or Baillet's) failure to specify the table for the *Corpus poetarum* in the narrative of discovery and searching, the same placement seems quite clearly implied for that book, too (VDC 109–11, 134–37). The table is the one piece of furniture mentioned in the dream narrative—indeed, the one object of any sort, other than the two books (the *Dictionary* and the *Corpus poetarum*) and the two persons (the dreamer and the Unknown). It seems more important that the books are placed on the table than that the dreamer sits at it.

Descartes's own Olympian interpretations make nothing of this seemingly inconsequential book table, but that does not mean that it was insignificant. The association of table and books meant something quite definite and quite personal to him. It meant the books that first inspired him, insofar as mere books ever inspired this least bookish of philosophers. Not the published works of Aristotle, nor those of any other ancient, nor those of any modern; the books that inspired Descartes were the manuscripts which Cornelis de Waard edited as Beeckman's *Journal,* but which that most private of authors first called his *tafelboeckje,* or "Table Books."[1] Descartes esteemed Beeckman above other thinkers for having joined physics and mathematics accurately. It does not matter that Beeckman had published nothing; it does matter that Descartes had examined his Table Books.[2] His friend and mentor had encouraged him to pursue related studies, and many aspects of his own Little Notebook suggest emulation.

DE III.1–4 and passim: There are *two* books (and two poems within the second book). This doubling may have meant almost anything, but there is only one meaning that takes into account the hovering figure of Isaac Beeckman, his great expectations for René Descartes, and the latter's promise to the former. On the eve of his departure from Breda, the young genius had responded to the exhortations of his older mentor by saying that *if* he stopped somewhere in the course of his travels, *then* he would settle down for work on his *Mechanics* or his *Geometry*.[3] Two weeks later, Beeckman had exhorted him to do just that, showing a great deal more interest in the former project than in the latter—and grievously offending him by what was probably supposed to have been no more than a little salutary correction for the disproportion between promise and performance.[4] That had been 6 May; now it was 10 November, six months later, and Descartes had finally stopped somewhere *and* finally returned productively to his studies. Of course, the two books had yet to be written.

Back at his work table after a prolonged absence, the dreaming traveler-author discovers *two* books, which appear before him as if by magic. The fortuitous production of two dream books by an aspiring author represents the wishful thinking so common in dream life that Freud himself regarded it as the essence of all dreams.

DE III.2, 10–11, 16: The first of Descartes's two books is a *Dictionary*. In the dream narrative, it inexplicably appears, disappears, reappears, and disappears once again; it is pleasing because it is potentially useful; and when it reappears, it is incomplete (VDC 105–8, 131–39, 151–52). According to his interpretation, "the *Dictionary* could only mean all the sciences gathered together" (VDC 158–59), an explanation that is interesting because it seems so arbitrary and because it is so closely related to Descartes's known waking aspiration to establish a universal mathematical science,[5] his dream-day conviction that he had discovered "the foundation of the wonderful science" (VDC 35–36), and his day-after belief that "it was the Spirit of Truth that had wanted to open unto him the treasures of all the sciences by this dream" (VDC 189–92).

The earliest rules from Descartes's *Regulae*, which seem to come from just this period, and Leibniz's *Cogitationes*, which copied materials from the Little Notebook, are the principal sources on Descartes's contemporaneous determination to go his own way and to show himself and the unity of the sciences to an admiring world.[6] Even before the dreams of 10 November 1619, he had indulged in wishful thinking, properly speaking. He had fantasized while awake that he was ready to "ascend onto the great stage," to emulate the most "ingenious inventors," to make his own unguided discoveries, to follow his own untutored rules (CP 1–9, 13–16). He had also laid claim to personified science as his own and envisioned the unity of the sciences (CP 1–12, 29–38).

In the same context, the *Praeambula*, Descartes had also expressed a very similar wish in a more obscure way. CP 17–28 has attracted most interest for its references to the "R[osi]- C[rucians]" as false claimants to wonderful sciences, but it is much more important for an obscure reference to himself as the pseudonymous author of the truly wonderful but wholly imaginary *Treasury of Mathematics:* "Polybius Cosmopolitanus' *Thesaurus Mathematicus* teaches the true ways of resolving all difficulties of this science and demonstrates that the human mind can go no further in this respect" (CP 17–20). This book of waking fantasy, a "treasury of mathematics" answering *all* questions in the *science* of mathematics, recalls the "incredibly ambitious" project of a universal mathematical science that Descartes confessed to Beeckman in March, the awakened dreamer's claim that the Books Dream promised him "the *treasures* of *all* the *sciences*," and the earliest announcement of the Method in the *Regulae*.[7]

Baillet preserved another passage from the early manuscripts that relates yet more particularly to the Books Dream. The proud discoverer of "the foundation of the wonderful science" was determined to declare his own intellectual independence and to satisfy at least himself concerning the originality of his attempt to rest everything on mathematics. The young Descartes closely associated the *Dictionary* with waking claims for both independence and originality:

> Just as we cannot either write a word in which there is anything but the letters of the Alphabet or fill a sentence with anything but words from the *Dictionary*, so we cannot write a book without some sentences that are found to be in others' works. But if what I shall say should be so coherent and so interconnected that each assertion

follows from others, I shall no more have borrowed these sentences as an argument from others, than appropriated the words themselves from the *Dictionary* [emphasis added].[8]

This passage paradoxically associates the most general reference work with the particular aspirations of this thinker-author.

As a useful if incomplete Table Book, twice positioned as such, the dream *Dictionary* recalls Beeckman's *Journal* and so his physico-mathematical science, which Descartes emulated in his own Little Notebook. As the source of all the words that Descartes could use to write a book of his own and as a compendium of "all the sciences gathered together" (VDC 164–65), it recalls his intellectual ambition and his aspirations for independence, originality, and universality. It is this last aspiration, known also from the *Cogitationes* (lines 29–33), from the *Regulae* (rules I and IV), and from the *Discourse* itself,[9] that accounts for his otherwise astonishing interpretation of his dream *Dictionary* and his most soaring claim for the whole dream (VDC 158–60, 187–92).

DE III.10–11, 16: The dreamer notes the evanescence and the incompleteness of the dream *Dictionary* only after the Unknown questions him about the *Corpus poetarum* (VDC 129–37, 137–39). Although Beeckman's Table Books were distinctively "incomplete," these elements are better taken quite simply as an expression of the dreamer's anxiety over work that he himself had barely begun, let alone "completed," as a restless traveler suddenly become inspired discoverer. If I am right, the whole point of the mysterious appearances and disappearances of the two dream books, especially the incomplete *Dictionary*, is that Descartes did not have in hand complete books of his own.

Much remains mysterious. Is the *Dictionary* best seen as an ordinary reference work, as the Table Book of Beeckman, or as the more complete and coherent book-in-the-mind of Descartes? Freud's answer would be that dreamers do not think in terms of exclusive alternatives, either/or.[10] Dream elements are often if not always overdetermined, in that one dream image condenses two or more dream thoughts.[11] This helps explain why, even in the most favorable clinical circumstances, no interpretation can claim to be exhaustive.[12] So much the worse for anyone who cannot accept analyses that are anything but clear and distinct, mathematically certain and demonstrative. Persons are not propositions.

DE III.4: The *Corpus poetarum* provides a perfect illustration of the characteristic ambiguity of dreams. There is a first certainty about this book and its meaning for Descartes—and also a second certainty or virtual certainty that seems to contradict the first. The first certainty, recognized by that worthy teacher-librarian-historian, Adrien Baillet, is that this dream book was a real book, one he could pull down from his shelves, Pierre des Brosses's *Corpus veterum poetaraum latinorum* (1603 and 1611). The second (virtual) certainty has not been recognized: for a seventeenth-century Frenchman so recently trained in the law(s), *the* one great *Corpus* was the *Corpus juris civilis*, the body of Roman civil law codified under Justinian and edited by modern jurists.[13]

The *Corpus* of the laws comprised the *Codex constitutionum*, the *Digesta*, the *Institutiones*, and the *Novellae*, and it was this Roman written law, not any French customary law, that Descartes had studied, however happily or assiduously.[14] There is still another virtual certainty, because there was another *Corpus* of another law, the *Corpus juris canonici*, the body of canon law, comprising no fewer than six lesser compilations. Descartes had been qualified in this law, too, just three years to the day before the dream day.[15] That the dreamer would have associated the *Corpus poetarum* with the *Corpus juris* is a simple matter of languages, Latin as well as French,[16] and education, legal as well as humanistic.

DE III.5: The aleatory opening of the dream *Corpus* to the particular poem ("Quod vitae sectabor iter?") may also have had generally vocational and specifically legal connotations. The practice of random book opening as a form of spiritual direction on the great question of ways in life was very old even then. The great exemplar was St. Augustine, who had heard singsong voices in the garden at the crucial moment of his conversion: "Take it and read it. Take it and read it." He had no doubts: "I must interpret this as a divine command to me to open the book and read the first passage that I should come upon."[17] This was enough: "So I went eagerly back to the place where . . . I had left the book of the Apostle. . . . I snatched up the book, opened it, and read in silence the passage upon which my eyes first fell [Romans 13:13–14]: 'Not in rioting and drunkenness, not in chambering and wantonness, not in strife and envying, but put ye on the Lord Jesus Christ, and make not provision for the flesh in concupiscence.' I had no wish to read further. There was no need to."[18] This Patristic tradition of divine guidance by aleatory reading best explains how Descartes could have convinced himself that the random reading of a *question* from *Ausonius* could have been "the good advice of a wise person or even of Moral Theology."[19]

But there was more than this to "the opening of the book" for the dream reader of the *Corpus*. The standard format for examinations of legal competence in the courts was to select laws for exposition "by the fortuitous opening of books."[20] Take, for example, the entry of Joachim Descartes into the Parlement of Brittany. Having purchased the office, Joachim appeared before the court. On 5 February 1586, the judges informed themselves of "the life and morals of the candidate," and he, in turn, selected a passage "by the opening of the book," that is, by the chance opening of the *Code*, a part of the *Corpus*. In his case, it happened to be a law concerning contracts for purchase and sale. On 14 February, Joachim returned to defend his thesis on this law:

> Messire Joachim Descartes . . . entered the chambers and answered on the law *"Si mater tua . . ."* from the *C[odex] de contrahenda emptione et venditione,* on the volumes of the *Digest* [the parallel commentary of the Roman jurists], and on practice. Then he retired [so that the judges could deliberate on his competence]. After determining his sufficiency, the Court decreed that he should be received for the exercise of the aforementioned office [of *conseiller*]. He returned and took the oath as is required and customary.[21]

The surviving documentation concerning René Descartes's licentiate on 10 November 1616 does not specify the process by which the testamentary law was selected, but there must have been the customary "opening of the book."[22]

DE III.5, 13: What did the dream Descartes find in his dream *Corpus?* A question, not an answer: "Quod vitae sectabor iter?" From Leibniz in the late seventeenth century to Adam in the early twentieth, the best-qualified students of Descartes in other ways have been most impatient with the dreams except, notably, for the citations from Ausonius, particularly "What way in life shall I pursue?"[23] This is the single most striking feature of the Olympian dreams. It recalls two historical facts about Descartes's education at La Flèche. He had *lived* his intellectual life in Latin for eight or nine formative years, and he had *loved* the poetry before going on to hate the philosophy.[24] Had he made the rational decision to reorient his conscious thinking methodically from these bookish traditions when he went to bed on the night of 10 November 1619? Probably so, although the evidence from the *Olympica* suggests a willingness to exempt the poets from the oblivion to which he hoped to doom the philosophers (VDC 159–72; CP 93–101). In the third and decisive dream, there was the *Corpus poetarum*, the accurate recollection of two verses, the correct identification of the poet, and the sense of having known the anthology especially well (VDC 126–28).

By the hypermnesia that characterizes all dreaming, the sleeping Descartes would have had fuller access to some levels of memory. Psychoanalytic authors have particularly emphasized this fact about dreams, but pre-Freudians were also well aware of the phenomenon, and non-Freudians have investigated it.[25] While asleep, dreamers often remember inherently trivial details from childhood experience as well as from the most recent past. On reawakening to a world in which mere dreams are so regularly underestimated and waking thought is overestimated, they are then surprised at the uncanny precision of memories that can be verified by directed inquiry. Much more commonly, of course, they forget that they have remembered, in large part because the dream memories, when and if briefly reviewed, mean so little on the morning after. On awakening, it is goodbye to the fragments from the past and hello again to the daily imperatives of the present. Descartes's situation as he awakened was exceptional, not just in that there were no "daily imperatives" of family or work to distract him but also in that he had *anticipated* a spiritual revelation in dream form (VDC 235–38).

Descartes dreamed and remembered that he had dreamed two verses: "Quod vitae sectabor iter?" and "Est et non." Why these initial verses? In his Interpretation III, phase 1, he explains that the first, a poetic *question* on alternative ways of life, "represented the good advice of a wise person or even of Moral Theology" (VDC 173–78). What good advice? What wise person? What moral theology? He is also somewhat orphic in Interpretation III, phase 2, on the meaning of the poet's "Yes and no." According to the awakened dreamer, these "Pythagorean" words meant "Truth and

Falsehood in human understanding and the profane sciences" (VDC 183–87). Had he been explaining himself to others, Descartes could have elaborated on the most prominent features of his most important dream on the night after his most enthusiastic discovery and before his most prayerful meditation on "the most important affair of his life" (VDC 1–38, 241–52). But he wrote for himself, and he did not elaborate.

The two verses seem to have little or no meaning within the dream narrative itself. They remain very obscure as interpreted. Still, the dreamer's recollection of the real verses from his real anthology indicates the source for what might be a better understanding of the two memorable poems and their meaning to him. Even the sleeping Descartes may have remembered more than the initial lines incorporated into his narrative. *If* the rest of the poems include material that is internally coherent and externally relevant, material that makes good sense of the otherwise puzzling verses for this particular dreamer at this particular time, *then* there is good reason to suppose that the sleeping man remembered more than the awakened man recorded.[26]

In pursuit of Descartes, I follow the tracks of his memory back into the poetry of Ausonius. Pierre des Brosses's anthology of the Latin poets does include both verses, just as the dreamer claimed.[27] Des Brosses printed the first fifty lines of the poem formally cited as Ausonius's *Eclogue* 2.[28] Hugh G. Evelyn White's prose translation of the first nine lines follows. Here the poet reviews vocational alternatives, beginning with the law:

From the Greek: A Pythagorean Reflection on the
Difficulty of Choosing One's Way of Life

What path in life shall I pursue? The courts are full of uproar; the home is vexed with cares; home troubles follow us abroad; the merchant always has fresh losses to expect, and the dread of base poverty forbids his rest; the husbandman is worn out with toil; frightful shipwreck lends the sea a grim name; the unwedded life has its sore troubles, but sorer is the futile watch and ward which jealous husbands keep; to serve Mars is a bloody trade; the tarnished gains of interest and swift-mounting usury slaughter the needy. . . .[29]

However favorably Descartes judged the more than philosophical wisdom in these verses, Ausonius's "Pythagorean reflections" offer nothing more profound than this: Damned if you do, damned if you don't.

The rest of *Eclogue* 2 teaches that it is bad to be young, bad to be old; bad to be human, bad to be divine; bad to be chaste, bad to be licentious; bad to have friends, bad not to have them; and so on. Whether or not you have honorable offices, great learning, many clients, powerful patrons, living heirs, or generous habits, you will suffer. Therefore, the summit of Greek wisdom was reached in the "Pythagorean" judgment that birth is the greatest misfortune and death is the greatest blessing.

DE III.6, 8, 10, 12: The second poem, *Eclogue* 4, nominally recommended by the dream Unknown, was actually selected by the sleeping mind of the real Descartes. It is probably no more thoughtful than the first, certainly no more scientific. Lines 1–14 read:

The Pythagorean "Yea" and "Nay"

"Yes" and "no": all the world constantly uses these familiar monosyllables. Take these away and you leave nothing for the tongue of man to discuss. In them is all, and all from them, be it a matter of business or pleasure, of bustle or repose. Sometimes two parties agree on one word or the other, but often they are opposed, according as men easy or contentious in character and temperament are engaged in discussion. If both agree, forthwith "Yea, yea" breaks in; but if they dispute, then disagreement will throw in a "Nay." From these arises the uproar which splits the air of the courts, from these the feuds of the maddened Circus and the widespread partisanship which fills the tiers of the theater, from these the debates which occupy the Senate. Wives, children, fathers, bandy these two words in peaceful debate without unnatural quarrelling. . . .[30]

Ausonius's last eleven lines in *Eclogue* 4 concern academic debate, as if it were typically mere wrangling over matters as clear to the unlearned as "day" and "night." The Latin *dies* is inherently ambiguous, meaning either the hours of daylight only or the twenty-four hours of light and dark. Now, if there are lighted torches or lightning flashes at night, is that the "day" in the "night"?[31] It is a case of "yes" and "no." According to Ausonius, the two monosyllables rule us all.

Why did Descartes recall *these* poems? The fragmentary quotations in the dream narrative and the peculiar explanations in the dream interpretations raise more questions without providing the materials for answers. How could the first line of *Eclogue* 2 be (mis-)read or (mis-)remembered as "good advice"? And how could the first line of *Eclogue* 4 be (mis-)read or (mis-)remembered as a promise of scientific understanding?

The "philosophical" content of the two poems is not at all impressive. The diligent searcher for moral wisdom in the first of them finds at best a cynical devaluation of human choices and at worst a nihilistic prescription for suicide; the reflective reader of the second finds at best a resolutely trivializing attack on forensic and academic rhetoric and at worst an angrily anti-intellectual denunciation of all negation, perhaps all affirmation, too. Such sophistry can hardly have contributed much to the formation of one of the greatest thinkers.

Nor can the artistic appeal of the poetry explain its privileged place in the Olympian dreams. Those few specialists who have chosen to focus on the work of Ausonius offer the most disparaging assessments:

> Whatever the salient characteristics . . . may be, intellectual fresh-
> ness, imagination, and a broad human outlook were not amongst
> them. . . . From first to last, his verse is barren of ideas: not a gleam
> of insight or of broad human sympathy, no passion, no revolt. His
> attitude toward life is a mechanical and complacent acceptance of
> things as they are. . . . Insensible, broadly speaking, to sentiment
> and unappreciative of the human sympathy that should pervade
> true poetry, Ausonius regarded the art . . . as the rhetorical treat-
> ment of any subject in verse . . . , [the less poetic] the subject, the
> better.[32]

His poetry is in fact this bad. Ausonius's prosaic muse inspired him to write on the letters of the alphabet, the days of the week, the monosyllabic nouns in the Latin language, and so on. His verses are sometimes ingenious, but their appeal to the young philosopher is puzzling.

Why Ausonius? Why these verses? The questions are answerable only in terms of *Descartes's dreams*. Anyone else's waking estimate of the philosophical content or artistic appeal of this poetry is beside the point. The particular dreamer's particular situation and the general characteristics of sleeping mentation are the decisive considerations. In general, dreams seem to condense and displace unconscious thoughts, judging from the fact that free associations, expanding on the several dream elements and refocusing interpretive attention, so regularly disclose coherent patterns of meaning relevant to real lives. The now-dead Descartes unwittingly specified the source for a functional equivalent of clinical associations for the two verses; to reopen his *Corpus poetarum* to his poems is to reopen his memory.

In the immediate context of the first quoted verse, there is the tumult of the courts and the anxieties of home, which even follow the traveler on his journey (*Eclogue* 2.1–3). This makes sense for the young Descartes in November 1619. It is relevant to his real life and coherent with the rest of this analysis. Consider now the immediate context of the second quoted verse, which seems so different in his narrative and his interpretation. Again, surprise of surprises, there is a reference to the clamor of the courts and, not long afterward, reference to domestic disagreements (*Eclogue* 4.1– 10, 13–14). There may be more in one context or the other— fears of the sea, rejection of soldiery, distaste for intellectual contention—but to have found in the two contexts the same most closely associated themes of court troubles and home troubles is to have approached as near the truth of the matter as the available evidence permits.

What way in life would René Descartes pursue? Not the courts, despite the family. The no to the law echoes as loudly as the yes to the search for truth, perhaps more loudly. On the anniversary of his licentiate and just before the Saint Martin's Day-after ceremonials and oath taking in the courts, this cadet son said no to the world of father Joachim Descartes, *conseiller* in the sovereign judicial court of Brittany and father of one *conseiller* already made, another in the making. This no to the law was also a yes to the sciences, but nothing is simple, and the anti-academicism explicit in *Eclogue* 4 may be significant.

By definition, one satisfactory associative interpretation can never preclude the possibility of another. There is at least one alternative explanation for this dreamer's recollection of these two verses at this time. Both poems are "Pythagorean," and this may have been very important. After he awakened on 11 November, Descartes seems to have identified at least the second verse as such (VDC

183–87).[33] An obvious attraction of this ancient for this modern is the Pythagorean linkage of philosophy with mathematics. Inspired more immediately by a less celebrated mathematical physicist, Beeckman, Descartes had begun his career as a modern Pythagorean one year earlier.

Eclogue 4, interpreted after awakening as a scientific revelation, somehow signified mathematical philosophy to the dreamer, whatever else it had meant for the poet. Descartes's first known work on mechanics, responding to Beeckman's question on the acceleration of a freely falling body, offered a solution that was generally geometrical and particularly Pythagorean. "Descartes reasoned that the pattern of increase of motion over time is as ever-larger Pythagorean triangles." That is, summing the units arrayed in equilateral triangles, he intuited that in the first "moment," the motion would be as 1, and in sequential "moments," it would increase from 1 to 3, 6, 10, 15, 21, and so on.[34] It was this work, the entitled but barely begun *Mechanics,* that Beeckman was most eager for him to continue and that Descartes tried to advance in the *Parnassus.*

It is also important that early moderns esteemed Pythagoras as a moral philosopher.[35] However, the Pythagorean lines in the first dream poem, as edited in the *Corpus poetarum* (which omits lines 51–64), were contextually remote from the initial line that he incorporated and thematically unrelated to anything else known to have been Cartesian. No Descartes, however young, could have found "the good advice of a wise person or even of Moral Theology" in the despairing couplet that taught the two greatest boons for miserable humanity to be these: never having been born in the first place or, failing that, dying young (*Eclogue* 2.48–50).[36]

There was also traditional Pythagoreanism in a young man's choice between the branching ways. The letter upsilon (Y) was the Pythagorean letter, insofar as it represented just such a branching, and it was the Latin poets who had most to say about this, not the Greek philosophers.[37] Persius referred to this tradition in two poems, both of which are particularly relevant to Descartes's situation. In *Satire* 3, the poet exhorts an errant youth to choose the right branch at the Pythagorean divide, to arouse himself from his sleepy idleness, and to direct his steps toward a defined goal.[38] In *Satire* 5, the poet recalls his own youthful wanderings and the guidance offered by Cornutus, his adoptive parent, beloved friend, and esteemed mentor, who had straightened out his crooked morals and directed his reason when he had arrived "at the branching crossways."[39] In less memorable and less personally suggestive verses, Ausonius, the poet of this dream night, twice referred to the old tradition of a young man's Pythagorean choice between the two ways, the right in both senses and the left or wrong.[40]

The verse that the dream Descartes first recalled and evidently preferred was Pythagorean in this sense, "Quod vitae sectabor iter?" The question that concerned him was that of his route through life, the beginning of Ausonius's *Eclogue* 2, not life or death, the end of the poem. That he was really most concerned with some such choice is strongly suggested by the biographical circumstances and the immediate poetic context. He had to decide between the ways of his father, judicial office and honors, and of his friend, mathematical philosophy and liberty.

DE III.6, 9, and 6–16 passim: All this strongly suggests that the Unknown of Dream III is best understood as yet another Beeckman figure. The obscure dream personage himself is closely associated with the table books and most particularly with the second poem (VDC 118–22), the one interpreted by the awakened dreamer as a promise of scientific understanding (VDC 183–87). The dream Descartes's response to his presence and his poem is telling. He is most anxious to show off his own knowledge, identifying the poet quite correctly and boasting that he knows the poem and can find it in the *Corpus* (VDC 123–28). This is perfectly in keeping with his newly affirmed identity as a "searcher for truth."

Nevertheless, the knower-searcher-discoverer fails repeatedly even in his dreams on the night after having discovered "the foundation of the wonderful science": he cannot explain where he got either the *Corpus* or the *Dictionary* (VDC 128–34); he does not actually get to use the *Dictionary,* and he cannot comprehend its incompleteness (VDC 137–39); he cannot find the Unknown's poem in his search of the *Corpus,* although it is the other book that he then discovers to be incomplete (VDC 126–42); he cannot even relocate his own poem, to which he had opened the book before the Unknown appeared (VDC 115–18, 143–47); he does not recognize this handsomer edition with its engraved portraits (VDC 147–51); he cannot seem to retain either the books or the bookish Unknown, both of which slip away before the frustrated dream thinker can redeem himself (VDC 151–53).

The frustrations of Dream III begin with the appearance of the Unknown. Dream Descartes wants desperately to *show* him what he *knows*, and yet he fails repeatedly. The best explanation is that the waking Descartes *was not* perfectly confident about his own intellectual accomplishment and that, for all his egocentric pretensions, he *was* particularly sensitive to at least one other person's critical judgment. Beeckman's spirit seems to have followed him on his travels and into his retreat.

DE III.14–15: When searching in the *Corpus poetarum* for *his* poem (*Eclogue* 2) at the end of Dream III, having already found the verse at the beginning, dream Descartes finds instead some little copperplate portraits. This is puzzling, because there are no portraits of the sort in Pierre des Brosses's book (VDC 148–51), any more than there are such engravings in the other, greater *Corpus*, Denis Godefroy's collections of Roman law.

Whence the engravings, if not from either *Corpus*? What did they mean? Descartes's answer was that the nighttime dream portraits were prophetic tokens and that the day-after appearance of an Italian painter, a prophecy come true, somehow vindicated the rest of his supernaturalistic interpretation. Now knowing his future, he sought no further explanation (VDC 192–200). However illogical Descartes's daytime reasoning, the dreamer is always right, and this apparent nonsense actually offers useful associational evidence. The little portraits were somehow related to the *Corpus*, his vocation, and his future.

Miniaturism was indeed the dominant style of engraved portraiture in France at the beginning of the seventeenth century. Thomas de Leu best represents these engravers.[41] His subjects included men of letters and savants as well as magistrates and courtiers. Arts and sciences were inseparable from their social context, and many authors chose to devote an engraved frontispiece to the vanity of the dedicatee. Even more interestingly, when the engraving honored the author himself, even the reduced, two-dimensional portrait specified his social qualifications and, typically, depicted his familial arms.

Most interestingly, a very high proportion of the engravings from even the very finest masters were commissioned so that young men could submit their theses under the image of a powerful protector. Robert Nanteuil (d. 1678) perfected the art of engraved portraiture in the generation after Descartes's death. Of 221 known portraits by Nanteuil, just 1 was ordered by a print-seller with strictly commercial ends in view; another 25–30 were portraits of authors *cr* their patrons for the book trade; at least 190 remain: "Almost all of the others were presented with or were meant to be presented with theses. The subject in each case was the person to whom the thesis was dedicated."[42]

René Descartes, too, was ambitious, even if his ambitions differed from those of his father and his father's colleagues. Although this is only speculation, he may have wishfully portrayed himself in his third dream as an author—and then improved the picture by wishfully adding engraved self-portraits to the book in his dreams. But the shadows of the law over so much of the rest of the dreams and the place of magistrates in real-life portraiture suggest a darker view. The little portraits in the *Corpus*, which Descartes himself preferred to interpret as prophetic signs of a philosophical future, may be so many deeply engraved marks of his *robin* past. To go his own way, he had departed from his father's way, something a seventeenth-century son could not do lightly.

The Olympian Interpretations in Retrospect

Descartes's Interpretation III is so spectacular in its implicit assertion of just what it explicitly denies, a dream *vision* (VDC 196–99, 204–7, 232–35, 247–52; compare 159–62), that less attention has been paid to his interpretations of the preceding two dreams. Furthermore, Interpretations I and II are obscure and inconsistent. Nevertheless, Descartes's immediate reactions to all three dreams are essential parts of the story, and failure to consider them carefully has contributed to the most serious misunderstandings by the most respected scholarly authority.

Henri Gouhier hypothesizes that the first and second nominal dreams were actually only pseudodreams[43] conceived by the youthful philosopher as introductory parts of a treatise on spiritual symbolism that he projected but never completed.[44] If this were demonstrable, any attempt to analyze the Olympian dreams as historical records would be nonsensical. If it were so much as tenable, any such attempt would be rash. But it is not tenable. This hypothesis necessarily entails reading the first and second nominal interpretations as only pseudo-interpretations, also conceived as parts of the supposed treatise-in-the-making. This hypothetically necessary reading is in fact impossible, however, and, for this reason among others, the received explanation of the *Olympica* as something other than a historical dream record simply fails.[45]

Descartes's three interpretations are too incoherent to have been conceived as parts of a philosophical whole, and neither the first nor the second either focuses on physical figures for spiritual realities or prepares the Cartesian cogitations on symbolism known from several of Leibniz's notes (CP 88–91, 115–19, 131–35). With one exception, his copies of these Olympian afterthoughts followed his copy of a resolution that Descartes dated 23 February 1620 (CP 109–12). This strongly suggests that his utterly conventional interest in figurative expression was remote by over three months from the night of dreams and the Olympian record, which is datable to November 1619 (CP 104–6; VDC 241–61). The one exception, CP 88–91, is a very brief passage of no particular interest, which has probably been misplaced as a part of Interpretation III.[46] There apparently was a relationship between the Olympian dreaming and the post-Olympian philosophizing about spiritual symbols, but the dream narratives and interpretations were historical occasions for later philosophizing of this sort, not literary constructions founded on earlier philosophizing.

Consider Interpretation I in Baillet's version, which may be incomplete: Descartes lurches from one extreme to another, from a vulgar spiritualism to an equally vulgar materialism. The former clearly predominates, but there is no discussion of symbolic elements in this dream or of spiritual symbolism more generally. Somehow, physical pain and the sharper prick of guilt convinced the dreamer on awakening that he had just received a demonic visitation (VDC 73–77). Then he prayed for God's forgiveness, not just for the sins of his waking past but also for the evils of his bad dream itself (VDC 77–83). Finally, for two full hours of "various [unreported] thoughts," he pondered "good and evil in this life" (VDC 83–86).

All this was quite in keeping with the most respectable dream lore of Descartes's time. The notion that demons were responsible for some dreams was a commonplace, sanctioned rather than repudiated by the most modern lay authorities.[47] The closely related notion that the sleeper who succumbed unconsciously to dream temptations had offended God was another such commonplace, on which that most "modern" student of dreams, Scipion du Pleix, could and did cite that greatest of the Latin Fathers, Augustine.[48] On 11 November 1619, Descartes would have been the very last man to interpret his dreams by the book, but he does seem to have shared fundamental assumptions about dreaming with more bookish authorities. With respect to the spiritualism of Interpretation I, he simply behaved like a seventeenth-century believer who really had dreamed bad dreams and really had meditated on them.

The same awakened dreamer also reacted to the same dream by rolling over in bed, turning from his left side onto his right. This implies that he also credited, however contrarily, a naturalistic explanation of the same lateral weakness or pain that suggested to him that his dream had been the work of a maleficent spirit. The troubled thinker apparently attributed his left-sidedness in the street scene to his left-sided posture in sleep. He thought that, to cure himself of his imagined debility, he had only to reposition his body in the bed, rolling from left to right (VDC 73–77).

What is so striking about this aspect of Interpretation I is that the truly great thinker should have so closely juxtaposed such contrary explanations of his own dreaming, explicitly spiritualistic in references to the "Evil Spirit" and his own sinfulness, implicitly materialistic in his change of bodily position. This systematic contradiction overshadows the illogic of the more "scientific" explanation taken by itself. That illogic is a matter of the troubled side, right or left. The dream trouble to be explained had certainly been on the *right side* (VDC 43–47), but the discomfort on awakening must have been experienced on the *left side,* judging from both the sleep posture on the left and the corrective repositioning to the right (VDC 73–77).

A dream doctor could explain this apparent inconsistency as a reflection of the actual conflicts that complicated Descartes's vocational decision and of the systematic contrast that generally opposes the distinctive amorality of unconscious mental life and the moral ideals upheld in conscious thought. In the street scene, the dreamer *unconsciously* rejects "the right," the law as an honored profession and the father's will as a legitimate imperative, but in the school scene, he encounters the friend who best represented the alternative vocation and for whom he had strongly ambivalent feelings. In Interpretation I, the awakened dreamer *consciously* moralizes, and, in the course of this thinking, he turns over in bed, symbolically reaffirming his commitment to "the right."

Had Descartes been reflecting dispassionately on spiritual symbols as such, he would have left a very different sort of record. This was a world in which only *some dreams* were thought to be spiritual, whereas *other dreams* were corporeal, and only *some* spiritual dreams were divine, whereas *others* were demonic.[49] Gouhier's hypothesis would require Descartes to have fabricated a figurative interpretation for a spiritual-divine pseudodream; this, however, is just what he did not record. Rather, Interpretation I confusedly presupposes that Dream I is both spiritual-demonic *and* corporeal, not spiritual-divine, and it does not interpret as spiritual symbols even those visual elements from the dream that suggest the most familiar figures, especially the various images of impeded progress in the street scene. The obscurity and confusion of the first interpretation are evidence against artificiality and so for historicity, not just of the interpretation but also of the dream itself.

Interpretation I also shows how much the concerns of the particular dream troubled the particular man. His assignment of moral blame to an evil spirit seems to have served him at the time as a psychological defense, projecting the blame from himself onto another. His implicit reduction of experienced dream troubles to mere effects of sleep positions would have entailed a radically different understanding of the dream, but it, too, seems to have served much the same purpose, defending the troubled man against the unconscious rebuke of his own dream.

Dream II and Interpretation II are even more telling in this respect. On reawakening from his Thunder Dream, Descartes discovered that he could generate entoptic flashes at will by blinking his eyes (VDC 90–102).[50] That ended his search for a substantive interpretation. Thunder was a familiar symbol of God's retributive anger, one used by Descartes himself in recording the fact of his *prior* meditation on his sins *in this immediate context* (VDC 79–83).

It is especially impressive, then, that Descartes should so unreservedly have embraced a naturalistic anti-interpretation for this little dreamlet, perhaps a hypnagogic hallucination,[51] and so categorically have denied any symbolic interpretation. His dubious (if comforting) philosophical exercise protected him against what would otherwise have been an almost inevitable (if painful) continuation of his meditations on his sins and their likely consequences. Given the "thunderbolts of heaven" from Interpretation I, anyone else interpreting the dream thunder in Dream II would have to hear it associatively as a sign of self-rebuke. The evident arbitrariness of the troubled man's explaining his aural hallucination by the visual pseudoflashes of Interpretation II is a sign of desperately defensive rationalization.

Descartes's recorded reflections after Dream I and after Dream II are quite unlike the second thoughts on these dreams that follow Dream III. In Interpretation III.3, his retrospective presumption is that *God* had warned him about his sinful past by the first two dreams (VDC 200–205) and had heralded His descent and His promises for a blessed future by the Thunder Dream (VDC 189–92, 223–25), not that an *evil spirit* had lured him into temptation, or that *his body* had lain in sleep on the wrong side, or that *his eyes,* closed in sleep, had somehow blinked with a terrible crash suggestive of thunder. It is as if the author of Interpretation I and II had not yet heard the good news of Interpretation III. This *is* good news. The interpretive discrepancies are so gross as to reassure critical readers about the historical integrity of the record. Philosophical invention would have been much more systematic.

Even the parts of Interpretation III devoted to Dream III are not truly "philosophical" in any senses other than that the interpreter was a philosopher-to-be and that he pronounced his own blessing on his own philosophy-in-the-making. He did attempt explanations of the most prominent objects in the dream, the two books and the two poems, but only as the occasions for the most arbitrary claims on behalf of his thought. This dream was "very soothing and very agreeable," because "the Spirit of Truth" had revealed to him his future (VDC 189–92, 196–200, 223–25):

1. *He* would bring together in a book "all the sciences" (VDC 158–59);
2. *he* would unify "Philosophy and Wisdom," an ambition that seems to link science and morals (VDC 160–62);
3. *his* choice of a way in life was sanctioned by "a wise person or even . . . Moral Theology" (VDC 173–78);
4. *he* would enjoy "the favors of Revelation and Enthusiasm" (VDC 181–83);
5. *he* would determine "Truth and Falsehood in human understanding and the profane sciences" (VDC 183–87);
6. *God* had given *him* "the treasures of all the sciences by this dream" (VDC 189–92).

And how could he be sure of all this? Because, as a sign, one of the dream books had included engraved portraits, and, in fact, an Italian painter did pay him a visit on the next day. Q.E.D.

Interpretation III, phases 1 and 2, reveals a great deal about the dreamer and suggests something about the meaning of his dream. Had he been willing to consider the dream as a product of "his human mind," he could have said much more of historical interest about his past. However, he became more and more convinced that the dream had been a divine vision of his future (VDC 154–58; compare 187–200, 223–25, 235–40), and for that reason he had nothing to say about anything but his state of mind at that moment. This is enough: it was *the* moment, the personal rebellion that sparked the Cartesian Revolution.

Claims 1, 4, 5, and 6 obviously concern Descartes's aspirations as the young discoverer of "the foundation of the wonderful science." More conventional sources also document the strength of his youthful convictions that the sciences were *one* and that he could find truths by a *regular method*.[52] There was more to Descartes's career than formal thinking, however. There was also a truly marvelous willpower and a boundless self-confidence that had nothing to do with the rationality of his fundamental ideas. The *Olympica* allows us to retrace these traits as far back as the wishful thinking of his dreams and the spiritualism of his last interpretation. An analysis of these materials offers previously unsuspected glimpses of what had come before that.

Claims 2 and 3 concern vocational choices, though this has never been obvious. The greatest interpretive challenge of the dreams has been to understand the pervasive anxiety and guilt of the young thinker. Why did Descartes feel this remorse? It was not a matter of bad thoughts. It therefore must have been a matter of the wrong way of life, at least as judged by his father, who represented the law, and perhaps also his friend, who represented a search for truth to which Descartes had not committed himself decisively enough. The dreams themselves betray his anxieties and his self-doubts. Interpretation III, phase 3, is most valuable for its partial recognition that Dreams I and II concerned his past life and wrong-doing (VDC 200–205, 220–23). Even here, his interpretations of the gift melon and the contrary wind smack of rationalizations and stop short of historically particular associations (VDC 206–29). An analysis founded on such associations goes further: Isaac Beeckman was trying to lure him into a scholarly retreat; Joachim Descartes was trying to force him into the law. Self-serving reflections on his dreams helped him decide between these ways of life, allowing him to make up his own mind while reassuring himself that his will was God's will, that his truths were God's truths (VDC 173–200, 223–25, 235–48).

Conclusions: The Dreaming Man
and the Thinking Thing

These conclusions concern the historicity of the dreams, the validity of this analysis, and its significance for students of Descartes's thought. First, historicity: Descartes really dreamed his Olympian dreams on the night of 10 November 1619. Furthermore, the evidence indicates that he recorded them accurately and that Baillet paraphrased his record reliably. Twentieth-century scholars have denied all this. To reaffirm the reality of these dreams and the worth of this evidence is in itself to restore the major event of and the best source on the most crucial period in the formation of Descartes's mature personality as a revolutionary thinker.

Second, validity: Descartes finally satisfied himself that he could discriminate between meaningless dreams and meaningful thoughts. With respect to manifest dream narratives, he was right about meaninglessness, but with respect to latent dream thoughts, he was wrong. The Olympian dreams were meaningful even by his own rationalist criteria. Historical inquiry directed toward the analysis of these dreams offers a wholly new perspective on the young Descartes. To look backward from the *Olympica* is to glimpse a more broadly and more deeply human figure than the lifeless construct familiar from the *Discourse*.

Third, significance: Descartes's thoughts still matter; his dreams, as such, do not (although the feasibility of an empirical and critical dream analysis is a methodological question of both considerable interest to students of dream psychology and at least limited interest to students of history as such). Dream psychology can be historical; this history must be psychological. And Descartes? He tried hard to be philosophical, systematically basing his thought on his self-knowledge as a *thinking thing*, emphatically *not* a *dreaming man*. Nevertheless, inquiry into the episode of the Olympian dreams offers a new, broader, and deeper understanding of *this* man at *this* crucial period, and so it also has implications for the critical understanding of his most celebrated thoughts, particularly the revolutionary rejection of others' thought by the rule of *évidence* and the rationalist conception of self essential to the *cogito*. This is of the most general interest, given the fundamental importance of these ideas for Cartesian thought and the significance of Cartesian thought for the history of modern Western civilization.

Historicity

Descartes himself eventually formulated philosophical criteria by which to distinguish his dreams from his thoughts. In the *Meditations,* the following concise generalization concludes his metaphysics: "For now I find a very notable difference, in that our memory can never bind and join our dreams to one another or to the rest of our lives."[1] These are the criterion of internal incoherence and the criterion of external irrelevance, respectively. *On the manifest level,* the earlier Olympian narratives satisfy these later criteria for real dreams, not thoughts.

The criterion of internal incoherence comes first. Consider either sequence, Dreams I and II or Dreams II and III. What binds and joins the Thunder Dream to Dream I's school scene beforehand or to the Books Dream afterward? On the manifest level, nothing, absolutely nothing. Setting aside the noisily disruptive second dream, what would bind and join even the first and third dreams, the school scene and the Books Dream? Not time, place, action, settings, props, actors other than the dreamer, or even notable characteristics of the dream Descartes himself.

Even the individual dreams fail to cohere. I have numbered but, significantly, not named Dream I. Its school scene is bound to its street scene only loosely by the dream Descartes's search for a refuge and a remedy. These two more nearly coherent scenes are themselves somewhat disjointed. The dream walker's troubles give a measure of unity to the street scene, but the ghosts vanish without leaving a trace, and the lateral weakness and the whirlwind suggest radically different disabilities:

DE I.1: RD encounters frightening ghosts as he walks the streets.
DE I.2: RD's weakness on his right makes him lean to his left.
DE I.3: RD feels shame at his inability to straighten up.
DE I.4: RD is spun around three or four times by a whirlwind.
DE I.5: RD is alarmingly unable to advance and fears falling.

At a touch, the school scene disintegrates into four pairs of dream elements:

DE I.6: RD enters a school's grounds seeking refuge and remedy.
DE I.7: RD voluntarily approaches a church for prayer.

DE I.8: RD unwittingly snubs an Acquaintance and tries to return.
DE I.9: RD is involuntarily driven back by a contrary wind.

DE I.10: RD is greeted by the Other Person and promised a present from N.
DE I.11: RD interprets the present as a melon from a foreign land.

DE I.12: RD sees others, upright and steady, around the Other Person.
DE I.13: RD is still leaning and unsteady, despite the abated wind.

Dream II, "a sudden, loud noise," is so abrupt that it is not properly either coherent or incoherent. Dream III is stereotypically dreamlike, the narrator's focus shifting rather erratically from book to book, verse to verse, poetry to engravings, and so on. The appearances and disappearances of the books and the Unknown are obvious signs of incoherence, and no one narrative line is followed to a satisfying end, logically or dramatically:

DE III.1: RD discovers a book on his table, its origin unknown.
DE III.2: RD happily identifies this book as the useful *Dictionary*.
DE III.3: RD discovers a second book, its origin also unknown.
DE III.4: RD identifies the second book as the *Corpus poetarum*.

DE III.5: RD opens the *Corpus,* by chance, at "Quod . . . iter?"
DE III.6: RD notices Unknown, who recommends "Est et non."
DE III.7: RD boasts knowledge of this poem and its place in the volume.
DE III.8: RD searches for "Est et non" in the *Corpus poetarum.*
DE III.9: Unknown asks, "Whence these books?" RD cannot explain.
DE III.10: RD loses the *Dictionary* and fails to find "Est et non."
DE III.11: The *Dictionary* reappears, now somehow incomplete.
DE III.12: RD finds Ausonius but not "Est et non" in the *Corpus.*
DE III.13: RD recommends "Quod . . . iter?" as a finer poem.
DE III.14: RD searches for this poem and finds engravings.
DE III.15: RD admires this edition and contrasts it with another.
DE III.16: Books and Unknown disappear without awakening RD.

Loose ends left dangling at the end—hardly a proper conclusion—of Dream III include not only the appearances and disappearances of the books but also the usefulness and incompleteness of the dream dictionary; the contents, structure, and ornamentation of the dream anthology; and the appearance of, disappearance of, and everything else about the mysterious Unknown.

The criterion of external irrelevance comes second. So little evidence survives about the young man's actual situation that most questions concerning the relevance of the manifest dream elements are strictly unanswerable.[2] Descartes himself, who wanted to relate his own dream narratives to his life, past and future (VDC 77–83, 197–205, 220–23), specifically bound and joined situation and narrative only with respect to DE III.14, the Italian painter actually encountered on the day after serving to explain the dream engravings imagined in the night before (VDC 192–96).

Descartes defined relevance in restricted senses when he conceived this criterion for distinguishing thinking from dreaming; by the irrelevance of dream experience, he meant that it transpires apart from continuous real space and time. His single illustration recalls Dream III, adding what is virtually his seal to an argument for historicity based on his criteria:[3]

> For now I find this very notable difference: our memory can never bind and join our dreams to one another [the criterion of internal

incoherence] or to the rest of our lives [the criterion of external irrelevance] as it usually combines aspects of our waking experience. Indeed, *if someone were to appear before me quite suddenly and then disappear in the same manner* when I was awake, *as do the images that I "see" while sleeping,* so that I couldn't tell where he had come from or where he was going to, it wouldn't be unreasonable for me to conclude that this wasn't a true man, but a specter or phantom conjured up in my own brain, *like those that I imagine [in my dreams] when I sleep.*

But when I perceive the things of which I become aware distinctly with respect to the place from whence they come and the place in which they are and with respect to the time when they make their appearance, and when I can integrate this awareness within the continuity of the rest of my life, there being no interruptions, I can be completely certain that I perceive them in waking life and not in sleep. Therefore, I ought not to doubt the truth of these things in any way at all, my senses, my memory, and my critical reason being in perfect accord [emphases added].[4]

Until he finally satisfied himself with these two criteria, the mature Descartes fretted over the distinction between his thinking and his dreaming, worrying that what seemed to be grand thoughts might be only petty dreams, after all. *His* philosophical purpose was to establish rational certainties, and so, *for him,* it was important to exclude all possibility that his metaphysical first foundations included mere fantasies.[5] Given his historical experience of fundamental thoughts and Olympian dreams at the beginning of winter 1619, he was right to be concerned, but it would never have occurred to him to worry that apparent dreams might have been actual thoughts.

In a modern version of the world turned upside down, scholars have stood the hero-philosopher on his head, concluding that his Olympian dreams were so many waking thoughts. Why have they done this? Part of the explanation must be that respectful Cartesians have seen that these dreams, taken at face value as dreams, show the great thinker's historical first foundations in fact to have included what a detached observer would reject as mere fantasies. Pseudodreams, however—the Olympian dreams reinterpreted as allegorical inventions—could be shelved far from the mature philosophy and cataloged separately in a sort of limbo library as mere juvenilia, soon outgrown.[6]

The reclassification of Descartes's real dreams as only philosophical fictions has been accepted by the most authoritative scholars. Nevertheless, this reclassification rests on serious misrepresentations of the historical evidence, on a virtually complete ignorance of dream psychology, and on a very partial understanding even of the supposedly influential allegorical traditions. In this case, it has been a nonpsychological history that has haughtily disregarded the evidence; the first task of a psychologically sophisticated history must be to reestablish it. My first major claim is to have vindicated the historicity of the dreams themselves, the accuracy of Descartes's report, and the reliability of Baillet's version. Appendices 1–3 add the necessarily technical argument.

Validity

Descartes's *latent dream thoughts* on 10 November 1619 concerned his rejection of the law in favor of "the search for truth," an apparently simple, even inevitable vocational decision that was actually complicated by uneasy relationships with both his father, the *conseiller* Joachim Descartes, and his friend and mentor, the savant Isaac Beeckman. The validity of this analysis can be measured by a somewhat modified version of the Cartesian criteria for meaningful thinking that were first conceived to disqualify all dreaming. I redefine relevance in terms of personal experience, emphasizing social and emotional life.

It makes better sense historically to begin with the redefined criterion of external relevance. On 10 November 1619, Descartes was an unsettled twenty-three year old distinguishable from other unsettled twenty-three year olds in at least the following ways. First, he was the son of an honorable family of Poitevin magistrates just then becoming a noble dynasty of Breton magistrates, and he had received the legal education that qualified him for an official career.[7] Second, he had been befriended by a personally timid but intellectually bold Dutch savant who had introduced him to the mechanistic understanding of physical phenomena, winning his love, inspiring his work, and urging its publication.[8] Third, he was a genius with grandiose ambitions to play a leading role on the great stage, to go his own way, to follow fixed rules, and to unify the sciences by a method modeled on geometrical reasoning.[9]

The dream date, 10 November 1619, and the initial reference to the contemporaneous discovery of "the foundation of the wonderful science" justify historical recourse to the *Discourse*. There, good evidence relates intellectual discovery (the fundamentals of a method) to vocational decision making (the search for truth chosen over the law).[10] Beeckman's *Journal* shows that Descartes's first encounter with his later mentor and dearest friend had come on the same date one year earlier (10 November 1618). Other evidence also suggests that he closely associated his intellectual development with the Feast of Saint Martin. This evidence includes his dated marginal notation from the *Olympica* on the "wonderful discovery" (11 November 1620) and Baillet's derivative account of his philosophical presentation to the learned company at the Papal Nuncio's (reportedly on or about 11 November 1628) and his commissioning then and there to write up and to publish his formal thought.[11]

The Saint Martin's date also had a prior special meaning for this lawyer-nonlawyer and son of a judge: records from Poitiers show that the culmination of Descartes's legal education had come on the same date three years earlier (10 November 1616), and massive evidence demonstrates that the annual *rentrées* of Saint Martin's Day-after (12 November) began the judicial year in the French courts with impressive ceremonies that included the oath taking of lawyers and judges.[12]

On the latent level, when interpreted, the several elements of the street scene (DE I.1–5) both cohere (Descartes's first criterion) and relate to the rest of his life (his second criterion). The street scene visually represents philosophical methods or ways and vocational choices or paths, the former through etymological resonances and the latter through symbolic images. The dream Descartes acts out a part that is in every respect non-*droit:* he cannot put weight on his *right* foot; he cannot hold himself up*right;* he cannot advance in a *straight* line. Dreamed fear, shame, and disability express what can only have been real-life anxiety, and the peculiar and manifestly incoherent dream explanations of the dream walker's troubles suggest the latent meaning of the anxiety. Some of it must represent doubts about how to pursue the right way as a thinker, but there were also deeper problems. In his latent dream thoughts, he was rejecting the law in favor of a search for truth, and his father would surely have objected that this was the wrong way in life, whereas his friend had already objected that he had not committed himself fully enough to this search.[13]

On the latent level, when interpreted along the same lines, the school scene also meets both Cartesian criteria for meaningful thinking, namely, those of coherence and relevance. Beeckman was to begin a quietly distinguished career as a teacher in the very month of Descartes's dreams, so that the school setting is particularly appropriate for a dream encounter on the anniversary of their historical first encounter. Cogitations concerning friendship, rebuke, and opposed passions (CP 74–87) seem to have come from a record of waking thoughts that followed this dream in the *Olympica* (VDC 83–86).

The approach-avoidance acted out by the dream Descartes in DE I.7–9 visually represents inclinations so strongly opposed that the proper terms are love and hate; the dream Acquaintance makes historical sense only as a Beeckman figure. The peculiar episode of the gift melon from a foreign land (DE I.10–11) recalls proverbial wisdom likening present-day friends to melons, there being much fewer really good ones than bad ones, and it being so difficult to select a good one from among the many others. Beeckman, the foreigner and the true friend in word, had proven false in deed, or so Descartes thought. The school scene ends with the melancholy vision of the Other Person "in the midst of the school courtyard," a company "clustered around him," unimpeded and untroubled. The dream Descartes looks on, standing apart, still afflicted with his troubles (DE I.12–13). On the manifest level, all this is both incoherent and irrelevant. On the latent level, its meaning is both coherent and relevant.[14]

Dream II provides the neatest example of *latent* meaningfulness even in a case of the most obvious manifest meaninglessness.[15] This dream followed two hours of nighttime wakefulness in which Descartes had confessed sins meriting "the thunderbolts of heaven" as God's punishment, prayed for forgiveness, and meditated on "good and evil" (VDC 77–86). He fell asleep once again, only to hear a dream noise that he took to be thunder. It is no wonder that, on awakening, he was terrified. He had passed judgment on himself, and his fearful dream expressed a guilty man's apprehension of merited punishment. Descartes does not explain the historical occasion for guilt or fear, of course, but the most coherent and relevant analysis is perfectly plausible: trepidation at his defiance of his father's presumed will on the matter of his "way in life," the law as a career preferred by the father-judge and rejected by the son-searcher-for-truth. Both knew the Fourth Commandment.[16]

Finally, *on the latent level,* the Books Dream, too, coheres and relates in much the same way, although, following Descartes's waking intuition, I suppose a reorientation from past in Dreams I and II (rejection of the law and familial tradition) to future in Dream III (affirmation of the search for truth as his own way). The two dream books recall Descartes's promise to Beeckman that he would complete his *Geometry* and his *Mechanics.* The close visual association of the books and the table also recalls Beeckman, who called his inspiring scientific notebooks "Table Books."[17]

As the title for the first of Descartes's dream books, the *Dictionary* recalls his pensée on his authorship and originality, and both its extreme elusiveness and its curious incompleteness (DE III.11) recall his real failure to produce a completed book, despite his grand aspirations, Beeckman's exhortations, and his promises. The nominally sleeping interpretation of the dream *Dictionary* as "all the sciences gathered together" (VDC 158–59) is arbitrary only on the manifest level. The latent meaning coheres with the rest of his dream thoughts and relates to his real life: Descartes wanted to complete and publish his own book of universal science, and he wished that he had done so.[18]

As the title of the second dream book, the *Corpus poetarum* recalls the great *Corpus* of the civil law, and Descartes's aleatory opening of this dream book (DE III.3–5) recalls the customary procedure used for examinations like those that had terminated his legal training just three years earlier in the first of the known Saint Martin's events. Even the dream engravings admired in the *Corpus* (DE III.14–15) may well have had a legal reference, given the custom of submitting theses under the protective regard of a patron's image.[19]

The first dream poem, Ausonius's "Quod vitae sectabor iter," explicitly raises the vexed issue of career choices (DE III.5). The nominally sleeping interpreter supposes this versified question to settle the matter in a way that is both wise and moral. Having staked his claim to a universal science, the dreamer's evident concern was to vindicate his choice of a way of life, the search for truth. This implies that he had already experienced or anticipated others' opposition to his choice, but that he was determined to go his own way as a philosopher (VDC 158–78).[20]

The second dream poem, Ausonius's "Est et Non" (DE III.6), seemed to the awakened dreamer to be a Pythagorean reference to "Truth and Falsehood in human understanding and the profane sciences" (VDC 183–87). Pythagorean mathematicism was broadly related to Descartes's own philosophical and scientific aspirations, most generally his conception of a mathematically inspired method and more particularly his geometrical solution to Beeckman's free-fall problem. The dream Unknown who gives him this poem a year to the day after the historical first encounter with Beeckman recalls this friend and mentor; the dream Descartes responds with claims of special knowledge, with a determined but frustrated effort to exhibit that knowledge, and with a superior poem of his own choice on a way of life as a truth seeker.[21]

Descartes's distinction between waking thought and dreaming nonthought was important enough to him that he placed it at the conclusion of his *Meditations*. He was right that there is an essential difference between thinking and dreaming, and his criteria were good ones. He was wrong, however, to conclude from the incoherence and irrelevance of manifest dreams that there is no such thing as truly meaningful dream thought.

In interpreting dreams, Freud first discovered personally significant patterns in each analysand's associations for separate dream elements. He reasoned that neither he, as a willfully passive and merely receptive analyst, nor the free-associating analysand could artificially fabricate or arbitrarily select associations to fit these significant patterns. They could come only from the dreamer's unconscious mind. These patterns imply previously unsuspected latent thoughts distorted by these processes of dream formation or thought transformation: condensation, displacement, and visual representation.[22]

Apart from the special case of his self-analysis, Freud's experience as a dream interpreter was restricted to the confines of the clinic and limits of the analytical hour. When he pronounced against the very possibility of interpreting the Olympian dreams, because there was no living dreamer to volunteer free associations, he did so as the jealous guardian of his own new science.[23] He could not have imagined a scholarly enterprise that would devote years to the historical analysis of one night's dreaming three centuries earlier. He probably knew nothing about the Descartes family or the Beeckman friendship, and he had almost certainly never considered any of the best sources on Descartes's youthful thought.[24]

The crucial question of validity cannot be answered by the dictates of Freudian theory or the limitations of clinical practice. The facts of the matter are these: the coincidence of the philosopher's epochal intellectual discovery with a troubled vocational decision is a conclusion of ordinary historical inquiry; even the limited sources available provide associations that satisfy Descartes's standards for meaningful thinking; and the most prominent dream elements in the most important dream, Ausonius's verses in Dream III, were drawn from Descartes's sleeping memory of a real anthology that we can still pull down from the shelves and reopen so as to observe latent content "before" the transformative processes of the dream work, condensation and displacement.

On the manifest level, the two verses recorded by Descartes do not cohere with one another or the rest of the dreams. On this level, I cannot establish their relevance to the rest of his life. There must be a latent level, however, one obscured by processes of condensation and displacement, because the poetic context, which expands the recorded text and redirects analytical attention to unrecorded elements, exposes a meaningful pattern:

> *Eclogue* 2: What way in life shall I pursue? The courts are full of tumult; the home is vexed with cares; home troubles follow us abroad. . . .

> *Eclogue* 4: "Yes" and "No." Everyone uses these monosyllables all the time. . . . From them comes the clamor of the courts [and other contests]. . . . Fathers hear these words from . . . children, who repeat them in peaceful expressions of particular inclinations without giving offense. . . .

Significance

There is no need to defend Descartes the man against any threat from his own Olympian dreams. They simply do not provide evidence of weak-mindedness, craziness, or anything else abnormal or pathological, despite the extreme embarrassment betrayed by sympathetic historians and the unholy glee of the unsympathetic.[25] Nothing in the manifest dreams or the latent thoughts seems especially shameful or morally reprehensible, whatever the worth of Freud's intuition that the dream melon was the symbol of a sexual fantasy. Even the most orthodox Freudian could conclude from this only that a Descartes who so fantasized in his dreams exhibited unconscious drives that could have been inferred from psychoanalytical theory alone.[26] So the dreams cannot sully the honor of Descartes the man.

The significance of the dreams for Descartes the thinker is another matter. Any redirection of attention from the late reports on thinking to the early reports on dreaming at the most crucial period in the philosopher's development is at least implicitly anti-Cartesian. This was true in the seventeenth century, when readers knew only the irrational narratives and enthusiastic interpretations, and it remains true at this point in the twentieth, when any analysis would have to emphasize latent thoughts, troubling emotions, and significant conflicts within an unconscious mind. The philosopher was later to make so much of his "essential" rationality, his perfect self-consciousness, and his personal autonomy and superiority to all "cares and passions," particularly at the beginning of winter 1619, that an analysis of dreams could be an occasion for battering his head with batons taken from his own hands.[27] However, there does not seem to be any point to an attack on a long-dead philosophical doctrine in the name of a psychological history.

The true significance of the Olympian dreams is that they can help explain the personality of Descartes the man as it was related to the ideas of Descartes the thinker. Two traits seem particularly distinctive. First, there was the youthful rebelliousness with which he declared his independence from the venerable claims of intellectual tradition, authority, and community. Second, there was the absolute conviction with which he identified himself as an autonomous thinker committed to the search for truth. Both had lasting consequences for the formal philosophy that he articulated only in later years.

Descartes's philosophical rebellion was at first a personally memorable historical event at the beginning of winter, 1619, a one-time rejection of all prior opinions in what amounts to a declaration of intellectual independence. In the *Discourse,* the second part begins with the celebrated sentence that sketches the scene in the heated chamber; then comes "thought," the quintuple analogy meant to establish the superiority of all independent thinking: *like* the architect . . . , *like* the city-planner . . . , *like* the law-giver . . . , *like* the scholar . . . , *and like* the young man coming of age.[28]

The personal aggressiveness of all this is inseparable from its intellectual radicalism. In the the second, third, and fourth of these analogies, Descartes implicitly condemns the disorderly cities, customary laws, and scholarly traditions that characterized his time and place. He was not a social-political revolutionary, but he was quite ready to pass judgment on the laws of Poitou, Brittany, Paris, and so on. And he had made up his mind on the sciences taught at La Flèche, Poitiers, and the other colleges and universities. Significantly, his judgment on the sciences comes fourth, not fifth.

Descartes's quintuple analogy culminates in the image of a young man coming of age and casting off dependence on others. He had been legally subject to his father at the age of twenty-three, and he was still implicitly rebellious in what amounts to a vindication of self-emancipation seventeen years later:

> And likewise, I also thought that we have all been children before reaching adulthood. For a long time, we were necessarily subject to our appetites and our teachers. They often disagreed, and neither the one nor the other always counseled us for the best. Thus, it is almost inevitable that our judgment shouldn't be as pure [impure appetites?] or as firm [infirm teachers and teachings?] as if we had had the complete use of our reason from the time of our birth and had followed no other counsels.[29]

Immediately after introducing the emancipated youth as a final model for the independent thinker, Descartes returns to his first analogy, the architect. This image seems quintessentially constructive, but in his hands it becomes destructive: "To be sure, we never see all of the houses of a city leveled simply so that they can be rebuilt in another way . . . , but we do see individuals tear theirs down in order to rebuild them, sometimes out of necessity, when the foundations are infirm."[30] The mature Descartes writes as if he had been perfectly justifed in what amounts to a one-day career as a philosopher-wrecker.

Joachim Descartes might have had something to say to his second son had he heard this sort of argument in 1619. Images of the philosopher-legislator, the philosopher-youth, and the philosopher-architect or -wrecker struck particularly close to home. As narrated in the *Discourse,* the searcher for his own truth who could have boasted only a beginner's credentials in the two laws of the schools, Roman law and canon law, makes a philosophical case against the sort of law actually applied in Joachim's court, the ordinances and edicts of the kings of France and the customary laws of Brittany. This would have been bad enough, but worse still would have been the claim of a younger son who was still legally a minor that he would have been better off, hypothetically, if he were to have had the full advantage of his own "pure" and "firm" reason from the time of his birth, so that he could have avoided all the pitfalls of guidance by anything or anyone else! And worst would have been the awful image of the philosopher-wrecker adopted by this willful youth who seemed to want to destroy his *house!* Whose house? What house?

Descartes's truly rebellious conclusion follows. It is his Declaration of Independence, and the words published in 1637 probably are faithful to a historical event in 1619:[31] "With respect to every opinion that I had ever accepted, I couldn't do better than to undertake, for once and for all, to reject them. Afterward I could either restore them or replace them, when I had taken their measure by the tools of reason."[32] This one event matters so much because the mature Descartes prescribed what amounts to a lesser reenactment for every methodical thinker with respect to every intellectual problem: "The first [precept or rule of the Cartesian method] was never to accept anything as true unless I knew it to be evidently such. This meant to take care to avoid haste and prejudgment and to include nothing in my thinking other than that which was so clear and so distinct in my mind that there was no reason to doubt it."[33] It would be equally justifiable to say that his first rule was to reenact his youthful rebellion on each occasion of methodical thinking—and that this rule regularized and legitimated just what had been irregular and illegitimate in his personal history.

It is impossible to overstate the significance of Descartes's first rule. Although it is now termed the rule of *évidence,* a constructive reading, it is also a rule of doubt, with radically destructive potential. When Jean Le Rond d'Alembert honored "the illustrious Descartes" as the philosophical forefather of the French Enlightenment, for instance, it was as a courageous rebel chieftain who had thrown off the yoke of "scholasticism, opinion, authority, and, in two words, prejudice and barbarism." He had, so to speak, plotted the revolutionary destruction of "arbitrary and despotic power." The rebel's most enduring heritage was his methodical doubt.[34]

This is not to reduce the Cartesian Method or its truly fundamental rule of *évidence* to whatever status is proper for the plottings of rebel chieftains or the posturings of rebellious sons. Instead, it is to open up the rationalist's heated chamber to the cooling drafts of historical analysis. It is to respect the weight of the evidence that associates the great philosophical breakthrough to a higher truth with the yet-to-be-proven-great philosopher's quite personal and quite passionate embrace of a vocation that might please his intimate friend but would displease his father. However complex or profound its origins, the rule has proved to be fruitful. I myself began even this inquiry by doubting away the scholarship reviewed critically in the appendices. But no one, certainly not a Cartesian appalled by my work, should doubt that the rule was also radical in its defiance of authority, tradition, and consensus.

The lesson of the Olympian dreams is that Descartes's intellectual breakthrough at the beginning of winter, 1619, was not clearly and distinctly set off from the rest of his life—and that his life was not quite so simply rational as he liked to think. A youthful rebellion against the way of life dominant in his father's house had come at the same time as his own intellectual discovery of "the foundation of the wonderful science." Only an abstract, ahistorical, and rationalistic historiography has separated the life from the work—to the greater glory of the latter. The analysis of the dreams serves us best by obscuring and complicating once again what Descartes reduced into the clear and distinct thought of his retrospective *Discourse*.

The thinking of the self-proclaimed master of methodical reason was conditioned by his past, his relationships, and his emotions. He himself coupled the retrospective story of his Declaration of Independence with the enunciation of a universal rule of *évidence* or doubt. An earlier and much less elegant version of that rule, tentatively datable to 1619–20, survives in the *Regulae*,[35] but the rational mind was never all in all, and analysis of the Olympian dreams now suggests deeper anxieties about the rectitude of his vocational course, his way in life as a searcher for truth, and even about his capacity as a thinker. It also suggests a deeper determination to break from what had been the familial pattern of judicial office holding.

Descartes would become a full-time thinker. That this was an identity, not merely a rewarding or satisfying occupation, is clear from the autobiographical elements in both his historical *Discourse* and his fictional *Recherche de la vérité*. That the identity went back to the season of the Olympian dreams is perhaps clearest in that fragment from the *Praeambula* in which Descartes makes himself the possessive husband for a science personified as a woman and made respectable by marriage to him (CP 10–12). Much later, his most celebrated thought and his philosophical first principle was the *cogito:* "I think, therefore I am." After the existence of self comes the nature of self; Descartes the thinker knows himself as "a substance whose entire essence or nature is only to think."[36]

The first readers of the *Discourse* rightly objected to the rationalistic exclusivity of this conception of the self. To know the self first or best or solely as a thinking thing is not to disprove the existence of other aspects of the self. But Descartes was adamant. He refused to accept the criticism or to reconsider his claim as only one stage in an ordered argument about the nature of the self.[37] In the *Meditations*, he argues that he is in fact "a thinking thing," nothing less, nothing more: "Thought is an attribute that belongs to me. It alone can't be taken away from me. I am, I exist. That is certain, but for how long? As long as I think. Perhaps, if I were to cease to think, I would thereby cease to be or to exist. . . . Therefore, strictly speaking, I am only a thinking thing, that is, a mind, an understanding, or a reason . . . I really am something, something that exists. But what? I've just said, a thinking thing."[38]

The *cogito* is best understood historically as an intuition, *René Descartes's* intuition *after* the episode of the Olympian thoughts and dreams. His very existence was unimaginable except insofar as he could affirm himself to be a thinker, nothing else. Philosophically, thinking was his essence. Psychologically, it was his identity. Thinking abstractly, and perhaps in other ways, too, he could not accept that he had been brought into personal existence as his father's son—and he could not imagine that he could be denied his chosen manner of life as an independent intellectual without risk of personal annihilation. He was a Thinking Thing. His identity had been forged in the course of his thinking, to be sure, but his thinking was that of a rebellious son and a restive pupil. Unlike his father, he would not be a magistrate. Like his friend, he would be a searcher for truth, a thinker in his own manner, more mathematical and more philosophical. And so it was to be.

Perhaps it is an error, yet another rationalizing error, to try to vindicate this sort of inquiry by reference to specific philosophical ideas. There was no right or straight way leading from the Olympian dreams to the numbered rules or the metaphysical propositions of the *Discourse* and the *Meditations*. Nonetheless, this does not mean that the great thinker was wrong to have supposed that the most important way station on his personal route toward philosophical maturity had been the heated chamber. There, he thought constructively. There, his dreams helped him resolve, at least partially, emotional conflicts related to his father and his friend. And there, he received what he took to be God's blessing, a divine commissioning to pursue his own chosen way.

The formal thinker whom we know so much better, the philosophical author of the mature works, was always to be aggressively independent. Further, he was to be the archrationalist. These very general intellectual traits were buttressed by if not founded on his quite particular and subrational passions. And we must not forget the inspiration of his superrational faith, however the d'Alemberts and Diderots preferred to interpret his work a century after his death. The unique advantage of René Descartes's Olympian dreams, both narratives and interpretations, is that they can usher us back into the heated chamber, wherein the great man at the threshold of his adulthood and of our modernity looked backward as well as forward, down as well as up, with his eyes fully closed for at least part of the fateful night and day.

THE HISTORICAL EVIDENCE
ON THE OLYMPIAN DREAMS

he Olympian dreams of 10 November 1619 somehow inspired Descartes with greater confidence in his new discovery of a "wonderful science," but these same irrational narratives and enthusiastic interpretations have appalled later Cartesians, who have rightly supposed that the dreams might shadow the thoughts of that epochal season. Adrien Baillet evidently disapproved of the dreams, but he had the documentary evidence, and, ever the copyist, he uncomprehendingly incorporated a version of the *Olympica* into his biography. It was left to the scholars of the twentieth century to deny the historical evidence on the dreamer in an apparent effort to defend the honor of the thinker.

First, in 1908 Charles Adam denied the reliability of Baillet's translation, the one surviving source on the dream narratives. The great editor thus built an outer wall that protected the great thinker from his own dreams. *Second,* in 1924 Henri Gouhier denied the accuracy of Descartes's lost dream reports. The great historian thus constructed an inner wall that could hold even if the outer wall failed. *Third,* in 1952 Paul Arnold denied the very historicity of the dreams themselves, which might not have mattered had Gouhier not then extended and endorsed the argument while qualifying it. This was to raise a seemingly impenetrable central keep for Descartes the thinker. None of these imposing walls was well designed or well built, however, and when these defenses are probed, they come tumbling down.

Appendix 1:
The Technical Question of
Baillet's Translations

Charles Adam, the historical excluder for whom the Olympian episode represented weak-minded "enthusiasm," Rosicrucian "illumination," and momentary "mysticism," was also the editorial includer to whom Baillet's *Vie de Monsieur Des Cartes* offered versions of many texts not otherwise available, including the *Olympica*.[1] Adam's combined authority as the scholarly biographer and editor has given his prefatory remarks great weight, but in the following five ill-considered sentences he couples weak arguments for the completeness and authenticity of Baillet's version of Descartes's *Olympica* with what at least seems to be a prohibitively strong argument against his translation:

> This discourse [the *Olympica* introduced as one of the "little treatises" in the Little Notebook], the length of which is not indicated in the Inventory [*sic*], does not seem to have been very long, because it was [only] a part, along with many other things, of the Little Notebook, Item C. Thus, we have it all, or almost all, in the six or seven pages of Baillet, volume 1, pages 80–86. *To be sure, Baillet has his own way of translating, always amplifying the texts and adding many details of his own invention; we have seen examples of this in our volume 1, pages 217–18, and volume 10, pages 49–50* [emphasis added]. Nevertheless, what he gives us here, clearly indicating his source, the *Olympica*, includes such particular circumstances and such sin-

191

gular details that he does not seem to have invented anything. Thus, we can believe that we possess, thanks to him, at least the essential of this discourse by Descartes.[2]

The drift of Adam's argument is meant to support Baillet's reliability. However, the rock struck at midstream, placed with some care by the ambivalent excluder-includer himself, sinks his arguments for completeness and authenticity, too. If Baillet always amplified and even invented, then the relative length of his version of Descartes's *Olympica* is not reassuring about completeness but rather alarming about authenticity. I shall return to the rock after having considered these other matters.

The completeness of a dream narrative is practically inconsequential for an interpreter, given the logic of Freud's essential rule. This precludes interpretive attention to narrative wholes and requires instead the analysis of the several elements. Thus, it hardly matters that Adam's loosely quantitative argument for completeness in his first and second sentences is much too impressionistic. Greater precision on length would have been possible, but it would hardly have helped to reassure critical readers. The evidence of Baillet's incompleteness is just too good, namely, the Olympian materials from the *Cogitationes Privatae* that have no complement in the *Vie de Monsieur Des Cartes*: CP 74–76, 77–87, 88–93, 102–3, 113–14, 115–23, 124–28, 129–30, 131–35, 136–38. So represented, these ten passages seem to add up to substantial omissions. However, the last six of them (CP 113–138) apparently followed the resolution that Descartes dated 23 February (CP 112) in the Little Notebook. Baillet was right to omit them from his historical narrative of the more spectacular thinking and dreaming at the beginning of winter. Other known omissions are more unfortunate, but, by the logic of Leibniz's selective note taking, they are from Descartes's interpretations or afterthoughts, not his narratives.

Authenticity does matter, and Adam attempted a qualitative argument for it in the last two sentences previously quoted. The narrative of the dreams seemed to him so circumstantial, so detailed, and so very strange that no waking biographer could have invented it. He concluded that Baillet had added nothing of his own to what he had taken from Descartes's Little Notebook. This is not a very forceful argument, even freed from the rocky middle sentence asserting contrarily that Baillet-the-translator was "always" also Baillet-the-inventor.

Had Adam wanted to construct a stronger argument for authenticity, he could have done so. All seventeenth-century readers, whatever their attitudes to Cartesian philosophy, regarded the episode of the Olympian dreams as an embarrassment for Descartes's reputation. Baillet, too, shared this opinion and distanced himself from the narratives and interpretations, even as he incorporated a version of Descartes's text into his own book. His introductory references to Descartes's supposed mental agitation, disturbance, contention, exhaustion, fever, and enthusiasm leave little doubt about his own judgment (VDC 1–32).

VDC 33–38 marks the descent from questionable thoughts to questionable dreams. Lines 39–42, 66, 73, 75–77, and 200–219 all suggest Baillet's own opinion that Dream I was a matter of Descartes's "imagination," no more. Lines 92–102 and especially 220–35 distance Baillet from either of the awakened dreamer's two contrary interpretations of Dream II, one naturalistic and the other spiritualistic. Lines 181–92, which report Descartes's claim for Dream III as a personal revelation, also insinuate his own contrary opinion.[3] Finally, at lines 226ff., 241ff., 268ff., and 286ff., Baillet's summary remarks on "enthusiasm," "agitations," "indecision," and "disorder" warn against any inclination to excuse the cerebral philosopher by blaming the pedestrian biographer for the whole unfortunate business.

On the first page of his preface Baillet says he began the historical project for which he is now best remembered only out of obedience to "authority." He had the full blessing of the Cartesian establishment and most particularly of Jean-Baptiste Legrand, the heir of Chanut and Clerselier. He also had the willing cooperation of the philosopher's family, the Breton nephews and niece. To all, he promised a true, exact, and faithful portrait of the moral hero of *le juste milieu,* the philosophical hero of *l'esprit géométrique.*[4] It is simply not plausible that this specially commissioned portraitist would have *invented*—or inventively *multiplied*—ignoble dream warts with which to disfigure the heroic thinker's countenance.

There are at least two sorts of tests that might expose Baillet's unhistorical interventions, if any, into what he represents as Descartes's historical dream report from 1619. Psychologically, we can look in the narratives for anything that does not conform to what is now known about dream life. There is nothing of the sort.[5] Historically, we can look in the interpretations for anachronistic "anticipations" of positions characteristic only of a mature Cartesianism. There are none. Although these tests are hardly conclusive, they do shift the burden of proof decisively from Baillet's defenders to his attackers.

Now I strike Adam's rock, the central, concessive sentence. The real weakness of the associated arguments for Baillet and the apparent strength of this argument against him explain why Gaston Milhaud and, in turn, Jacques Maritain were persuaded that Adam had made the case against Baillet's version of Descartes's dreams.[6] But he had not. The rock is not what it was cracked up to be.

Adam proposes only two examples of Baillet's supposedly habitual amplification, addition, and invention. The first is his account of the initial encounter between the young Descartes and his mentor, Isaac Beeckman, on the streets of Breda in 1618. The second is his account of the mature Descartes's initial presentation to a socially distinguished and philosophically sophisticated audience, including Cardinal Bérulle, in Paris in 1628.[7] These examples are not to the point, however. Baillet's admittedly questionable performance as a historian in these two cases says little or nothing about the reliability of his version of the Olympian dreams. Neither the occasions in Descartes's life nor the sources available for Baillet's use are closely comparable.

The two occasions of Baillet's unreliable amplifications are similar in that both concern dramatic revelations of the young Descartes's mental powers. In Breda in 1618, he first showed himself as an all-powerful mathematician to Isaac Beeckman, then a man of no particular station or reputation but within about a year the conrector of the Latin school of Veere and within a decade the rector of the Latin school of Dordrecht, the preeminent school in Holland.[8] In Paris a decade later, he first showed himself as an all-powerful philosopher to Cardinal Bérulle, Father Mersenne, and others gathered at the Nuncio's residence.[9]

Even in their relatively paltry biographies from the 1650s, Daniel Lipstorp and Pierre Borel had realized some of the potential of these two occasions. Adrien Baillet would realize more, doing better by the standards of a baroque history that prized dramatic

194

scene painting and rhetorical speech making.[10] Of course, modern-day historians will judge this to be doing worse by the standards of what has become a less literary and more scientific discipline. But no matter.

These two instances do not justify Adam's dictum concerning Baillet's unreliability, still less any extension of that dictum to disqualify his paraphrase-translation of Descartes's *Olympica*. In the case of the great thinker's first intellectual triumphs, there was a worthy performance before a worthy audience. It was one thing to improve such stories in the telling, "amplifying" and "adding" inventively for heightened effect. In the very different case of the great thinker's irrational dreams and enthusiastic interpretations, with no worthy performance and no worthy audience, it would have been something else entirely. In this unique instance, it would have been to debase the hero precisely at the point of his dramatic break with the past. Improvement for the respectful biographer would have entailed reductions and subtractions from the dreamer's account of the embarrassing episode, not amplifications and additions.

Baillet's documentation was also very different for the two anecdotes of genius revealed and the one night of genius befuddled. On the encounter with Beeckman, he had Lipstorp's unprepossessing sketch and whatever else oral traditions and written memoirs from Legrand may have added.[11] On the presentation at the Nuncio's, he had Borel's error-ridden sketch of a sketch, the whole of a letter from Descartes to Ville-Bressieu that is now known only in part, and, again, whatever else oral traditions and written memoirs may have added.[12] On the Olympian dreams, he had nothing from any prior biographical writing, nothing from the correspondence, and apparently, nothing from Cartesian traditions other than everyone's unsatisfied curiosity about the meaning of "the foundation of the wonderful science" or "wonderful discovery."[13] For the better as well as for the worse, however, he did have Descartes's own narratives and interpretations, the absolutely authoritative account of an episode that was too important and too well documented to ignore.

Adam's ill-considered sentences on Baillet's version of Descartes's *Olympica* reflect his own uneasiness with the dreams. When it is not a question of Descartes's darker-than-night dreams, the sky brightens over Baillet for Adam's very respectful ackowledgment of very great debts:

> We can say that the two volumes published by Baillet have passed almost entirely into the eleven volumes of our edition and into this [biographical] volume 12. In large part, his work was an assemblage of documents, the originals of which are now lost, and which we know only by the excerpts that he published. Many of [his] pages have been cut into pieces, each of which has its place in [this edition] of the correspondence or the works. . . . Moreover, he fulfilled his biographical responsibilities conscientiously.[14]

The real quarrel of the modern Cartesians seems to be with the historical fact of Descartes's dreams, not with the supposedly unhistorical quality of Baillet's reporting.

Adam's weaker arguments for Baillet's completeness and authenticity have had nothing like the impact of his apparently stronger argument against Baillet's translations: "To be sure, Baillet has his own way of translating, always amplifying the texts and adding many details of his own invention."[15] This concessive sentence from an argument nominally intended to *affirm* the historical reliability of Baillet's version of Descartes's *Olympica* has been pulled from context and used to *deny* his reliability,[16] but it has never been tested systematically.[17] Leibniz's *Cogitationes,* Baillet's margins, and Descartes's own *Regulae* provide Latin originals from the philosopher's manuscripts for such a test of Baillet's paraphrase-translations.

First, Leibniz's *Cogitationes* have always been accepted as verbatim copies of Descartes's originals. However, Leibniz's disdain for the dreams was such that he left only one passage corresponding to Baillet's version of the interpretations:

AT, X, 217 (CP 93–101):	AT, X, 184 (VDC 163–72):
Mirum videri possit, quare graves sententiae in scriptis poetarum, magis quam philosophorum. Ratio est quod poetae per enthusiasmum et vim imaginationis scripsere: sunt in nobis semina scientiae, ut in silice, quae per rationem a philosophis educuntur, per imaginationem a	Il ne crooit pas qu'on dût s'étonner si fort de voir que les Poëtes, même ceux qui ne font que niaiser, fussent pleins de sentences plus graves, plus sensées, et mieux exprimées que celles qui se trouvent dans les écrits des Philosophes. Il attribuoit cette merveille à la divi-

poetis excutiuntur magisque elucent.

nité de l'Enthousiasme, et à la Force de l'Imagination, qui fait sortir les semences de la sagesse (qui se trouvent dans l'esprit de tous les hommes, comme les étincelles de feu dans les cailloux) avec beaucoup plus de facilité et beaucoup plus de brillant même, que ne peut faire la Raison dans les Philosophes.

Adam assesses the reliability of this paraphrase thus: of CP 93–101 he says that this "sentence [is] translated almost word for word by Baillet"; of VDC 163–72 he says, "We have the Latin, of which this is the translation almost word for word."[18]

In addition, Baillet's account of Descartes's postdream vows depends so closely on a passage that Leibniz also excerpted as to allow the construction of one other Olympian parallel:

AT, X, 217–18 (CP 104–12):

Ante finem Novembris Lauretum petam, idque pedes e Venetiis, si commode & moris sit; sin minus, saltem quam devotissime ab ullo fieri consuevit.

AT, X, 186–87 (VDC 248–78):

Pour tâcher d'intéresser cette bien-heureuse Mère de Dieu d'une manire plus pressante, il prit occasion du voyage qu'il méditoit en Italie dans peu de jours, pour former le voeu d'un pèlerinage à Notre-Dame de Lorette. [*"Olympic. Catres. ut supr."*] Son zèle alloit encore plus loin, et luy fit promettre que, des qu'il seroit à Venise, il se mettroit en chemin par terre, pour faire le pèlerinage à pied jusqu'à Lorette; que si ses forces ne pouvoient pas fournir à cette fatigue, il prendroit au moins l'extérieur le plus dévot et le plus humilié qu'il luy seroit possible, pour s'en acquitter. Il prétendoit partir avant la fin de Novembre pour ce voyage. . . .

Omnino autem ante Pascha absolvam tractatum meum, et si librorum [*sic* in Foucher de Careil; corrected to "librariorum" by Adam, following Baillet] mihi sit copia dignusque videatur, emittam, ut hodie promisi, 1620, die 23 Septembris [*sic* in Foucher de Careil; corrected to "23 Febr." by Adam, following Baillet].

Le têms de son quartier d'hyver s'écouloit peu à peu dans la solitude de son poêsle; et pour la rendre moins ennuyeuse, il se mit à composer un traité, qu'il espéroit achever avant Pâques de l'an 1620. ["*Ibidem. 'Die 23 Febr.'*"] Dès le mois de Février, il songeoit à chercher des Libraires pour traiter avec eux de l'impression de cet ouvrage.

Baillet's amplification here is evident, but the real problem is one of historical judgment, not language skills. Invention may be the proper pejorative both for his surprising claim that Descartes had planned to break winter quarters in Germany for a trip across the mountains to Italy and for his astonishing notion that, very soon after 11 November, Descartes's enthusiasm so yielded to boredom that work on his "treatise" became nothing more than a way of filling the empty days of winter.

Baillet himself would surely have been surprised by this critical exercise. He was not editing translated documents; he was trying to tell a coherent story drawn insofar as possible from the documents. But he hurried, and when it came to fitting the pieces together, he hazarded inferences without alerting his readers. He *knew* that the historical Descartes had not traveled to Italy or published a treatise in the winter of 1619–20, but he had also discovered in the *Olympica* that the dreams had inspired vows or resolutions concerning travel and publication. What to do? He inferred explanations, patched together a chapter, and tried to compartmentalize the regrettable episode.

Baillet's transitions at the beginning and the end of the episode of the Olympian dreams *are* problematic, and the critical reader of VDC 1–32 and VDC 241ff. must be very cautious. The reliability of his version of the documented episode itself is another matter, however, and it is enough to observe simply that Baillet *does not* smooth out the irrationality of the dreams or the enthusiasm of the dreamer for a better fit with the rational thinker from the *Discourse*. He *does not* visibly intrude to impose an artificial coherence or superficial plausibility on Descartes's incoherent and implausible *Olympica* or to explain his idea of what really happened and what it truly meant.[19]

Second, Baillet's margins in other contexts give three Latin texts that he apparently copied verbatim from the Little Notebook and then incorporated into his French narrative. His marginal citation was in each case "Fragm. Mss." As does Henri Gouhier,[20] I assign all three to the *Experimenta:*

Baillet's margin, II, 449 (cp. Leibniz, AT, X, 215):

Adverto me, si tristis sim, aut in periculo verser, et tristia occupent negotia, altum dormire et comedere avidissime. Si vero laetitia distendar, nec edo, nec dormio.

Baillet's text, II, 449:

Il avoit aussi observé qu'il mangéoit avec plus d'avidité, & qu'il dormoit plus profondément, lors qu'il étoit dans la tristesse ou dans quelque danger, que dans tout autre état; & que lors qu'il étoit dans la joye il ne pouvoit ni manger ni dormir.

Baillet's margin, II, 531:

Non est quod Antiquis multum tribuamus propter Antiquitatem; sed nos potius iis antiquiores dicendi. Jam "enim senior est mundus quam tunc, majoremque habemus rerum experientiam."

Baillet's text, II, 531:

Je ne vois pas, dit il, qu'il faille tant faire valoir l'Antiquité dans ceux qui portent la qualité d'Anciens. C'est un nom que nous méritons mieux qu'eux, parce que le monde est plus ancien maintenant qu'il n'étoit de leur têms, & que nous avons plus d'expérience qu'eux.

Baillet's margin, II, 545:

Ut nulla scribere possumus vocabula in quibus aliae sint quam Alphabeti litterae, nec sententiam implere, nisi iis verbis constet quae sunt in Lexico: *sic* nec librum nisi ex iis sententiis quae apud alios reperiuntur. Sed si illa quae dixero ita inter se cohaerentia sint atque ita connexa, ut unae ex aliis consequantur, hoc argumento erit me

Baillet's text, II, 545:

M. Descartes voulant bien accorder que ce qu'il disoit avoit déja été dit par d'autres, croyoit qu'il en étoit de même de luy, que d'un homme qu'on accuseroit d'avoir pillé l'Alphabet & le Dictionnaire, parcequ'il n'auroit pas employé de lettres qui ne fussent dans le premier, ni de mots qui ne se trouvassent dans le second. Mais il ajoutoit que

non magis sententias ab aliis mu-
tuari, quam ipsa verba ex Lexico
sumere.

ceux, qui reconnoîtroient l'enchaînement de toutes ses pensées qui suivent nécessairement
les unes des autres, avoüeroient
bientôt qu'il seroit aussi innocent du vol qu'on luy impute,
qu'un habile Orateur que l'on
rendroit plagiaire de Calpin &
du vieux Évandre, pour avoir
emprunté les mots de l'un, & les
lettres de l'autre.

Baillet was perfectly capable of precision. In the first of these three pairs of passages, his Latin copy served Adam as a basis for correcting errors in the flawed copy from Foucher de Careil's *Cogitationes*.[21] Baillet's French paraphrase of this text is also perfectly reliable. He recast Descartes's Latin text into indirect discourse, reordered it intelligibly, and, with these qualifications, rendered it almost word for word.

The other two sets of parallel texts pairing Latin from Baillet's margins with French from his narratives have already been endorsed with only one qualification by the most meticulous scholar.[22] Henri Gouhier notes that Descartes's *dixero* in the last passage establishes a future tense imperfectly translated by Baillet's *il disoit*, but Baillet was adapting the passage for his final defense of the Cartesian corpus against charges that the mature thinker had repeated or "plagiarized" others' works. For young Descartes in 1619, the point had been that what he *would say* in the future *would be* truly original; for Baillet in 1691, the point was that what Descartes *had in fact said* before his death *had in fact been* truly original. His change of the tense made perfect historical sense.[23]

Third, Descartes's *Regulae*, which Baillet knew only from the Latin manuscript, survives in two early publications, a Dutch translation (1684) and a Latin edition (1701). Rule IVb includes an extended autobiographical passage that Baillet paraphrased in translation on successive pages. This allows at least the comparison of this one block of the young Descartes's autobiographical Latin prose with Baillet's biographical French adaptation. Charles Adam and Giovanni Crapulli have already made the comparison, and I need only report their findings. Adam endorses Baillet's reliability in this case: "Baillet translates almost all of rule IV in his volume 1, pages 112–15. Even though it was not published within quotation marks, this long passage is nevertheless a rather faithful translation, as anyone can verify by comparing it with the Latin text."[24] The more recent and more critical editor of the *Regulae* concurs. Crapulli's conclusion suffices: "He [Baillet] does not translate in the strict sense of the word, but his paraphrase follows the text closely, so much that we can sometimes use it in the course of our textual criticism. . . . For the most part, Baillet follows the text very closely, almost to the point of translating."[25]

In the effort to test Adam's unfavorable judgment of Baillet's reliability as paraphraser-translator of the *Olympica* I have reviewed three sets of parallel texts, those based on Leibniz's *Cogitationes*, Baillet's margins, and the Dutch and Latin *Regulae*. In every case, the historian's failure to punctuate quotations as such would have licensed him to range widely from the Cartesian originals. Reservations concerning his historical judgment do not affect the conclusion: in every instance, he incorporates virtual translation under the guise of paraphrase.

A skeptic might still wonder whether Baillet would have allowed himself greater liberties as the paraphraser-translator of something as essentially free-form as the text of a dream or a dream vision. His *Vies des Saints* includes such material, and his sources survive for critical review. He himself singles out the remarkable dream vision of St. Perpetua. In this case, we must consider Baillet's version in the light of both a prior French version by Sébastien Le Nain de Tillemont and the Latin source, the *Passio* attributed to Perpetua herself.[26] It should now come as no surprise that the much-maligned "copyist of copyists" distinguishes himself, if at all, by a seemingly uncritical—but perfectly reliable—willingness to incorporate others' texts. He depends so obviously on de Tillemont's accessible and apparently authoritative translation of the source that it is easy to conclude the minor variants represent only his own unreliable amplifications and inventions. But no. Baillet also went back to the source, and his few departures from de Tillemont's translation reflect his return to Perpetua's original.

Adam's critical rule, that Baillet invariably amplified and invented, cannot be used to deny the reliability of his version of the Olympian narratives and interpretations. *Baillet's* rule was to translate literally "in those cases where exactitude has seemed necessary the better to support what would [otherwise] have seemed more doubtful and more difficult to accept."[27]

APPENDIX 2: THE TECHNICAL QUESTION OF DESCARTES'S DREAM REPORTS

Henri Gouhier raised a second issue, more fundamental even than Baillet's reliability, when he denied Descartes's accuracy as a dream recorder:

> What is surprising [about the dreams] is the precision with which they are told. It is rather natural that Descartes should have reconstituted the last in full detail, but the second and especially the first?
>
> It is a commonplace observation that our dreams are more or less reconstructed by our awakened consciousness. Reconstruction gives them a logic and a precision that they may not have had. As we reflect on a dream, details appear, and, in the words of [Victor] Egger, "we become artists unaware." Paul Tannery, one of Descartes's editors [with Charles Adam], abandoned the study of dreams, judging that waking intelligence introduced too many foreign elements into their reconstitution. [Gouhier's footnote: "(Marcel) Foucault, *Le rêve* (Paris, 1906), p. 4; cf. ch. 4."]
>
> The psychologists understand these difficulties very well, and we must not forget them when we consider the content of the third dream, [which the awakened thinker has] so rationalized, and especially when we read the narrative of the first [dream, which the awakened thinker has] over-burdened with episodes reproduced down to the last detail: "He had to lean to his left side; [he

felt a] great weakness on his right side; [he was buffeted by] gusts that [. . .] spun him around three or four times on his left foot;" etc.[1]

"The psychologists" seem here to have passed judgment for the revolutionary thinker but against the lost *Olympica*. As Gouhier expounds it, their rule is that any detailed dream report is "always suspect." Three sequential dream narratives are "much more suspect."[2] This terrible law of suspects permits no defense and no appeal. It condemns Dream I and Dream II: "Only the third dream deserves our attention."[3] It condemns even Dream III, because the dreamer can have reported it only after awakening and thinking about it: "It is wrong to distinguish the dream from its interpretation."[4] Thus, even in his dream narratives, the Descartes of the heated chamber was the Thinking Thing.

Victor Egger comes first in Gouhier's crucial paragraph on the psychologists and the *Olympica*. Egger's memorable phrase on the dream reporter as an "artist unaware" expresses his doubts about a once-celebrated dream report, Louis-Alfred Maury's Guillotine Dream.[5] Egger managed to convince himself that Maury must have experienced his dream in about 1840, that he could not have recorded it before about 1852, and that he must have recounted it orally in the twelve-year interim.[6] In this supposedly long period of supposedly numerous retellings, Maury must have "completed, organized, and systematized" the narrative:

> [T]he observation of dreams is particularly difficult, and the only way to avoid all error in this respect is to set down on paper what one has just experienced and observed. If not, one quickly forgets. . . . Total forgetfulness isn't serious, but partial forgetfulness is perfidious. If one then begins to relate [orally] what one has not forgotten, one risks completing by imagination the incoherent and disjointed fragments furnished by memory. *In the involvement of an oral retelling, the logic of real life partially replaces the fantastic sequences of the dream state, and one becomes an artist unaware*[7] [emphasis added].

Here is the "artist unaware" from Egger's psychology who eventually blundered into Gouhier's history. In context, it is clear that the italicized judgment concerns only *oral* dream narratives. The solitary Descartes in his heated chamber made a *written* dream record within a matter of hours, days, or weeks, not months or years.[8] There is no evidence of oral performances during the winter of 1619–20, and it is as hard to imagine the reclusive Frenchman seeking out an alien audience for his most intimate secrets as to imagine an assembly of Germans or others eager to hear all about the young stranger's dreams.

If anything, Egger's dream psychology tells for Descartes's accuracy, not against it. Egger was confident that, on awakening, he retained the "natural and direct memory" of a dream from the preceding interval of sleep. He could write it down without becoming "an artist unaware." He was "an attentive observer": "At each awakening, whether in the night or in the morning, we always remember some dream, but this memory is extraordinarily fugitive, and, if we do not fix it immediately, it vanishes. *We can fix it simply by attention, that is, by deliberately committing it to memory or, better yet, by setting it down in writing*"[9] [emphasis added].

Paul Tannery is the other person named in Gouhier's paragraph as an authority on dreaming. Tannery's abandonment of dream studies serves as a warning to lesser Cartesians that even Descartes's editor could not succeed in the study of even his own dreams. However, Tannery was simply not a dream psychologist. This most distinguished historian of science, mathematics, and philosophy repeatedly and emphatically expressed disclaimers, even in the three brief notes that he published on the subject of his amateurish dream researches. He conducted one fruitless experiment, devoting to it some fifteen minutes a day for less than a month sometime at the end of the 1870s. That was all.[10]

As a curious amateur, Tannery tried to discover whether one of his dreams could be the source of memory traces in another dream later in the same night. His research method was to sleep facing an unshuttered window in the hope that the morning sun would arouse him sufficiently to note the contents of his dreams, if any. He would then try to return to sleep, hoping both for later dreams in which earlier elements might recur and for later awakenings by his solar alarm to note any recurrences. This research design was badly flawed: even if he had awakened from a second dream with recollections of recurrent dream elements, he could never have been sure that the memory traces in that second dream recalled the first dream itself and not the ensuing interval of wakefulness in which he had so carefully noted its contents. He was right to close the shutters on this primitive sleep laboratory.

Tannery's first relevant publication came "over fifteen years" after his one month of dream studies.[11] He acknowledged that he had never "pursued these observations methodically"; he had never formed the habit of "regularly writing down dreams"; he had found apparent recurrences in sequential dreams only "very rarely (once or twice)"; he had forgotten the details of even this rare instance or two; and, although he had begun to assemble materials on dreams at a time closer to his observations, he had finished by "destroying most of his notes."[12] Tannery's abandonment of dream studies reflects his particular frustrations at his inability to discriminate his memory of the dream itself from the functioning of "awakened intelligence," no less but also no more.[13] To have allowed it any psychological authority has been a grave historical error.

Marcel Foucault's *Le rêve* (1906) must bear a uniquely heavy burden. His hasty review of the literature was apparently the sole basis for Gouhier's knowledge of Egger's and Tannery's papers. More importantly, his problematic synthesis provided the theoretical rationale for Gouhier's rejection of the Olympian dream narratives. Foucault attempted to formulate a single principle of dream recall, "the law of logical evolution":

> Dreams recorded immediately are made up of discontinuous tableaux and are very incoherent. Dreams recorded later are much more continuous and coherent. Thus, the ensemble of the representations that the sleeping mind furnishes to the awakening mind follows a very clearly discernible evolution: it goes from incoherence to coherence. . . . The logical work done during waking has as its purpose to put into order that ensemble of chaotic events, to make of them a succession of facts as much as possible like our experience of the real world. . . . We can characterize the evolution of the dream during waking as a "logical evolution."[14]

Foucault attracted readers of his own generation by combining notions from post-Cartesian philosophy and post-Darwinian biology into a single psychological theory. However, he could not offer a single instance of the successive reports of one dream, his own or anyone else's, that might have illustrated if not demonstrated

the hypothesized law of logical evolution.[15] His theory is now out-
moded, and his research was always inadequate, but some of his
ideas are better than others, and some of the best tell in Descartes's
favor as the Olympian dream recorder:

> Thus, the dream that has not been fixed [in the dreamer's memory]
> in any way is forgotten very easily, even if it has been clearly in
> mind for a moment. *The dream that has been fixed, whether in a
> spontaneous manner, by reason of its emotional character, or in an artificial
> manner, by the grace of our attention, is forgotten much less easily. Even
> the fixed dream may very well disappear or be distorted. Therefore,* if we
> want to seize the dream and to hold it in the form in which it came
> to our consciousness at the beginning of our awakening, *it is in-
> dispensable to record it in writing immediately*[16] [emphases added].

Even old Foucault, with his archaic notions of instantaneous,
disconnected dream tableaux, reports successes in "fixing" dreams
during nighttime awakenings for daytime recording the next morning. How is this to be done? By "attention." And what else favors
recall? "Strong emotion," which can unify dreams within sleep and
awaken the dreamer for conscious recall. Finally, what must the
conscientious student of dreams do on awakening? "Record them
in writing immediately."[17] Descartes's Olympian dreams and dream
records meet these criteria almost perfectly. Descartes's Olympian
dreams, especially the most suspect Dreams I and II, were strongly
emotional. He awakened after each dream to consider it attentively.
And he did record his dreams in writing, whether or not he did
so "immediately."

Gouhier deserves high praise for having paid any attention at
all to dream psychology and for having done so as early as 1924.
No other qualified Cartesian has ever followed his good example.
Furthermore, Egger, Tannery, and Foucault were all curious and
intelligent men, and what they had to say about dreams is still of
interest to the historian of psychology. However, Gouhier paid
insufficient attention even to his own chosen authorities and no
attention at all to the two greatest advances in twentieth-century
dream psychology: the Freudian revolution and the discovery of
rapid-eye-movement or REM sleep.

Freud willingly granted that he had no way to elicit indubitably
accurate dream reports, but having raised this obstacle in one
paragraph, he strode around it in the next: "We can help the

defect of the uncertainty in remembering dreams if we decide that whatever the dreamer tells us must count as his dream, without regard to what he may have forgotten or altered in recalling it."[18] Freud's decision to accept the dreamer's report as his dream reflects his primary clinical interest in the individual patient, not in waking memory as such. Therefore, he gave accuracy a new meaning. The analysand's associations for reported dream elements matter absolutely, whereas the analyst's attempts to discriminate true memories of dream experiences from false alterations in dream reports do not matter at all. Indeed, 556 pages into the greatest book ever written on dreams, Freud remarks off-handedly that "the dream is in any case a matter of no importance."[19] That is, the manifest dream is only a screen.

Freud's method requires the redirection of scientific attention from the problematic dream report, suspected as an uncertain compound of memory, forgetfulness, and invention, to the awakened dreamer's statements, taken as they are given. In the long history of human thought on dreams and dreaming, this is the Great Revolution. The scientists no longer rule; their reason is no longer an absolute law for all thought of all subjects, as it was for century after century. The subjects are the new sovereigns, however rational, nonrational, or irrational the implications of the evidence that they hand down to the scientists.[20] After Freud's *Interpretation of Dreams*, Egger's, Tannery's, and Foucault's once-reasonable voices seem to speak the language of a merely rationalist Old Regime. These philosophical gentlemen contemned dreams and dreamers while arrogating a privileged status for their own waking reason.[21]

Gouhier could have learned from Freud's revolutionary work, although *Die Traumdeutung* (1900) had not yet been translated into French by the date of *La pensée réligieuse de Descartes* (1924). Still, he could hardly have foreseen the consequences for his historical work of the second great breakthrough in twentieth-century dream studies, Eugene Aserinsky's discovery of REM sleep in 1953, only five years before the publication of *Les premières pensées de Descartes* (1958). The most relevant psychophysiological findings are scattered in later English-language journals.[22]

The discovery of REM sleep showed that we all dream much more than had ever been supposed, doing so in regular stages of sleep that can be monitored, and this finding suggested two lines of research relevant to any evaluation of Descartes's dream reports. First, there are questions of memory. Descartes must have dreamed at least three times on 10 November 1619, but could he have remembered his three dreams on 11 November? What factors favor morning-after recall in the laboratory, and do these factors seem to pertain to the reports from the heated chamber? Second, there are questions of sequential dreams. What characteristics do—or do not—seem to relate the several dream reports of a given night? Do Descartes's dream narratives as a set conform to generalizations based on more extensive data more systematically studied?

With respect to the first issue, dream recall, there have been both experimental studies relating nighttime dream reports to morning-after recall and theoretical attempts to identify the factors that favor successful recall. I begin with two experimental studies, one involving many subjects, each for one night's monitored sleep, the other involving one subject for many nights' sleep.

Frederick Baekeland was the principal investigator in the first of these studies, which involved twenty healthy young male subjects. Their sleep was monitored for one night in the laboratory, during which each subject was awakened for nighttime reports by a bedside buzzer five minutes after the beginning of the first REM period and ten minutes after the beginning of each subsequent REM period. After the terminal awakening and report, each was asked, without any prior warning of this experimental interest, for detailed recall of the nighttime reports. All twenty subjects were awakened experimentally at least four times, but the experimenters chose to study the morning recall of only the first three such reports, because "terminal reports were generally perfectly recalled."[23] Of the twenty, nine remembered all three earlier reports; twelve remembered at least two, and fifteen remembered at least one.[24]

Two factors that significantly favored morning-after recall were, first, greater length of the nighttime dream report and, second, greater time elapsed between the experimental awakening and resumed sleep.[25] Both factors relate to the known circumstances of Descartes's Dream I, which Gouhier has most suspected. This narrative includes thirteen dream elements by my count. Successfully recalled "longer" dreams in Baekeland's study averaged fewer than eleven dream elements. Furthermore, the spontaneously awakened Descartes reported that, before falling asleep once again, he had pondered this dream, his sinful past, and good and evil for "almost two hours." Experimentally awakened subjects who successfully recalled dreams in the laboratory did so after "longer" periods of wakefulness averaging only about a quarter of an hour. Thus, with respect to Dream I, which was rather long and which was followed by a very long period of nighttime wakefulness, laboratory findings tend to validate the implicit historical claim of morning-after recall.[26]

The second empirical study of morning-after recall is even more compelling. A middle-aged chemist who "had remembered only a few dreams in his whole life" began analysis. While a clinical outpatient, he tried to record his dreams regularly every morning, but he averaged only about one dream report for every five or six nights. This was enough to intrigue him, and he agreed with a team of Swiss investigators headed by C. A. Meier to spend ten weeks of five nights each in a laboratory, where he tape-recorded 166 dream reports after experimental awakenings at the end of 198 REM periods. Every morning, he attempted to recall his nighttime reports.[27]

Having so much material from one very intelligent and actively cooperative subject permitted Calvin Hall, the principal data analyst and a confirmed empiricist, to determine the characteristics of remembered dream reports. In this study, three interactive factors favored memory: recency, length, and intensity. That is, significantly more of the dream reports from the last quarter of a night's sleep were recalled; significantly more of the dream reports extending sixteen or more lines when transcribed were recalled; and significantly more of the intensely emotional dream reports were recalled.[28]

The criterion of recency would have favored morning-after recall of Descartes's Dream III, and the criteria of length and intensity would have favored recall of Dreams I and II, respectively. Because of the experimentally observed correlation between greater length and better memory, there is no reason to suspect Dream I as too long or too detailed to have been a real dream report. The chemist recalled eighty-seven percent of all longer dream reports and almost ninety percent of those that were at least moderately intense.[29]

I have yet to define recall. Calvin Hall has probably collected more dream reports than any other researcher of this most-productive generation. His conclusion is this: "Generally speaking, when a dream was recalled in the morning, it was virtually the same as the dream recorded during the night. The average length of recorded and recalled dreams was exactly the same."[30] The experimental evidence tells in Descartes's favor as a morning-after recaller and recorder. After two hours of anxious nighttime reflection on Dream I, it would have been anomalous for him *not* to have recalled it the next morning.

Theoretical discussions of dream reports now begin with the acknowledgment that the most imaginative researchers with the most sophisticated equipment still have discovered no way to enter the sleeper's private dream world. They end with the counsel that, practically speaking, the waking dream report is the dream itself. Classical memory theory now provides the theoretical framework for understanding what we remember and what we forget.[31] The following factors seem to be most important: the serial order of the dream in the night, the length of the nighttime dream report, and the intensity of the nighttime dream report.

With respect to serial order, there is a recency effect that favors the last report (Descartes's Dream III) and a primacy effect that favors morning-after recall of the first nighttime report (Descartes's Dream I). John Trinder and Milton Kramer have observed both recency and primacy effects, and their experimental observations provide additional evidence for the memory advantages of length (Descartes's Dreams I and III) and intensity (Descartes's Dreams I, II, III).[32]

Finally, David B. Cohen has devoted several papers to the elaboration of an adequate theory of dream recall. He emphasizes two factors, the *salience* of the dream (vividness, bizarreness, emotionality, activity) and the absence of recall *interference* after awakening (distraction, inattention). Salience seems to be little more than intensity by another name; interference, however, adds a great deal to the factors from classical memory theory.[33] Cohen found that the experimentally directed performance of even the least engag-

211

ing task, like checking the weather report, interfered significantly with subsequent dream recall.[34] The complete absence of distractions and the focus of all attention in the heated chamber would have favored Descartes's recollection on the morning of 11 November.

Having reviewed recent experimental and theoretical studies of dream recall, I turn to experimental and clinical studies of sequential dreams. Qualified psychophysiologists have presented extensive illustrations of successive reports from single subjects on single nights. There is no important difference of opinion on the interrelationship of such reports. Typically, there is little or none on the manifest level. A search for continuity may show that similar or identical elements do occur in quite different contexts, but the rule is that the sequential reports from a given night are separate dramas, not the several acts of a single drama. It does not affect this argument that clinical and clinically inspired interpreters have discerned coherent *latent* meanings in dream sequences. The rule is *manifest* incoherence, dream to dream.[35] As I previously argued in the conclusion, this is just what we find in the Olympian dreams.

Henri Gouhier was troubled by what he took to have been the lessons of a now-superseded psychology, which suggested to him that Descartes's so-called dreams were just too detailed and too unified to have been actually dreamed. When he looked back on the Olympian narratives, he saw or thought he saw that the philosopher's waking interpretation after the third dream report had inspired an artistic "reconstitution" of all three reports taken as a set. At most, he was willing to accept Descartes's Dream III. He was particularly firm in rejecting the detailed narrative of Dream I.[36]

Gouhier was mistaken, however. He suspected the "surprising precision" of the Olympian narratives, but the following parts of Dream I are left *imprecise* and *undetailed*: the ghosts, the streets, the school, the Acquaintance, the Other Person, Monsieur N., the foreign land, and the clustered individuals. Descartes's report says nothing specific about *what* the dreamer seeks at the beginning or finds at the end, *whence* he is coming or *whither* he is going, *when* the story transpires, or, especially, *whom* he encounters.

Allan Rechtschaffen directs the Sleep Research Laboratory at the University of Chicago, a center of this new psychology since the initial discovery of REM sleep there in 1953. He has examined Descartes's narratives at my request. Forewarned of Gouhier's suspicions, his opinion is this: "There is nothing in the reported material to preclude its having been dreamed. We sometimes get such long, detailed, apparently well remembered dream reports from young adult subjects awakened from long REM periods. Such reports may have a prolonged story line which is punctuated by the sudden appearance of apparently discordant elements—such as in Dream I."[37]

Dream II only makes matters worse for anyone who would dismiss the dream reports as too detailed, too precise, or too coherent. There is no detail, no precision, and no coherence. What waking art could explain the ominously "sudden, loud noise," a brontological boom, with *nothing* before and *nothing* afterward in Dream II itself and *no* apparent relationship to the narrative either of Dream I before or of Dream III afterward?

Neither art nor logic unifies the disparate materials of the *Olympica*,[38] and there is no psychologically valid reason to suspect the accuracy of its reports. How could so good a historian ever have come to Henri Gouhier's conclusions? A necessary part of the explanation is bad psychology, borrowed from Foucault, but this cannot be the whole explanation. We must also take into account the rationalist biases that Gouhier, Foucault, and so many others have shared. Only this can explain the fact of this borrowing and the willingness of Gouhier and other good Cartesians to take the last step in discrediting the historical evidence on the dreams.

Appendix 3: The Technical Question of Rosicrucian Allegories

Paul Arnold announced to the world in 1952 that Descartes's Olympian dream reports were only a fictional product of his imagination, *not* a factual report of his experience. He claimed that the *Olympica* (1619) was so much like Johann Valentin Andreae's *Chymische Hochzeit: Christiani Rosenkreutz* (1616) that it, too, must have been conceived as a literary allegory.[1] Arnold had neither professional training nor prior standing as a historian, and he knew nothing about dream psychology. His only approach to Descartes was by way of an otherwise skeptical interest in an old polemical tradition that had tried to damn Cartesian philosophy by suggesting a Rosicrucian affiliation for the philosopher. Yet his work quickly punctuated "Descartes's 'Dream' " in the scholarly bibliography of Cartesian studies.[2]

Arnold asserted "an exact parallel" between "the whole of the events occurring in the first and the second dreams" from the *Olympica* and "the whole first day" of the *Chymische Hochzeit*.[3] Only the alleged parallel could justify Arnold's further claims, namely, that Descartes did not actually dream at all but fabricated pseudodreams modeled on Rosicrucian allegories and that the Cartesian method somehow originated from "the young philosopher's encounter with the teachings of Rosicrucian Illuminism in its purest form, directly descended from medieval mysticism, in the *Chemical Wedding of Christian Rosenkreutz*."[4]

Arnold's exposition, repeated but only slightly varied in a series of publications, is very unsystematic and lacks any form of citation, but I will try to represent it formally enough for reassessment. For the *Olympica*, I use numbered dream elements (e.g., DE I.1 for Dream I, dream element 1). For the *Chymische Hochzeit* (abbreviated as CH), I cite pages from Lazarus Zetzner's 143-page edition, one of the three editions (all published in Strassbourg in 1616) that Descartes could conceivably have used, adding references to Ezechiel Foxcroft's highly regarded English translation, *The Hermetick Romance or the Chymical Wedding* (abbreviated as HR), published in 1690.[5]

Dream I

DE I.1: RD encounters frightening ghosts as he walks the streets.

CH: Arnold includes the element in his extended citation from VDC but makes *no claim* of a parallel in CH.

DE I.2: RD's weakness on his right makes him lean to his left.

CH: Arnold includes the element in his extended citation from VDC but makes *no claim* of a parallel in CH.

DE I.3: RD feels shame at his inability to straighten up.

CH: Arnold includes the element in his extended citation from VDC but makes *no claim* of a parallel in CH.

DE I.4: RD is spun around three or four times by a whirlwind.

CH: Arnold seems to associate DE I.4 with DE I.9 and to claim a parallel to contrary wind at CH 19 (HR 25).

DE I.5: RD is alarmingly unable to advance and fears falling.

CH: Arnold claims a parallel to CR's "exhausting" march and "very difficult" climb at CH 18, 19 (HR 24, 26).

215

DE I.6:   RD enters a school's grounds seeking refuge and remedy.

CH: Arnold claims a parallel to CR's objective, the mountaintop castle reached at CH 19 (HR 26).

DE I.7:   RD voluntarily approaches a church for prayer.

CH: Arnold includes the element in his extended citation from VDC but makes *no claim* of a parallel in CH.

DE I.8:   RD unwittingly snubs an Acquaintance and tries to return.

CH: Arnold claims a parallel to the first porter at the castle, who greets CR and gives him a token at CH 20–21 (HR 26–28).

DE I.9:   RD is involuntarily driven back again by a contrary wind.

CH: See DE I.4. Arnold claims a parallel to the contrary wind that prevents CR's from turning back at CH 19 (HR 25).

DE I.10:   RD is greeted by the Other Person and promised a present from N.

CH: Arnold claims a parallel to the second porter, who has anticipated CR's arrival, at CH 22–23 (HR 29–30).

DE I.11:   RD interprets the present as a melon from a foreign land.

CH: Arnold claims a parallel to the "enormous globe" *or* "golden ball" (CH 59–60, 111ff.; HR 78–81, 148ff.).

DE I.12:   RD sees others, upright and steady, around the Other Person.

CH: Arnold includes the element in his extended citation from VDC but makes *no claim* of a parallel in CH.

DE I.13:   RD is still leaning and unsteady, despite abated winds.

CH: Arnold includes the element in his extended citation from VDC but makes *no claim* of a parallel in CH.

Interpretation I:

Arnold claims a parallel: RD's "two hours of reflection, terror, and prayer" following his Dream I are "just like" CR's "night of reflection, terror, and prayer" following his arrival at the castle (CH 34–35; HR 44–46).

Dream II:

Arnold claims a *double* parallel: RD's Thunder Dream recalls not only the trumpet blast, the myriad lights, and the Lady who enters CR's chamber, invites him to the royal wedding, and then exits to more blasts (CH 3–4; HR 4–5) but also a later fanfare and the "little lights" announcing the entrance of the Virgo into the castle banquet hall (CH 29; HR 39).

Interpretation III, Phase 3:

Arnold seems to claim a parallel: RD interprets the gift melon as a figure for mysterious "charms of solitude"; to Arnold this suggests "the fruits of meditation, the goals of contemplation, and spiritual illumination."

Arnold's argument for allegorical invention and so against historical dreaming pairs one text that has puzzled Cartesians, the *Olympica*, with another that has been unknown to them, the *Chymische Hochzeit*. To be successful, an argument of this sort requires the most disciplined efforts to avoid at least four fallacies related to comparison. First, the fallacy of selectivity: this involves using incomplete or unrepresentative selections from the texts under scrutiny. Second, the fallacy of misrepresentation: this involves misrepresenting texts in order to pair them, exaggerating likenesses and minimizing differences. Third, the fallacy of divergence: this involves claiming parallelism between texts that are accurately represented but not truly similar. Fourth, the fallacy of discontinuity: this involves reordering the sequence of elements or episodes in the sources for the sake of an alleged parallelism. Arnold's argument is fallacious in every respect, failing at every stage.

First, the fallacy of selectivity with respect to the *Olympica:* Arnold makes no claim concerning the elements DE I.1, 2, 3, 7, 12, and 13. It is impossible to determine whether he means to make a claim for DE I.4. This means that he has selected from the *Olympica* only six or seven of the thirteen dream elements—and quietly excluded six or seven, apparently because even he does not think that they conform to any parallel from the *Chymische Hochzeit.* This is already a particular embarrassment for a scholar who introduces his argument with the claim of an "exact parallel" including "the totality of the events that occur in the first and second Cartesian dreams."[6]

With Arnold, I turn to the *Chymische Hochzeit:* "As for the events related in the first dream, they are found in order in Andreae, during the whole first day. . . ."[7] A scholar aware of Arnold's work but otherwise unfamiliar with the *Chymische Hochzeit* might be startled to learn that *not one* of the alleged parallels to elements of Descartes's Dream I from Andreae's allegory refers to the narrative of Christian Rosenkreutz's Day I. That first day and night (of an allegorical week) include two great events, a very elaborate angelic invitation to the royal wedding and a very elaborate dream vision concerning escape from the prison of sin. Neither event could possibly have inspired either the street scene or the school scene of Dream I.[8]

Second, the fallacy of misrepresentation spoils Arnold's claim with respect to DE I.4 (if, indeed, it is a claim), DE I.5, Interpretation I, and Dream II. There is no whirlwind in the *Chymische Hochzeit,* and Christian is never spun around three or four times by anything else. Descartes's ghosts, his hemiplegic weakness, his leftward lean, and his whirlwind spins all seem parts of the explanation for the dreamer's inability to advance and his fear of falling. None of this follows the allegory of the *Chymische Hochzeit.* Christian Rosenkreutz does dream that both his feet are bound in the shackles of sin, and when he awakens, he finds real wounds, physical marks of his spiritual infirmity (CH 13, 17, 28; HR 16–17, 26, 37). However, he begins his pilgrim journey singing lightheartedly with the birds and skipping light-footedly with the fawns (CH 14–15; HR 19–20). Unlike the dreaming Descartes, the waking Rosenkreutz *hastens* on his way (CH 16, 18, 19, 22; HR 21, 25, 26,

29–30), called by an angel and sustained by grace (CH 3–5, 18–19; HR 4–6, 25–26).

Misrepresentations of the Olympian materials spoil Arnold's "parallel" for Descartes's Interpretation I, the two hours of wakefulness Descartes spent pondering a dream he attributed to an evil spirit and meditating on his sins. The esotericist uses identical language for the nighttime experiences of Descartes and Rosenkreutz (CH 34–35; HR 44–46),[9] but Andreae's model Christian is notably contrite when he considers his sins and "comforted" with the prospect of "future gain" (CH 33, 35; HR 44, 46). His penance is an expiation, and his real humility is rewarded with an allegorical dream vision of the false pride *of others* and the damning consequences *for them* (CH 34–35; HR 45–46).

The first of Arnold's two "parallels" for Descartes's Dream II best illustrates the extreme carelessness with which he misrepresents material from Andreae's allegory. He says that the Lady-angel who brings the wedding invitation to Rosenkreutz at the beginning of Day I is heralded by a trumpet blast and "thousands of little lights."[10] Only some such "sudden, loud noise" and "sparks of fire" would make Andreae's remarkable episode of angelic invitation at all comparable to Descartes's Dream II (sound but no lights) and Interpretation II (lights but no spiritualia). However, both sound and lights are Arnold's inventions, not Andreae's. The allegorical Lady-angel enters carrying her trumpet, not blowing it, still less hurling thunderbolts; she merely taps Christian on his back to gain attention (CH 3–4; HR 4). Furthermore, although her sky-blue robe is decorated with golden stars, she is simply not preceded by any "little lights," let alone "thousands" of them (CH 3; HR 4).

Third, the fallacy of divergence: unfortunately, it is possible to avoid gross misrepresentation while claiming as an "exact parallel" to a given element an episode that is not even similar. This also is most easily illustrated in the case of an alleged allegorical model for Descartes's Thunder Dream. Arnold's second "parallel" is the second entrance for Andreae's Virgo Lucifera (whom Arnold confuses with the Lady-angel). Here, indeed, are both a fanfare and thousands of tapers. However, there are also two bright torches and a "gloriously gilded Triumphant Self-moving Throne," as well as brief but weighty sermonettes on God's grace and man's sin (CH 29–32; HR 39–43). Rosenkreutz understands them perfectly and remains penitent. Descartes would have had to be a very dull fellow to need all this foofaraw to suggest his "sudden, loud noise"— and then to interpret his "sparks" contrarily with his own prideful science.

Divergences also disqualify Arnold's "parallels" for DE I.6, 8, 10, and 11. The mountaintop castle to which Rosenkreutz gladly runs is in no way comparable to the urban school into which Descartes stumbles. Arnold unaccountably takes the two porters at the castle gates (CH 20–23; HR 26–30) to have inspired Descartes's Acquaintance and his Other Person,[11] although there is nothing in Rosenkreutz's encounters to suggest the snubs, reversals, and vague promises so closely associated with these obscure figures in Descartes's Dream I, and there is nothing in the dream narrative to suggest the porters, gates, and castle in the Christian allegory.

A solution to the riddle of Descartes's gift melon (DE I.11) would allow us to salvage at least something from the ruins of this failed argument. Arnold offers two solutions, which are so dissimilar as to constitute his own reduction to absurdity of the argument for parallel texts and, consequently, for Descartes's *Olympica* as allegorical fiction modeled on Andreae's *Chymische Hochzeit*. One is a half-recessed terrestrial globe, thirty feet in diameter and hollow, on the outer surface of which pilgrims can find their native countries marked in gold and on the inner surface of which they can view planetarium shows (CH 59–60; HR 78–81). The other is a hanging golden globe that, when heated, cooled, and cut open, yields up a "great, lovely, snowy-white egg" (CH 111ff.; HR 148ff.). Both globes are wonderful to behold, but could either have inspired the gift melon from a foreign land that the less imaginative dreamer never gets to see?

The one dream element from Dreams I and II that I have yet to consider, the contrary wind that blows the dream Descartes back toward the church (DE I.9), does have an analogue in Andreae's contrary wind (CH 19; HR 25). In the allegory, Rosenkreutz advances toward the castle, pauses to break bread with a pretty white dove, rushes off to chase away a filthy black raven, and then, when he turns back to retrieve his bread and his other possessions, feels the contrary wind (CH 18–19; HR 24–25). It is at least possible to compare these passages. Andreae's pilgrimage, sacramental bread, and spiritual dove all establish a context in which the contrary wind is only incidental to the scriptural theme of turning back. Andreae drew this from Genesis 19:17 and 26 (Lot's wife) and Luke 9:57–62 (Jesus' exhortation: follow me and do not look back) and 17:28–32 (Jesus' admonition: "Remember Lot's wife" and do not turn back).[12] There is no such context and no obvious scriptural reference for Descartes's DE I.9. There is the fallacy of discontinuity, however. Despite his professions of an orderly sequence, Arnold's adoption of *this* "parallel" forces him to turn back as a reader of the *Chymische Hochzeit!*

Arnold's argument fails at every stage, as reflected in an orderly review of his claims with respect to the several dream elements and the corresponding fallacies:

DE I.1:   No claim; fallacy of selectivity.
DE I.2:   No claim; fallacy of selectivity.
DE I.3:   No claim; fallacy of selectivity.
DE I.4:   If no claim, fallacy of selectivity;
              if claim, fallacy of misrepresentation.
DE I.5:   Claim; fallacy of misrepresentation.
DE I.6:   Claim; fallacy of divergence.
DE I.7:   No claim; fallacy of selectivity.
DE I.8:   Claim; fallacy of divergence.
DE I.9:   Claim; fallacy of discontinuity.
DE I.10:   Claim; fallacy of divergence.
DE I.11:   Claim; fallacy of divergence.
DE I.12:   No claim; fallacy of selectivity.
DE I.13:   No claim; fallacy of selectivity.
Dream II: Claim; fallacy of misrepresentation.

This is not a very impressive performance, but it somehow impressed such learned scholars as Henri Gouhier and Gregor Sebba. Gouhier actually embraced and extended Arnold's arguments, cautiously tabling the *Chymische Hochzeit* for further consideration but enthusiastically holding up the *Raptus philosophicus* as a second allegorical model and vaguely suggesting "Scipio's Dream" as a third. Sebba exhibited an uncritical admiration of Arnold's work and implicitly adopted his hypothesis when he defined the relevant section of his bibliography.[13]

What makes Arnold's tentative references to the *Raptus philosophicus*[14] so much more important than his more confident references to the *Chymische Hochzeit* is that both Gouhier and Sebba recommended them particularly to scholarly Cartesians. Despite Gouhier's professed regard for Arnold's "meticulous" research and analysis, he did have his doubts about the "curious comparisons" and "ingenious parallels" between the *Chymische Hochzeit* and the *Olympica*.[15] He also stopped just short of accepting the full force of Arnold's argument against all historical dreaming.[16] It is wrong to exaggerate these reservations, however, whether on the subject of literary parallels or of historical dreams. Arnold had what seemed to be a decisive impact in both respects.

First, consider the impact of Arnold's esoteric "parallels." Gouhier called attention to Arnold's work and particularly to the "more impressive" comparisons that his predecessor had drawn between the *Raptus philosophicus* and Dream III:

> *In the first place, in the two cases, it is a question of a dream.* The author [this term seems to refer to the first-person narrator and central character of the *Raptus philosophicus*, not its unknown author] is at a crossroads, [and] he wonders which is the right way to go. Finally, he decides to take a narrow road, overgrown and almost untraceable. After many adventures (the encounter with a lion who threatens to kill him, with birds who return to life after having been killed by a crow, etc.), a woman appears, asking him: "Where are you going? What spirit leads you here?" She then shows him a book "in which there was written, but not methodically, everything that exists in heaven and on earth. . . ." A young man dressed in white, who has preceded the candidate from the start, then reveals to him that this woman is "Nature . . . , who is now quite unknown to the savants and the philosophers." *Thus, in the two stories, the dreamer poses for himself the question of the way of life, and he sees a book containing the sum total of human knowledge*[17] [emphases added].

In this restatement of Arnold's "comparison," Gouhier offers only two sentences that directly liken the *Raptus philosophicus* to the *Olympica*, Dream III, namely, the first and the last, here italicized. Everything else pertains to the *Raptus* alone. The first sentence and the last claim that the *Raptus*, too, like the *Olympica*, presents what is at least nominally a dream. This is incorrect. A *raptus* is a "rapture" or "ravishment," and this *raptus* begins and ends without the assertions of sleeping, dreaming, and awakening that frame so many other allegories. Here, we read only this: "Now, it happened one night that I could neither sleep nor rest. . . ."[18]

It is also quite misleading to say that the Rosicrucian narrator "poses for himself the question of the way of life," for as Gouhier himself goes on to state, his objective, known from the start, is to enter the Fraternity of the Rosicrucians. Furthermore, for the candidate to be asked "Where are you going?" as he makes his symbolic ascent up the narrow path is hardly the same as for Descartes the aleatory reader to open his anthology at Ausonius's poem.[19]

Finally, it is very misleading to liken the allegorical book of esoteric wonders, the *Azoth*, to Descartes's two dream books, the useful Dictionary and the familiar *Corpus poetarum*. Nature personified hands down the *Azoth*, and in it the narrator finds all this and more: necromancy, geomancy, pyromancy, hydromancy, chaomancy, and astrology.[20] Descartes's commonplace volumes become symbols of all the sciences and of philosophy and wisdom (if not of all the many "mancies") only retrospectively, not in the narrative but in its ensuing interpretation.

Gouhier does qualify his endorsement of Arnold's supposed "parallels," but he also adopts the more general hypothesis of Rosicrucian readings without the sort of critical hesitation that Arnold himself expressed. For example, there is a language problem. In Descartes's day, the *Chymische Hochzeit* and the *Raptus philosophicus* were unavailable in any language other than German. There is, however, no good evidence that the young Descartes, even as a traveler in Germany, read any books in that language.

Indeed, at the time, as well as later, Descartes wrote as if he were not much of a reader in any language. In the *Praeambula*, the Cartesian wisdom that begins with the fear of the Lord does not end in veneration of print: "When we have read a few lines, . . . we know [all there is to know] about most books. . . ."[21] In the *Discourse*, Descartes describes a sweeping rejection of books as such. We can see good evidence of this aversion to reading even in the exceptional case of Raymon Llull's *Ars brevis*, a Latin book, a short book, a known book, and a relevant book—and one that he asked Isaac Beeckman to read for him![22]

Unaccountably, Henri Gouhier, the more critical historian, destined for Étienne Gilson's armchair in the Académie française, never confronted the problems of the alien language and of the unbookish philosopher. Following the apparent implications of Arnold's work without sufficient reflection on all that remained unclear, he simply accepted Descartes's familiarity with the Rosicrucian literature as a matter of fact.[23] In particular, he endorsed and extended Paul Arnold's most cautious parallels with respect to Dream III and the *Raptus philosophicus*.

Second, having reconsidered the impact of Arnold's rash claims of esoteric literary parallels for the *Olympica*, let me reconsider the impact of his work on the question of the historicity of the dreams. Given the extreme casualness with which he used his sources and the fallaciousness of his arguments, it is astonishing that he could have convinced better-qualified scholars. But convince them he did. In Gouhier's case, there appears to be a gradual slide toward qualified agreement rather than an immediate or unqualified assent. In 1956, he defended the historicity of "*at least* one dream" (emphasis added), even if he was already willing to concede perfect certainty only for what I have labeled Interpretation III, phase 1. In 1958, it was "one dream" or at least "one fragment of a real dream." By 1972, however, it was *only* one dream: "Only the third dream seems to us to correspond to a dream really dreamed."[24] Because Gouhier went so far toward accepting Arnold's proposed Rosicrucian parallels for this same third dream, by his own argument he effectively mooted his continued acceptance of even one historical dream.

What accounts for the success of Arnold's hypothesis? It cannot reflect the strength of his very weak argument that Dreams I and II parallel the *Chymische Hochzeit*. It does not reflect the strength of his more tentative suggestion that Dream III also parallels the *Raptus philosophicus*. The sixteen elements of Dream III are listed in order at the head of chapter 8. Readers with sufficient patience may turn back to compare them with Gouhier's previously quoted paragraph of "more impressive comparisons," or better yet, with Arnold's much longer synopsis of the very rare and very strange *Raptus philosophicus*, or best of all, with that crucial document itself. My own conclusion is this: Arnold's hypothesis was the bad idea of a curious student of esoterica who was preoccupied with Rosicrucian literature, indifferent to Descartes except as someone already suspected of Rosicrucian sympathies, and ignorant of dream reports as such.[25]

But why did Arnold's bad idea convince others? The hypothesis that the *Olympica* is an allegory in the manner of Rosicrucian literature reclaims Descartes's otherwise irrational dreams and his embarrassingly enthusiastic interpretations as products of the Thinking Thing, who can thus be supposed to have narrated just a bit of a real dream and invented a lot of pseudodreaming as an artful introduction for the thoughts on spiritual symbols known from Leibniz's *Cogitationes Privatae*. The bad idea is still a bad idea, however, even as Gouhier restates it: maybe the model was not the *Chymische Hochzeit* . . . ; maybe it was not the *Raptus philosophicus* . . . ; but how about "Scipio's Dream" . . . ?

The idea of a Ciceronian model for Descartes's *Olympica* is no better than the idea of a Rosicrucian model, despite the fact that this former pupil of French Jesuits would almost certainly have been familiar with "Scipio's Dream." Although the rest of Cicero's *Republic* had been lost, this concluding piece of moralistic fiction had survived along with Macrobius's *Commentary*, and it was very widely read and very highly esteemed in the Renaissance.[26] Descartes must have been familiar with the classical precedent for philosophical instruction in dream form. However, presumed familiarity cannot validate Gouhier's variant on Arnold's hypothesis.[27] The great problems with this bad idea have to do with literary form and philosophical content. Descartes's *Olympica* violates every relevant principle for the use of philosophical fictions. Along with Cicero's text, Macrobius presented rules for the genre. First, he can approve only those fictions that "encourage the reader to good works." Second, among improving fictions, he can approve only those that "rest on a solid foundation of truth treated in a fictitious style." Third, among improving and solidly founded fictions, he can approve only those that offer "decent and dignified conceptions of holy truths, with respectable events and characters, . . . beneath a modest veil of allegory."[28] Strike one, strike two, strike three, and the *Olympica* is out as properly Ciceronian allegory—or, for that matter, *as any other sort of allegory*.

Allegorical invention is possible only in the context of a *community of belief* based on an *established truth*.[29] Its success depends absolutely on a shared tradition, within which the reader brings to the task of interpretation the same higher truths that the author has expressed in figurative composition. But no such shared tradition can possibly explain the Olympian dreams. This dreamer had been wholly caught up in the enthusiasm of what he took to be the discovery of a great *new* truth: "10 November 1619. When I was full of enthusiasm and was *discovering* the foundation of the wonderful science . . ."[30] The Olympian dream narratives could not have been written as an allegorical introduction to a *new* philosophy or "wonderful science," simply because allegory in the service of *novelty* makes no sense, there being no possibility of a shared reference to an authoritative tradition.

Notes

Introduction

1. Chanut, *Inventaire succinct des escrits qui se sont trouvez dans les coffres de Mons. Descartes après son décedz à Stocholm en Feb. 1650* (Paris, Bibliothèque Nationale, manuscrits français, n.a., 4730); in addition to this Paris copy, there is also a Leiden copy in the Bibliotheek der Rijksuniversiteit, where it is cataloged as HUG 29 a. Leibniz, *Cartesii cogitationes privatae*, in *Oeuvres inédites de Descartes*, ed. Alexandre Foucher de Careil, 2 vols. (Paris, 1859), 1:2-17. Baillet, *La Vie de Monsieur Des Cartes* (Paris, 1691), 1:50-51, 81-86. Charles Adam carefully edited all three documents in his *Oeuvres de Descartes* (Paris, 1908), 10:5-12, especially 7-8 (Chanut); 211-19 (Leibniz); and 179-88 (Baillet). Further references to this great edition will be made in text using only the initial letters of the surnames of Adam and his coeditor, Paul Tannery: AT. Following my translations of the three sources in part 1, I will refer to them in text by the initial letters of the titles and the line numbers in my versions (SI = Stockholm Inventory; CP = *Cogitationes Privatae*; VDC = *Vie de Monsieur Des Cartes*).

2. AT, 6:11. The word "then" in this passage can refer only to "one day" at the end of the first part; see AT, 6:10. The year is established by the later reference to his "twenty-three years"; see AT, 6:22. Descartes was born on 31 March 1596. For more on the chronological coincidence of thinking and dreaming, see part 2, chaps. 3 and 4.

3. AT, 6:18-19, 22-28.

4. For politics see AT, 6:13-15, 22-23; for religion see AT, 6:22-23, 28, 40-41, 60. With respect to the applicability of his method to these sensitive topics, Descartes seems to want it both ways. On the one hand, he reserves

these sensitive subjects as beyond the potentially corrosive reach of his egocentric rationalism with its methodical doubt. On the other hand, he advertises
on his first page that he has reaffirmed "the existence of God and of the
human soul" by the exercise of his methodical reason.

5. AT, 6:8–9, 27.

6. AT, 6:4–10.

7. AT, 6:11–13.

8. Baillet, *Vie*, 1:51; AT, 10:179.

9. Baillet, *Vie*, 1:84; AT, 10:185; VDC, 196–99. For the identity of "the
Spirit of Truth," see John 14:17, 15:26, 16:13.

10. Baillet, *Vie*, 51; AT, 10:7, 179.

11. Baillet, *Vie*, 1:50–51. Leibniz, "Notata quaedam G.G.L. circa vitam et
doctrinam Cartesii" and "Remarques sur *L'abrégé de la vie de Mons. des
Cartes*," both in *Die philosophische schriften* (Berlin, 1880), 4:310, 315.

12. Baillet, *Vie*, 1:82–84.

13. [Daniel-Pierre Huet, pseudonymously disguised as] G[illes] de l'A[unay],
Nouveaux mémoires pour servir à l'histoire du cartésianisme (n.p., 1692),
42–44.

14. Baillet, *Vie*, 1:81–83. Baillet correctly identified the anthology: it was
the *Corpus omnium veterum poetarum Latinorum*, compiled by Pierre des
Brosses and published in successive editions at Lyon (1603) and Geneva (1611).
Descartes might have used either edition, and the pagination differed slightly.
In the first (1603), the poem "Quod vitae sectabor iter?" is on p. 655 of vol.
2, followed by "Est et Non" on pp. 655–56, so that, strictly speaking, the
dream reader would have had to lose his way from the initial verse to another
on the same page! In the second (1611), the first of these verses is on pp.
658–59 of vol. 2, the second, on p. 659, so that the dream reader would
have had to lose his way between facing pages.

15. Jacques Maritain gave new life and scholarly substance to the satirical
tradition from Huet in an essay first published in 1920. Maritain waved aside
the narratives and focused on the interpretations, emphasizing that the dreamer's enthusiasm came at the very moment of the thinker's epochal days in
the heated chamber. See *The Dream of Descartes*, trans. Mabelle Andison
(New York, 1945), 13–29 and endnotes.

16. Baillet, *Vie*, 1:83–85.

17. See n.9.

18. Baillet, *Vie*, 1:85.

19. The initial publications are Adam, "Avertissement" to the *Olympica*,
in AT, 10:175; Gouhier, "Le songe de Descartes," in *La pensée réligieuse de
Descartes* (Paris, 1924), 311; Arnold, "Le 'songe' de Descartes," *Cahiers du
Sud* 35 (1952): 272–91.

20. In the notes of Leibniz, the biography of Baillet, and the satire of

Huet, the seventeenth century had sketched out three possible responses to the dreams from the *Olympica:* exclusion, compartmentalization, and derision. The historical works of the early twentieth century went no further, but at least they did not fully actualize the potential of scholarly denial. Charles Adam virtually excluded the dreams from his otherwise inclusive *Vie et oeuvres de Descartes* (Paris, 1910), 49–50. Gustave Cohen unhappily included a compartmentalized paraphrase of Baillet's paraphrase in his *Écrivains français en Hollande dans la première moitié du XVIIe siècle* (Paris, 1920), 397–99, and Jacques Maritain happily derided in "Le songe de Descartes," *Revue universelle* (1 December 1920), republished in book form under the same title in 1932. For later retrogression, see the appendices.

21. Retrospection limited Descartes's later and apparently more historical account of 1619 in several ways that are particularly relevant to my work. By 1637, Descartes had withdrawn completely from his family and his homeland, and he had also broken violently from Isaac Beeckman. He had so settled into his way of life as a "searcher for truth" that any alternative vocation was virtually inconceivable, not just for the present, but as a past possibility.

Exclusiveness is a more obvious limitation of the *Discourse.* Its historical account served philosophical purposes at the high cost of reducing the "life" to thought. The thinker excluded other people from his story, even those most closely associated with his intellectual life, to the point that the ungrateful former pupil lamented, "If I had only had just one teacher..." (AT, 6:16). A vigorous critic might contend that Descartes excluded himself as a social being, an emotional being, a developing being, or, in short, a human being.

The systematic biases of this retrospective and exclusive account are also evident. After 1628, Descartes based a formal metaphysics on his own certain existence as a thinking thing. His philosophy was systematically antihistorical insofar as it effectively doubted away the past and reduced existence to momentary consciousness; it was systematically antisocial insofar as it focused attention only on the rational self, the perfect God, and the physical world; and it was systematically antipsychological insofar as it insisted on his own fully self-conscious rationality.

Finally, persuasive and defensive purposes qualified even the rationally reductionistic "history" that Descartes did offer in the first and second parts of the *Discourse.* His discussion of his education at La Flèche must be read in the light of his own privately declared ambition to offer an alternative program for the schools of his day. His presentation of the four rules of the Method was designed to serve as an introduction to the scientific treatises published with the *Discourse.* And in all of this he was acutely aware of the trial and condemnation of Galileo for having taught similar principles and of the need to fend off any such troubles for himself.

22. AT, 6:31–33, 38–40.

23. AT, 9:22, 71.

24. Because of the use and abuse of Freudian personality theory in historical and cultural criticism, all "psychohistory" has become suspect. Freud's very name is a red flag, antagonizing historical empiricists, who are apt to lower their heads in bullish charges. Please note my Baconian epigraph and distinguish Freud's *method* of dream interpretation, which I have adapted, from all psychoanalytical *theories* of personality, which I have not adopted.

In the judgment of informed psychologists, Freud's most enduring accomplishment was his discovery of this method. For his own opinion as an older theorist, see the "Preface to the Third (Revised) English Edition" (1931), in *The Interpretation of Dreams*, trans. James Strachey (New York, 1965), xxxii. For that of his disciples, see especially Ernest Jones, *The Life and Work of Sigmund Freud*, 3 vols. (New York, 1953), 1:350–63; Alexander Grinstein, *Freud's Rules of Dream Interpretation* (New York, 1983), passim. For that of his most notable critics, see especially Carl Jung, "General Aspects of Dream Psychology" and "On the Nature of Dreams" (both revised 1948), in *Collected Works* (Princeton, 1960), 8:238–39, 284; Alfred Adler, "On the Nature of Dreams" (1936), in *The Individual Psychology of Alfred Adler* (New York, 1956), 357; Jean Piaget, *Play, Dreams, and Imitation in Childhood* (New York, 1962), 182. For that of the best qualified psychophysiological researchers, see Richard M. Jones, *The New Psychology of Dreaming* (New York, 1970), 3; William C. Dement, *Some Must Watch while Some Must Sleep* (San Francisco, 1972), 134; David Foulkes, *A Grammar of Dreams* (New York, 1978), 27–87.

25. Freud, *Interpretation*, 35, 128, and passim.

26. Ibid., 659–60 and more generally 196–253.

27. Ibid., 136, 486, 538.

28. Ibid., 133. See also Freud, "Freud's Psychoanalytic Method" (1904), "Recommendations for Physicians on the Psychoanalytic Method of Treatment" (1912), and "Further Recommendations in the Technique of Psychoanalysis" (1913), all in *Therapy and Technique*, ed. Philip Rieff (New York, 1963), 57, 118–19, 121–22, 147. For more popular exposition, see Freud's *Introductory Lectures to Psychoanalysis* (1916–17), trans. James Strachey (New York, 1977), 105–7, 113–15, 287–88 and n.1.

29. See Bacon, *Novum Organum*, 1:xcii, the passage that serves as this book's epigraph.

30. Descartes, AT, 9:71. Freud adopted these criteria in his letter to Maxime Leroy, translated in the latter's *Descartes* (Paris, 1929), 1:89; see also *Interpretation*, 128, 155, 192, 311–12, 561–64; *Therapy and Technique*, 219–23.

31. I include translations from the *Cogitationes Privatae* in chap. 1, along

with a brief discussion of the technical problems of exact provenance and relative chronology.

32. *Oeuvres inédites de Descartes*, 1:8–9, or AT, 10:216. This is a confusing and perhaps confused note. For a clearer presentation of the relevant evidence, see Chanut, Stockholm Inventory, AT, 10:7, and Baillet, *Vie de Monsieur Des Cartes*, 1:50–51, 81, 83–84. For Leibniz's attitudes, see "Notata quaedam G.G.L. circa vitam et doctrinam Cartesii," in *Die philosophische Schriften*, 4:310; "Remarques sur *L'abérgé de la vie de Mons. des Cartes*," *Philosophische schriften*, 4:315.

33. AT, 10:1–8, 179–88, 205–19.

34. AT, 10:175–76.

35. *Vie et oeuvres de Descartes* (Paris, 1910), 49–50.

36. Ibid.

37. Ibid.

38. Ibid., 55.

39. Baillet, *Vie de Monsieur Des Cartes*, 1:80–86. See below, chap. 2.

40. Cohen, *Les écrivains français en Hollande*, 393, 395.

41. Ibid., 397.

42. Ibid, 399.

43. Baillet, *Vie*, 1:85.

44. Gouhier drew his dream psychology from Marcel Foucault's *Le rêve* (Paris, 1906). Nothing in his brief discussions of the subject suggests formal use of anything beyond Foucault's inadequate review of earlier work. Unfortunately, he misrepresented even this archaic psychology. See appendix 2.

45. *La pensée réligieuse de Descartes* (Paris, 1924 and 1972), 313–15; *Les premières pensées de Descartes* (Paris, 1958 and 1979), 32–37. I use the second editions of both books.

46. See Arnold's "Le 'songe' de Descartes," 272–91; *Histoire des Rose-Croix et les origines de la Franc-Maçonnerie* (Paris, 1955), 273–99; "Descartes et les Rose-Croix," *Mercure de France* 1166 (1960): 266–84; *La Rose-Croix et ses rapports avec la Franc-Maçonnerie* (Paris, 1970), 150–63. Gouhier, "Descartes a-t-il rêvé?" *Revue internationale de philosophie* 36 (1956): 203–8; *Premières pensées*, 38–41, 138–41; *Pensée réligieuse*, 313.

47. Sebba, *Bibliographia Cartesiana* (The Hague, 1964), 20 (on Arnold's "Le 'songe'") and 18 (on Gouhier's *Premières pensées*).

48. Sebba, *The Dream of Descartes,* assembled from manuscripts and edited by Richard Watson (Carbondale, Ill., 1987), 8, 11, 18, 32–33, 36–37, 48–56. On the vortex, this recasts the hypothesis of Heinrich Quiring, "Der Traum des Descartes: Eine Verschlüsselung seiner Kosmologie, seiner Methodik and der Grundlage seiner Philosophie," *Kant Studien* 46 (1954–1955): 135–56. Sebba knew this paper and briefly reviewed it in the *Bibliographia*

Cartesiana, 21, where he rightly rejected it as an "impossible hypothesis." On the *cogito*, this recasts the hypothesis of Bertram Lewin, *Dreams and the Uses of Regression* (New York, 1958), 49–52. Sebba knew this published lecture, too, and took it much too seriously as a contribution to Cartesian studies in his notice in the *Bibliographia Cartesiana*, 20–21. The minimal documentation in Sebba's posthumous *Dream of Descartes* makes no reference to either predecessor.

49. I distinguish psychiatrists's essays on the Olympian dreams from psychological studies of dreaming. Sebba had read many of the former, but he paid no attention whatsoever to the latter. For his willingness to use Freud's letter as a lesson in the irrelevance of psychological analysis to the case of the Olympian dreams, see *The Dream of Descartes*, 2, 6, 8, 25, 31, 43, 44, 47, 51.

50. Beeckman does play a role in the interpretation, but there is no rigor in the use of Cartesian materials from his *Journal:* ibid., 24, 27, 29, 34, 36–38. As for Leibniz's *Cogitationes,* Sebba cites (and almost certainly both misattributes and misinterprets) only one brief Cartesian fragment: ibid., 34.

51. Freud to Leroy, published in French without a date in Leroy's *Descartes*, 2 vols. (Paris, 1929), 1:89–90. The argument for 1928 as the probable year of Freud's letter depends on a known terminus ante quem and an inferred terminus post quem. Leroy dated his "Avant-propos" 15 December 1928. Given Leroy's prolific and varied output in the middle and later 1920s, he could not have been free for work on Descartes before the beginning of that year:

1924: *Le socialisme des producteurs: Henri de Saint-Simon.*
1925: *La vie véritable du comte de Saint-Simon.*
1926: *Les spéculations foncières de Saint-Simon.*
1927a: *La ville française: Institutions et libertés locales.*
1927b: *La Société des Nations: L'ère Wilson.*
1927c: *Les premiers amis français de Richard Wagner.*
1928a: *Fénelon.*
1928b: "Introduction" to Descartes, *Le discours de la méthode.*

52. In chronological order: (1) Stephen Schönberger, "A Dream of Descartes: Reflections on the Unconscious Determinants of the Sciences," *International Journal of Psychoanalysis* 20 (1939): 43–57; (2) Iago Galdston, "Descartes and Modern Psychiatric Thought," *Isis* 35 (1944): 118–28; (3) J. O. Wisdom, "Three Dreams of Descartes," *International Journal of Psychoanalysis* 28 (1947): 11–18; (4) Bertram D. Lewin, *Dreams and the Uses of Regression* (New York, 1958); and (5) Lewis S. Feuer, "The Dreams of Descartes," *American Imago* 20 (1963): 3–26, and "Anxiety and Philosophy: the Case of Descartes," *American Imago* 20 (1963): 411–49. The first four authors

were psychoanalysts addressing, in the first instance, other psychoanalysts. The fifth, Feuer, was a professor writing for a journal of applied psychoanalysis of which Freud had been an honorary founding editor.

53. In chronological order: (1) John Rittmeister, "Die Mystische Krise des jungen Descartes," *Confinia psychiatrica* 4 (1961): 65–98; republished in *Zeitschrift fur Psychosomatische Medezin und Psychanalyse* 15 (1969): 206–24 (Rittmeister's work was accomplished if not published before his wartime death at the hands of the Nazis); (2) Marie von Franz, "The Dream of Descartes," in *Timeless Documents of the Soul* (Evanston, Ill., 1968), 55–147. This English version revised and extended work first published under the title *Zeitlose Dokumente der Seele* in *Studien aus dem Jung-Institut,* 3 (1952).

54. There is an apparent high-handedness in my listing all this work without discussing in detail the interpretations of the professional psychiatrists who have considered the subject. I have, however, paid the closest critical attention to all this work. Feuer's papers from the Freudian theoretical perspective and von Franz's little monograph from the Jungian theoretical perspective are the best of the lot, but it is a bad lot historically. Neither of these two authors deals successfully with the problems of extending associative methods, and neither focuses rigorously on the limited historical evidence on the young Descartes's life and thought. All this work, even at its best, is commentary informed by theory but not disciplined by empirical, critical method. All of it is spoiled by serious errors on points of fact and by a more general indifference to other source materials, especially Beeckman's *Journal* and Leibniz's *Cogitationes.*

55. These are the topics covered in Freud's *Introductory Lectures on Psychoanalysis,* delivered in 1916–17, here cited from the Strachey translation as republished by Norton (New York, 1977).

56. AT, 6:32–33. This claim seemed extraordinary even to the first readers of the *Discourse* (1637), but Descartes defended it vigorously.

57. No errors: Descartes's first claim came in the *Regulae,* AT, 10:371–72; the claim is implicit in the whole project represented by the *Discourse,* AT, 6:8–9, 12–13, 16–17, 18–19, 21, 27–28; it is explicit in the *Meditations,* AT, 9:46–49. No bad dreams: Descartes to Balzac, 15 April 1631, AT, 1:197; cp. to Balzac, 5 May 1631, AT, 1:204; Descartes to Elizabeth, 1 September 1645, AT, 4:282. No uncontrolled passions: *Passions of the Soul,* part 1: art. 45–46, 50, and part 3: art. 211, in AT, 11:362–64, 368–70, 485–88.

58. Ernest Jones, *Freud,* (New York, 1953–57), 1:384; 3:83.

59. Ibid., 3:139–43. Max Schur became Freud's personal physician at this time. See his *Freud: Living and Dying* (New York, 1972), especially 403–6.

60. Jones, *Freud,* 3:146.

61. Freud to Leroy (1928), in Leroy, *Descartes,* 1:89.

62. Descartes had explained that the internal incoherence and external irrelevance of dreams distinguishes them essentially from waking thoughts. See AT, 9:71.

63. For the necessity of a dreamer's associations, see Freud, *The Interpretation of Dreams,* 274 and passim.

64. Bacon, *Novum organum,* book 1: aphorisms 42 and 44.

65. Freud to Leroy, in Leroy, *Descartes,* 1:89.

66. Ibid., 1:89–90.

67. That there are "thoughtlike" dreams is amply confirmed by laboratory research. The questions of theoretical interest have to do with how to integrate such dreams with others in a coherent psychology. *None* of Freud's most familiar summary publications discusses "dreams from above": *The Interpretation of Dreams* (1900 and later editions); *On Dreams* (1901); *Introductory Lectures on Psychoanalysis* (1917); *New Introductory Lectures on Psychoanalysis* (1932); or *An Outline of Psychoanalysis* (1939). The very well read psychoanalyst would know only a single short paragraph in the "Remarks on the Theory and Practice of Dream-Interpretation" (1923), in *Therapy and Technique,* 207–8.

A layman's opinion: there seems to be no clear definition of the threshold distinguishing dreams from "above" and "below," or, in more modern terms, NREM and REM mentation, and there is no justification for Freud's contrary willingness to let the dreamer explain straightforwardly, without associations, in the former case but not the latter. For the place of NREM dreams in a more modern and more scientific dream psychology, see the authoritative and accessible exposition in David Foulkes, *The Psychology of Sleep* (New York, 1966), 99–120.

68. Given the modishness of the reading that makes the *Olympica* a work of spiritual symbolism in the Christian tradition, it is worth emphasizing that there was an older pagan tradition of dream interpretation by symbolic equivalents. The great classic of the genre is Artemidorus's *Oneirocritica.* In honor of Stekel's dream apples and *perhaps* Descartes's dream melon, I quote one example that gives the flavor of the whole: "Seeing and eating spring apples [in a dream] that are sweet and sun-ripened is a sign of good luck. For it indicates the pleasures of love, especially to men who are concerned about a wife or a mistress. For these apples are sacred to Aphrodite" (Artemidorus 1:73). There is a convenient translation with commentary by Robert White: Artemidorus, *Oneirocritica: The Interpretation of Dreams* (Park Ridge, N.J., 1975). For those of Descartes's generation, there was an equally convenient edition of the Greek text with a Latin translation by Nicolas Rigault, first published in Paris, 1603. See Claes Blum, *Studies in the Dream-Book of Artemidorus* (Uppsala, 1936), 14.

This sort of dream interpretation remained very popular in France well into our "Cartesian Age of Reason." See, for instance, the signed work of a perfectly respectable M. de Mirbel, *avocat* at the Parlement of Paris, *Le palais du prince du sommeil où est enseigné l'oniromancie autrement l'art de déviner par les songes* (Lyon, 1670). Mirbel's work was republished at the height of the Enlightenment: Nicolas Lenglet Dufresnoy, *Recueil de dissertations anciennes et nouvelles sur les apparitions, les visions, et les songes,* 2 vols. (Paris, 1751), 2:47ff.

69. Leroy, *Descartes,* 1:83–88.

70. Freud, *The Interpretation of Dreams,* as revised in successive editions beginning in 1909, 385–95. Stekel's papers on the subject in 1909 were followed by his *Der Sprache des Traumes: Eine Darstellung der Symbolik und Deutung des Traumes* (Wiesbaden, 1911).

71. Stekel, *Der Sprache des Traumes,* 79–88. Freud, *The Interpretation of Dreams,* 393, 415. Freud's intimate friend from the 1890s, Wilhelm Fliess, had pressed on him the notion that left-handedness and bisexuality were related: see Freud to Fliess, 29 December 1897, 4 January and 9 October 1898, and 15 February 1901, in *The Origins of Psychoanalysis,* ed. Marie Bonaparte, et al. (New York, 1957), 244, 245–46, 271, 330. For Freud, this was a question of personal as well as scientific significance, and, even after breaking from Fliess, he retained his interest in the theory. He himself alleged the instance of Leonardo da Vinci and referred respectfully to the idea that left-handedness was a sign of homosexuality in the concluding paragraphs of his unfortunate *Leonardo da Vinci and a Memory of His Childhood* (1910).

72. Stekel, *Der Sprache des Traumes,* 73, 150, 158. Freud, *Interpretation of Dreams,* 321, 407; *Introductory Lectures,* 156, 158.

73. Freud to Leroy, in Leroy, *Descartes,* 1:90.

74. For the meeting date, see Beeckman's *Journal,* excerpted in AT, 10:46–47. For the love, see Descartes to Beeckman, 24 January 1619, AT, 10:151–153. For the reflections on friendship and on passions, see AT, 10:217 (CP 74–87), which must correspond to material summarized by Baillet at AT, 10:182 (VDC 84–86). For the melon, see below, chap. 7.

75. The retrogression is a matter of ever more fundamental denial of the historical evidence: first, Adam denied Baillet's reliability as our source for the dream material from the lost *Olympica;* second, Gouhier denied Descartes's accuracy as the reporter of his own dreams in that lost work; third, Arnold denied the very historicity of the dreams themselves. All these denials rest on assumptions that have never been critically tested. None can withstand rigorous testing. See appendices 1–3.

Chapter 1

1. Charles Adam and Gérard Milhaud appended a very useful summary of Chanut's life from a Cartesian perspective in their edition of Descartes's correspondence; see *Correspondance,* 7 vols. (Paris, 1936–63), 5:328–31.

2. Baillet, *Vie,* 2:428.

3. Ibid., 2:428. For more on Clerselier, see *Correspondance,* 6:354.

4. The standard scholarly reference is Adam's great edition, AT, 10:7–8. A facsimile of the Paris copy of the manuscript is available in Samuel S. de Sacy's *Descartes par lui-même* (Paris, 1956), 61. There is also a Leiden copy of the same Stockholm Inventory, which is the primary authority for *"Praeambula"* rather than *"Perambula"* as the title of the last dossier cataloged. The reference in the manuscript collection of the Bibliotheek der Rijksuniversiteit te Leiden is HUG 29a, 33r. The deputy keeper of Western manuscripts, Dr. Ch. M. G. Berkvens-Stevelinck, has kindly provided the documentation necessary to confirm this reading. Borel and Baillet both read *"Praeambula."* The other seventeenth-century sources on the *Olympica,* Leibniz and Baillet, add helpful information. Both give the anniversary year, 1620, for the marginal notation on the "wonderful discovery" at the head of the *Olympica.* In addition, Baillet specifies that the note was in Descartes's own hand, using a different ink. See Leibniz, *Philosophische Schriften,* 4:310; Baillet, *Vie,* 1:50–51.

5. One departure from past scholarship, Adam's great edition in the *Oeuvres de Descartes* and Gouhier's meticulous analysis in his *Premières pensées de Descartes,* is to group SI lines 5–11 as a single entry, giving the length in pages as well as the title and marginal note of the *Olympica.* Adam's editorial paragraphing for Item C, which has no basis in the Paris copy of the Stockholm Inventory, has encouraged speculation that the "six sheets written" (SI 6) were one dossier, contents unknown, and "the discourse entitled the *Olympica"* (SI 9) was another, length unknown.

Other entries on the composite notebooks show that the cataloger of the Stockholm Inventory worked perfectly consistently from perfectly reasonable principles. He always counted and recorded the length of the component dossiers, whether in numbers of sheets, pages, or lines, and he always provided at least some summary indication of contents, such as a title if there was one. Therefore, unless he violated his own working principles twice in succession, first failing to indicate contents for the "six sheets written" and then promptly failing to indicate length for "the discourse entitled the *Olympica,"* we must conclude that this is a single entry on a single dossier.

Baillet, who worked directly from Descartes's Little Notebook, provides confirming evidence when he gives his page count for the *Olympica:* the biographer's "twelve pages" (*Vie*, 1:50) exactly equal the cataloger's "six sheets." Leibniz is the authority for the size of the sheets as octavos. This is the necessary implication of the manuscript notes published in AT, 10:208–9.

6. Current wisdom on the subject is that the *Praeambula* and the *Experimenta* followed the *Olympica*; see Gouhier, *Premières pensées*, 66–67, 71.

7. Ibid., 11–13.

8. Adam, AT, 10:205–10; Gouhier, *Premières pensées*, passim.

9. Baillet knew about these notes, but with Descartes's originals in hand, he would have had no occasion to seek out Leibniz's copies. See his *Vie de Monsieur Des Cartes*, xxvi.

10. *Oeuvres inédites de Descartes*, ed. A. Foucher de Careil. The material of greatest interest to my book is in 1:2–17.

11. AT, 10:203–48. Adam's "Avertissement," 205–10, recounts all this in some detail.

12. Henri Gouhier, *Premières pensées*, 16–17, 39–41, 71–78. For counterargument, see n.17. Ferdinand Alquié followed this misattribution in his edition of the *Oeuvres philosophiques de Descartes* (Paris, 1963), 1:28, 49–50; John Cottingham has done the same in his translation of *The Philosophical Writings of Descartes* (Cambridge, 1985), 1:1, 3–4.

13. *Oeuvres inédites de Descartes*, 1:8 and note, 9 and note.

14. Working from Leibniz's copies, Foucher de Careil left a paragraph break here, but not the blank lines that separate discriminable cogitations in his edition; ibid., 1:12. Working from Descartes's originals, Baillet specifically and repeatedly affirmed that Descartes vowed the pilgrimage to Loretto in November, 1619. See his *Vie de Monsieur Des Cartes*, 1:86 and 120.

Although Baillet worked from documents no longer extant, his authority on such chronological points is far from absolute. It does seem plausible that the young enthusiast should have vowed a pilgrimage in the first excitement and personal uncertainty of his "wonderful science" and his as wonderful dream visions. Despite Baillet's assurances, however, we may very well wonder whether Descartes had already planned a trip across the mountains for that early winter.

Descartes's two vows, to undertake the pilgrimage before the end of November and to complete the treatise before Easter, may both have been dated, despite Leibniz's apparent evidence to the contrary. His understandable casualness in this regard is clearest at CP 64–73. Descartes's "wonderful science" and his "way in life" were the great concerns of the beginning of the winter. Finishing a treatise, presumably something related to the "wonderful science," was another matter for another time, the end of winter.

15. Foucher de Careil, working from Leibniz's copy, gives "September";

Baillet, working from Descartes's original, gives "February." Adam correctly preferred the latter. See *Oeuvres inédites de Descartes*, 1:12; *Vie de Monsieur Des Cartes*, 1:86; AT, 10:218 and note b.

16. *Premières pensées*, 16, 66–71. Gouhier acknowledges indebtedness on this point to the work of Abbé J. Sirven, *Les années d'apprentissage de Descartes* (Albi, 1628), 60–61. Alquié, in turn, acknowledges indebtedness to Gouhier: *Oeuvres philosophiques*, 1:28, 45–47.

17. *Premières pensées*, 16–17, 71–73.

18. Ibid., 16–17, 39–40, 71–76. Gouhier's initial presentation of the matter promises a later demonstration. His first substantive discussion rejects the seemingly obvious attribution of CP 64–73 to the *Olympica*. His reasons are these: first, Leibniz's CP, lines 64–65, does not reproduce *exactly* either of the very similar texts from the *Olympica* quoted by Baillet (*Vie*, 1:50–51); second, Leibniz's CP, lines 66–67, could not have been a part of the dream narratives and interpretations paraphrased by Baillet (*Vie*, 1:83–84).

These arguments rest on the presumption of an unvaried, word-for-word copying, a presumption that is unverified and unverifiable. This apparently conservative principle leads inevitably to much greater difficulties. In the name of Leibniz-the-verbatim-copyist, Gouhier hypothesizes an error in copying dates and, more alarmingly, an intrusion of someone other than Descartes, perhaps *Leibniz,* into the Little Notebook to leave the marginalia then copied by Leibniz or for *Leibniz.* Thus, the presumption self-destructs. See *Premières pensées,* 74–75.

It is implausible in itself—and unparalleled elsewhere in the what remains of the Little Notebook—that, after having made an elaborate record of his dreams in the *Olympica,* Descartes should have gone back to the *Experimenta* for what would have amounted to not quite detached notes on his own notes for no known purpose. Furthermore, the "reverse" sequence of "upside-down" materials in Descartes's series 2 very strongly suggests that the *Experimenta* preceded the *Olympica.* Although it is always possible that the author could have gone back to fill some of the blank pages left in an earlier dossier after having substantially "completed" a later one, Occam's razor argues against supposing so without better evidence for it. Gouhier would agree with this use of the razor; see *Premières pensées*, 13, 16, 73.

Technically, the form of Leibniz's reference to Ausonius's poem as "carmen 7" virtually guarantees that the note represents his hasty summary of the *Olympica*, not his verbatim copy from the *Experimenta*. The poem in question, "Quod vitae sectabor iter," is in fact from *Liber VII* [*Eclogarum Liber*]. However, Descartes had it from Pierre des Brosses's *Corpus omnium veterum poetarum Latinorum*, which was organized on different principles. For des Brosses and Descartes, it was "Edyl XV": see *Corpus poetarum* (Lyon, 1603), 645.

Finally, Baillet makes a particular point of explaining in some detail that Descartes's initial text and marginal note in the *Olympica* on the "foundation of the wonderful science" or "wonderful discovery" had been an unsolved puzzle for all Cartesians who considered the manuscripts. He would surely have mentioned *another* text and marginal note posing the *same* fascinating but obscure problem. The fact that he did not do so virtually precludes an otherwise improbable duplicate entry in the earlier *Experimenta* with another similarly elliptical and identically formatted text and marginal note on the same "foundation." See *Vie,* 1:50–51. Leibniz objected to this passage from Baillet, implying that *he,* at least, had solved the puzzle. But even in a hypercritical mood, he did not suggest that Baillet had ignored other relevant cogitations from the Little Notebook. See *Philosophische Schriften,* 4:315, and compare 310.

Chapter 2

1. Baillet, *Vie,* 1:80–86; AT, 10:180–89.

2. Adam, AT, 10:174–75. Gouhier, *Premières pensées,* 31 and n.1. Gouhier, the ranking student of the *Olympica,* closely follows Adam in his suspicion that Baillet's "more or less paraphrased" version was only "approximate," having been "ornamented" or "amplified." He does not add new evidence or argument. See *Premières pensées,* 32, 40, 78, 117.

In passages not specifically concerned with the dreams, Gouhier offers a general rule for critical readers of the *Vie de Monsieur Des Cartes:* Baillet's documentary research was "conscientious," but his own historical constructions are "suspect." That is, we may trust Baillet's narrative only insofar as it rests on the enviable documentation that he had inherited from Descartes by way of Chanut, Clerselier, and Legrand. On the other hand, we must distrust his tendency to resort to speculation or imagination when this documentation failed him; ibid., 20, 124. Applied to the specific case of the Olympian dreams, Gouhier's own general rule ought to have reassured him, because Baillet certainly worked directly from a single, authoritative document.

Gregor Sebba is the most recent authority on Baillet's characteristics. Like Gouhier, he also looks back to Adam as the best judge of Baillet's work. Unlike Gouhier, however, *he* reaffirms an editorial judgment that is unequivocally favorable to Baillet, praising him for his factual detail, his narrative abundance, and "his meticulous regard for concrete reality." See Adam, AT, 1:xlv; compare *Vie et oeuvres de Descartes,* AT, XI1:iv. Sebba reaffirms the first of these judgments in "Adrien Baillet and the Genesis of his *Vie de Monsieur Des Cartes,*" in *Problems of Cartesianism,* ed. Thomas M. Lennon (Kingston, Ont., 1982), 48 n.94. Sebba's broad perspective on Baillet's development as a historian contributes to his own cautiously favorable judgment; ibid., 23 n.45, 51, 59.

3. Augustin Frion, *Abrégé de la vie de Mr. Baillet,* in Baillet, *Jugemens des savans* (Amsterdam, 1725), 1:xxv.

4. Baillet's quasi-enlightened attempt to revise hagiographical legends while still retaining a calendar of saints remains very interesting, however open to doctrinaire criticism from rationalists and believers alike. My references are to the imposing folios of 1701: Baillet, *Les Vies des Saints,* 4 vols. (Paris, 1701).

5. Adam, *Vie et oeuvres,* iii note a, and viii–ix. Sebba's "Adrien Baillet" represents decisive advances on all of this.

6. Baillet, *Vies des Saints,* 1:iv.

7. Ibid., iv–v.

8. The anonymous *Recueil de lettres critiques sur les Vies des Saints du Sr. Baillet* (N.p., 1720) shows that these are not just hypothetical objections. Traditional *dévots* were outraged by the apparent denial of saintly miracles and visions. Baillet seemed anxious to "decanonize" saints in a way that suggested unavowed "Jansenistic" intentions; *Recueil,* 50, 82–83, 110–11, 162–63.

9. Ibid., 381, 382–83.

10. Baillet, *Vie,* 1:ii.

11. For all of this, see Frion, *Abrégé de la vie de Mr. Baillet.*

12. Ibid., xxxvi.

13. For a chronological list of works, see Sebba, "Adrien Baillet," 20ff., especially 40; for the fun and games, see 18 n.20 and 43–44.

14. Baillet, *Vie,* 1:i–iii, viii, xxxv. When Baillet wrote of "my own ignorance and my own weakness," he was not, I suppose, trying on another authorial mask. Incidentally, Baillet's name is nowhere to be found on the title page, and the dedicatory epistle is signed with initials alone (his own).

15. Gilles Ménage was first and angriest, having been attacked for what amounted to a bad life as well as bad poetry in the *Jugemens des Savans* of 1686 (see 4:340–47). Ménage began the preface to his *Anti-Baillet* (1688) with a wonderfully scornful review of Baillet's qualifications: "Monsieur Baillet is a priest from the Diocese of Beauvais, the sometime regent of the fourth class in the College of the City of Beauvais, and now the librarian of Monsieur *l'Avocat général* de Lamoignon and the preceptor of Monsieur his son" (*Jugemens des Savans,* 7:v).

16. Boschet, *Réflexions sur la Vie de Monsieur Des Cartes,* in *Jugemens des savans,* 7:327–30 and passim.

17. Ibid., 331.

18. Ibid., 331–33 and passim.

19. Ibid., 334–37.

20. Ibid., 348–65.

21. Ibid., 362, with references to Baillet's *Vie,* 1:147, and 2:456.

22. Ibid., 327.

23. Ibid., 1:xii–xiii.

24. Frion, *Abrégé de la Vie de Mr. Baillet,* xxiii–xxiv, xxvii, xxviii–xxx, xxxi, xxxvi.

25. Ménage, *Anti-Baillet,* in Baillet, *Jugemens des Savans,* 7:v.

Part Two: The Dream Day

1. Herodotus 7:16; Lucretius *De rerum natura* 4:962–67; Cicero *De divinatione* 2:62:128; 67:140. For the place of this ancient observation in the "modern psychology" of the early seventeenth century, see especially the work of Scipion du Pleix or Dupleix, *Les causes de la veille et du sommeil, des songes, et de la vie et de la mort* (Paris, 1609), 71, 76, 83, 89, 118, 141–42. Dupleix the dream psychologist had already distinguished himself by publishing the first course of philosophy in the French language, and he would earn further distinction—and notoriety—as a complaisant Historiographer Royal under Louis XIII. The most interesting feature of his dream book is its eclecticism. This was the one great school on the subject in his time. It was, he thought, perfectly possible to dismiss most "ordinary dreams" as trivial reflections of the past, "the objects, plans, occupations, and thoughts that have concerned us in the previous day," while also crediting a few heaven-sent dream prophecies of the future. Compare Dupleix's remarks on "ordinary dreams" (118) with his preceding discussions of divine and diabolical wonders. Descartes represented the uncertainty and complexity of seventeenth-century attitudes on dreams and spirits insofar as he, too, dismissed most "ordinary dreams" as meaningless natural phenomena, having credited his own extraordinary dreams as deeply significant communications from spirits, either divine (Interpretation III) or diabolical (Interpretation I).

2. Freud, "Remarks upon the Theory and Practice of Dream Interpretation," in *Therapy and Technique* (New York, 1963), 206. Compare Freud, *Interpretation of Dreams,* 197; "Revision of the Theory of Dreams," in *New Introductory Lectures on Psychoanalysis* (New York, 1965), 11.

3. Freud, *Interpretation of Dreams,* 197–202, 591–95.

4. It is remarkable that Freud's analysis of the Dream of the Botannical Monograph, specially chosen to show the place of day residues, goes back not just to the experiences of the one previous dream day but also to those of "two days before," then "a few days earlier," and soon the previous decade and more. The one reference to young childhood in the associations to these dream elements that he chose to publish is exceptional and involves guilt rather than a wish; see *Interpretation of Dreams,* 202–9.

Chapter 3

1. Baillet, *Vie*, 1:51.

2. AT, 6:10–11.

3. AT, 6:22.

4. Étienne Gilson, "Commentaire historique," in *René Descartes, Discours de la méthode: texte et commentaire* (Paris, 1947), 156. Baillet made a fool of himself in his contemporaries' eyes by a tedious rehearsal of just such matters; see his *Vie*, 1:54–59.

5. *Vie*, 1:78. Compare Baillet's *Abrégé de la Vie de Monsieur Descartes* (Paris, 1706), 39. The two indications of place are perfectly compatible, but we have no idea what source Baillet could have had. At his worst, he could have dispatched his hero toward the Duke of Bavaria, having no other justification for his geographical precisions. At his best, he could have gotten the information from a once-credible but now-lost source.

6. Gilson, "Commentaire historique," 156, with references to Baillet, *Vie*, 1:50–51, and to Leibniz, *Cogitationes*, AT, 10:179 and 216. Gilson's commentary is not above criticism: Leibniz's genius could not have "confirmed" Descartes's date by copying it. In fact, he did not quite copy it. He seems to have made two passes at the one date, first noting the year and the month of the dream without the day and second noting the day and the month without the year. His references are more confusing in the *Cogitationes* than when quoted out of context: textual "Dream 1619, Nov." and marginal "*Olympica*, 10 Nov. . . ." See Baillet, *Vie*, 1:50–51.

7. Gouhier, *Premières pensées de Descartes*, 32.

8. In 1619, Descartes preferred to call himself a "Poitevin," and at this time his father was by adoption a "Breton." However, the baptismal register at La Haye-Descartes establishes the fact that his mother gave him birth in the Touraine. See Charles Adam's *Vie et oeuvres*, 1–5. Saint Martin's appeal was certainly wide enough to cover the several sins of provincial pride.

9. Descartes was clearly responsible for the disclaimer of perfect abstinence at VDC lines 244–47, which imply the St. Martin's Eve date, although it is possible that he left it for Baillet to name the festival and to mention the custom of popular drinking at VDC lines 240–44.

10. Arnold Van Gennep, "11 Novembre: saint Martin," in *Manuel du folklore français contemporain* (Paris, 1953), tome premier, 6:2823 and note; Sartori, "Martin, hl.," in E. Hoffmann-Krayer and Hans Bächtold-Stäubli, *Handwörterbuch des deutschen Aberglaubens* (Berlin, 1932–33), 5:1711–12. There were other traditional terms in the autumn defined by the liturgical calendar, specifically St. Michael's (29 September) and All Saints' (1 November), but the most important was St. Martin's.

11. Jean Fournée, *Enquête sur le culte populaire de saint Martin en Nor-

mandie (Nogent-sur-Marne, 1963), 67. These *dictons* express a folk wisdom that was not uniquely Norman or even French: "There is nothing specifically Norman about them."

12. Ibid., 67–68.

13. Sartori, "Martin," 1711.

14. AT, 6:10–14; these lines suggest suddenness; 16–20 suggest gradualness. Both Adam and Cohen were willing to suppose a rapid formulation of the four-rule method, although Adam supposes it to have been an unremarkable codification of commonplace notions already in hand in 1619, whereas Cohen supposes it to have been a final revelation in 1620: Adam, *Vie et oeuvres*, 55; Cohen, *Écrivains français*, 401. Weber's further study of the *Regulae* suggests that the Descartes of 1619–20 had not yet achieved the elegant simplicity of the later formulation known from the *Discourse.*

15. AT, 6:7.

16. AT, 6:14–15, 22–23, 40, 60, 74.

17. AT, 6:11–13. Descartes's fifth "ainsi . . ." was not so much an impersonal, logical conclusion as it was a first-personal imperative for an as-yet unemancipated young man. The whole is not so much a rational argument as it is a declaration of intellectual independence.

18. The first and second instances immediately precede the passage translated in my text: "We never see them level all of the houses in a city, for the sake of rebuilding them in another manner and improving the appearance of the streets. But we do see that individual proprietors [choose to] demolish their houses in order to rebuild them and that sometimes they have to do so, when the *foundations* aren't sound and there is danger of a collapse. Reasoning in this way, I convinced myself that it is hardly likely that an individual [subject] would plan to reform a state, changing everything and tearing it down to the *foundations* in order to build it up again, nor even that he would try to reform the body of the sciences or the order established in the schools to teach them" (AT, 6:13).

The third instance immediately follows: "And I firmly believed that I would succeed much better in directing my life in this way, than if I were to have built only on old *foundations,* relying on only the principles that I had been taught in my youth without ever examining them" (AT, 6:14). The fourth instance extends this imagery in the next paragraph: "My plan was never more far-reaching than to attempt to reform my own thinking and to build on a *foundation* that was all my own" (AT, 6:15).

19. AT, 6:13–14.

20. For "foundations" and the related principles of novelty, egocentrism, and mathematicism, see AT, 6:14, 15, and 7, respectively. That the mathematicism of part 2 (17, 18, 19) is "foundational" is evident from part 1 (7).

21. Jean-Paul Weber, *La constitution du texte des Regulae* (Paris, 1964), 3–17.

22. AT, 10:374–79. John Schuster, "Descartes's *mathesis universalis:* 1619–1628," in *Descartes: Philosophy, Mathematics, and Physics,* ed. Stephen Gaukroger (Totowa, N.J., 1980), 41–96.

23. AT, 10:371–72.

24. AT, 10:373–74.

25. See chap. 1.

26. For *"Praeambula,"* see the Leiden copy of the Stockholm Inventory and the two seventeenth-century biographers, both of whom had access to manuscripts: Pierre Borel, *Vitae Renati Cartesii compendium* (Paris, 1656), 17; Baillet, *Vie,* 1:50, and 2:403. Baillet's two identical readings in widely separated contexts are particularly impressive in that he himself also held and used Descartes's Little Notebook itself. See chap. 1, n.4.

27. Baillet, *Vie,* 2:449.

28. Ibid., 2:450.

29. Merton gives Bacon's two versions of the paradox in *On the Shoulders of Giants* (New York, 1965), 80–81. The first came in the English-language *Advancement of Learning* (1605), the second in the Latin *Novum Organum* (1620). *The Advancement of Learning* had not yet been translated into either of Descartes's working languages, French and Latin, and the *Novum Organum* was not published before the 1620s. Thus, Descartes could not have read either before the apparent date of the *Experimenta* (1619). This does not preclude the possibility of indirect influence.

30. Baillet, *Vie,* 2:531.

31. Ibid., 2:545.

32. Henri Gouhier has already brought these passages (back?) together, and this is just the place to acknowledge my indebtedness while pursuing my own argument; see *Premières pensées,* 145–47.

33. Freud, *Interpretation of Dreams,* 207–16.

34. AT, 6:4, 7–9.

35. Adam, *Vie et oeuvres,* 34–35.

36. Ibid., 564–65.

37. Ibid., 39–40. For a facsimile of the baptismal record, see Alfred Barbier, *René Descartes: Sa famille, son lieu de naissance* (Poitiers, 1901), 9.

38. Adam, *Vie et oeuvres,* 39–40 and note a.

39. Ibid., 40.

40. AT, 6:3, 27, 78.

41. AT, 6:3.

42. AT, 6:78.

43. AT, 6:78.

44. AT, 6:8–9, 27.

45. Gilson's commentary on the first passage is both spare and impersonal, on the second, spare and "personal" only in an uncritical sense in which "Descartes's very life was wholly devoted to thought and to the search for truth." See the "Commentaire historique," 119, 139–40, 254.

46. AT, 6:6.

47. Gilson, "Commentaire historique," 120.

48. AT, 6:8–9.

49. AT, 10:360.

50. Weber, *La constitution du texte des Regulae,* 34–47.

51. AT, 6:9. For Descartes's temporary role as a volunteer soldier or, more properly, as an observer of soldiers, see the references gathered by Gilson, "Commentaire historique," 143–46, 155–56. The question of arms as an actual or potential vocation is crucial to my thesis. I distance even the young Descartes from soldiery as a vocational identification.

First, in the *Compendium musicae* from the beginning of the year, 1619, the young author takes pains to distinguish himself as "a man without occupation or obligation" from the "ignorant soldiers" around him (AT, 10:141).

Second, in the correspondence that describes his activity and inactivity that winter, he shows no sign of pursuing or planning to pursue a military career. More to the point, insofar as these letters concern the summer, a campaigning season for real soldiers, they reserve for this gentleman-traveler the perfect freedom to come and go as he pleases. He seems to have been much more concerned to avoid "troubles" than to seek out battles, and he looks forward to stopping in order to write, not in order to fight (AT, 10:151–66, especially 158–59, 162).

Third, in the *Experimenta,* from later in 1619, there is just one autobiographical account of Descartes "in action" as a young cavalier, sword in hand. It has nothing to do with war. Rather, it portrays him as a traveler, facing down thievish sailors who may have offended him more by mistaking him for a *merchant* than by conspiring to rob and kill. There are no war stories, properly speaking (*Vie de Monsieur Des Cartes,* 1:102–3).

Seventeenth-century biographers thought of Descartes as the young son of an "old noble family"; they knew that these were war years; and they did not have anything like documentation for any other activities. All this was reason enough to award him a war record posthumously, marching the hero's ghost back and forth for the greatest moments, the Battle of White Mountain, the Siege of La Rochelle, and so on. See especially Borel, *Vitae Cartesii compendium,* 4. Modern biographers are skeptical; see Adam, *Vie et oeuvres de Descartes,* 60–61 and note a, 99 and note b.

La Rochelle remains a good possibility, although this would have been more spectacle than battle for Descartes. Borel's informant, the engineer Étienne de Ville-Bressieu, is credible. Furthermore, Descartes was relatively nearby, in Brittany at Elven (near Vannes), at the beginning of the crucial summer, 1628, and the Descartes family had business with the king at La Rochelle that July: see the documentation in Sigismond Ropartz, "La famille Descartes en Bretagne (1586–1762)," *Bulletin archéologique de l'Association bretonne* (1875): 95.

Even Baillet's assertion that Joachim Descartes had planned a military career for the cadet son of his first family may only be a surmise based more on familial pride and faulty traditions than on anything historical. It neither adds nor subtracts from this tradition that Adam follows along—without documentation. See Baillet, *Vie,* 1:35, 40; Adam, *Vie et oeuvres,* 40.

52. AT, 6:27.

53. Gilson, "Commentaire historique," 230–34, 256, 261; T. Keefe, "Descartes's 'morale provisoire': a reconsideration," *French Studies* 26 (1972): 129–41, especially 135.

54. AT, 6:27–28.

55. Renée Kogel, *Pierre Charron* (Geneva, 1972), 47. The great number of editions complicates citation. I cite only book and chapter numbers in most cases. The most useful edition for most purposes is that published in three volumes in Paris, 1836. I have also consulted the edition published "chez la venue Meist" in Paris in 1621.

56. Eugene F. Rice, *The Renaissance Idea of Wisdom* (Cambridge, Mass., 1958), 178–207.

57. The index to Gilson's "Commentaire historique" lists references on pp. 94, 121, 122, 173, 174, 179, 235, 291, 427, and 429. See Richard H. Popkin, "Charron and Descartes: The Fruits of Systematic Doubt," *Journal of Philosophy* 51 (1954): 831–37.

58. Charron, *De la sagesse* (1836) 1:101.

59. VDC, lines 163–64. For rule IVb, see AT, 10:376; for rule IVa, see AT, 10:373.

60. *De la sagesse* (1836) 1:xxxii.

61. Baillet, *Vie,* 2:545.

62. Leibniz, CP, lines 66–70; Adam, *Vie et oeuvres,* 49.

Chapter 4

1. Cohen, *Écrivains français en Hollande,* 395–96.

2. Gouhier pointed out this further coincidence only to dismiss the whole line of argument. *Premières pensées,* 75–76.

3. Ibid.

4. Adam, *Vie et oeuvres,* 39–40 and note a.

5. AT, 10:46–47; Beeckman, *Journal,* ed. C. de Waard, 4 vols. (The Hague, 1939–53), 1:xii and 257.

6. Note that the "Descartes" who appears by that name in the heading of Beeckman's account of the 10 November meeting in AT, 10:46, was Beeckman's much later marginal addition to his earlier record: "*Angulum nullum esse male probavit Des Cartes.*" See de Waard's "Note sur le manuscrit," xxviii. For the best edition of the successive namings in entries from 1618, see *Journal,* 1:237, 238, 244, 246, 247, 255, 257, 258, 263.

7. De Waard, "Note sur le manuscrit," iii.

8. AT, 10:46–47. Beeckman, *Journal,* 1:237.

9. AT, 10:48–51, 175. Italics mark my paraphrases of Baillet's paraphrases, as signaled by Adam. Oddly, the great historian-editor did not object to what I consider the worst anachronism, the antedating of the four-rule Method. Baillet was not editing or translating Lipstorp's text, however; he was retelling an anecdote, and most of his variants are either fully defensible or utterly trivial. The worst part of his performance from the perspective of history as a critical discipline is his uncritical reliance on the historically unreliable Lipstorp. It is copying, not invention, that limits—and distinguishes—"his own" work.

10. Baillet, *Vie,* 1:43–44. I have italicized the variants in Baillet's account, which make it something other and "less historical than" the more succinct Latin source from which he worked. I discuss this more fully later.

11. Daniel Lipstorp, *Specimina philosophiae cartesianae* (Lyon, 1653), 76–78. Adam edited the relevant materials from Beeckman, Lipstorp, and Baillet together in such a way as to emphasize Baillet's unreliability. Baillet's retelling does complicate matters, but I am inclined to exculpate him and to blame the oral tradition.

12. Baillet, *Vie,* 1:xiii–xv, xxvii–xxx; 2:216, 374–77.

13. There is also a less obvious but no less potent factor, as I will show in chap. 6. By the time that he could have communicated this self-serving anecdote to Schooten, Descartes had exploded in volcanic rage at Beeckman's claims to have anticipated him and to have taught him anything. See the two letters from Descartes to Beeckman, September–October 1630, AT, 1:154–69; AM, 1:144–63; *Journal,* 4:194–202.

14. Descartes to Beeckman, 23 April 1619, AT, 10:162–63; AM, 1:14; *Journal,* 4:62.

15. The best evidence for all this comes in the five letters from Descartes to Beeckman from the first half of 1619 and the one known response from Beeckman to Descartes. See AT, 10:151–69; AM, 1:1–23; *Journal,* 4:56–65.

16. Weber, *La constitution du texte des Regulae,* 47.

17. *Pace* Gouhier, *Premières pensées de Descartes,* 75–76.

18. Baillet, *Vie,* 1:163, 160–66.

19. Ibid., 1:161, 162, 164, 165.

20. The first fruit was "to show whether a proposition is possible or

not . . . with a certainty equal to that produced by the rules of Arithmetic";
the second was "to resolve infallibly the difficulty represented by this proposition."

21. Ibid., 1:163; AT, 1:213; AM 1:198.

22. Who else but Baillet would have preserved this wonderful detail by including it in Descartes's life? *Vie,* 1:230–31.

23. Adam, *Vie,* 95–98.

24. Baillet, *Vie,* 1:160.

25. See note 51 to chap. 3. Descartes may very well have visited the camps around La Rochelle in the summer of 1628, and he may have met then and there with the principals involved in the later Paris conference. However, he sought out Beeckman at Breda in Brabant on 8 October 1628, and, while with Beeckman, he declared his intention to return to Paris. Therefore, it is very unlikely if not quite impossible that he was at La Rochelle at the end of the siege. Beeckman, *Journal,* 3:94–95; 4:135.

26. The Mersenne correspondence cannot help settle the matter. In his notes, C. de Waard argues for a date sometime later in 1628, but he cites no hard evidence against a date on or soon after Saint Martin's, for instance, within the octave. See Marin Mersenne, *Correspondance* (Paris, 1945), 2:101, 114, 163–64, 221–22.

27. Descartes to Mersenne in response, end November 1633, AT, 1:270; AM, 1:241.

28. Descartes to Mersenne, two letters, both 11 November 1640, AT, II1:230, 238; AM, 4:198, 205.

29. Let me bury in a note what may be only a coincidence. Saint Martin's was also a particularly important anniversary date for Cardinal Bérulle, who is thought to have charged Descartes to publish a work that promised to establish truths of religion: it was on 11 November 1611 that Bérulle had founded the Oratory; see M. Houssaye, *Le père Bérulle et l'Oratoire de Jésus, 1611–1625* (Paris, 1874), 26–29. A coincidence? Who knows? All of this does suggest a very devout environment for the semipublic commissioning of René Descartes to write what became the *Discourse.* Despite his eventual identification with a form of philosophical doubt that became dangerous to the faith, there is no good reason to suspect his own public and private professions of religious belief.

30. Gustave Ducoudray, *Les origines du Parlement de Paris et la justice aux XIII et XIV siècles* (Paris, 1902), 89–90 and notes.

31. François-André Isambert, *Recueil général des anciennes lois françaises* (Paris, 1827, 1829), 11:221, 248–49; 14:414–16.

32. La Roche Flavin, *Treize livres des Parlements* (Bordeaux, 1617), 319.

33. Ibid., 330.

34. Ibid., 318.

35. Ibid., 320.

36. Ibid., 332. The Parlement of Brittany at Rennes, where Joachim Descartes was fast establishing his family as a judicial dynasty, did not sit according to the schedule most familiar to La Roche Flavin, who was an officer in the Parlements of Paris and of Toulouse. For Rennes, see the "Édit du roy Henry IV qui ordonne que les séances du Parlement, qui étoient chacun de trois mois auparavant, seroient de six mois, donné à Lyon au mois de Juillet l'an 1600," in *Édits, déclarations, et lettres patentes du roy, et règlements concernant le Parlement de Bretagne* (Rennes, 1754), 46–49. See also Noël du Fail, *Les plus solennels arrests et règlemens donnez au parlement de Bretagne,* 2 vols. (Nantes, 1715–16), 2:376–77. However, the places of René Descartes's birth, upbringing, and legal education (La Haye, Châtellerault, and Poitiers, respectively) were all within the jurisdiction of Paris. For him and those about him, "Saint Martin's" was the liturgical reference for what amounted to Law Day.

37. AT, 6:27.

38. AT, 6:23–24.

39. AT, 6:24–25.

Part Three: The Father and the Friend

1. AT, 6:3, 27.

Chapter 5

1. Descartes to Mersenne, 25 May 1637, AT, 1:376.

2. For details on the court and Joachim's office, see Frédéric Saulnier, *Le Parlement de Bretagne, 1554–1790* (Rennes, 1909), 1:xix–xxi, xxxi–xxxii, 295–96. Briefly, the Parlement was a sovereign tribunal, the highest court for civil and criminal cases in the province; a *conseiller* was one judge in the corporation of judges; the *non-originaires* were Frenchmen from provinces other than Brittany who were added to the native Bretons in the Parlement at Rennes in a royal effort to bind this recently independent province to the rest of the kingdom.

3. For the Poitevin family and its extensions, the invaluable reference is the work of Alfred Barbier, somewhat misleadingly entitled *Trois médecins poitevins au XVIe siècle: Les origines châtelleraudaises de la famille Descartes* (Poitiers, 1897). The doctors in question were all dead long before René Descartes's birth. Barbier's patient work in Poitevin archives gathered evidence for my emphasis on the law, not medicine, in the world that the philosopher

knew. For further references, genealogical charts, and a convenient synthesis of Barbier's work and that of others more concerned with the family outside of Poitou, see E. Thouverez, "La famille Descartes d'après les documents publiés par les sociétés savantes de Poitou, de Touraine, et de Bretagne," *Archiv für Geschichte der Philosophie* 12 (1899): 504–28; 13 (1900): 550–77; 14 (1901): 84–110. The immediately relevant baptismal records are most easily accessible in Thouverez, "La famille Descartes," 14 (1901): 91–92.

4. Louis de Grandmaison, "Nouvelles recherches sur l'origine et le lieu de naissance de Descartes," *Bibliothèque de L'école des Chartes* 60 (1899): 451–52.

5. P[ierre] or R[ené] Descartes to [Jeanne Sain, widow of Claude Brochard,] *la lieutenante de Poitou,* 12 May [1606–10], in Maxime Leroy, *Descartes* (Paris, 1929), 2:168–73. Charles Adam and Gérard Milhaud relegated this letter to an appendix in their edition of René Descartes's correspondence; see *Correspondance* (Paris, 1936), 1:473–74. The problem is that the signature is not necessarily that of the later philosopher: the initial letter can be read as a "P," an "R," or even, as argued by Adam-Milhaud, the terminal letter of the previous word, "filz."

Having closely examined this signature and compared it with others in the Musée Descartes at La Haye-Descartes, I venture only the technically unqualified opinion that this early signature is not enough like that of the more mature philosopher to justify a confident attribution. The Descartes in question could quite easily have been René's elder brother, Pierre. For authorship by René, there is the familial tradition. For authorship by Pierre, there is reference to a brother's health, and René is known to have suffered from chronic illnesses as a schoolboy. Even if Pierre did write the letter, it is good evidence on the role of the grandmother as a surrogate parent for the boys.

6. Sigismond Ropartz, "La famille Descartes en Bretagne (1586–1762)," *Bulletin Archéologique de Bretonne* (1875): 49, 92–95. Ropartz is wrong to suppose that we can date the second Joachim's birth—and the terminus ante quem for the first Joachim's remarriage—by counting back twenty-seven years from his formal reception by the Parlement in 1627. The twenty-seven-year minimum age was adopted later, and the court often admitted young men in their early twenties. See Saulnier, *Le Parlement de Bretagne,* 1:xxviii–xxix.

7. On La Flèche generally, see Camille de Rochemonteix, *Un collège des Jésuites aux XVIIe et XVIIIe siècles: le Collège Henri IV de La Flèche,* 4 vols. (Le Mans, 1889). There were, of course, holidays at La Flèche for the great feasts of the Church, but there were nothing like the indulgent vacations of our secular calendars. See Rochemonteix, 2:42–46; 4:209. The best presentation of Jesuit ideals on such matters can be found in François de Dainville, S.J., *La naissance de l'humanisme moderne: les Jésuites et l'éducation de la*

société française (Paris, 1940). For a more critical discussion of the *collèges* and their social role, see Roger Chartier, Dominique Julia, and Marie-Madeleine Compère, *L'éducation en France du XVIe au XVIIIe siècle* (Paris, 1976). For the letter of the law on calendars, curriculum, and everything else, see the *Ratio studiorum* in G. M. Pachtler, S.J., *Monumenta Germania Paedagogica* (Berlin, 1887), vol. 5, pt. 2.

8. Descartes to Charlet, 9 February 1645, *Oeuvres philosophiques*, 3:542–43.

9. Étienne Charlet, this long-remembered surrogate father from Descartes's schoolboy years at La Flèche, had two cousins who had held office in the Parlement of Brittany. See Adam, *Vie et oeuvres de Descartes*, 20 and note a, 564–65; Saulnier, *Le Parlement de Bretagne*, 1:220–21 and n.1. The second of these cousins, Jacques Charlet, must have been particularly close to Joachim. He was the son of a *conseiller* in the Présidial of Poitiers, where the Descartes were related by the Ferrands and the Brochards, and he himself entered the Parlement at Rennes as a *conseiller* just three days before Joachim and then went on to the Chambre des comptes at Nantes, where Joachim was to find his second wife.

On Jeanne Sain and the Brochards, see table 8. When René went on to Poitiers, he found his uncle and godfather, René Brochard, a former *avocat*, mayor, and *conseiller* in the Présidial court, whose brother-in-law Jean d'Elbène had become yet another *conseiller* in the Parlement of Brittany. See Barbier, *Trois médecins poitevins*, 122–23; Ropartz, "La famille Descartes," 33, 49; Saulnier, *Le parlement de Bretagne*, 1:288–89. Jean d'Elbène had been *lieutenant général* in Poitou and styled himself "sieur de Lavau et des Ormes Saint-Martin," where the Descartes also had landed properties.

10. For the two Gilles Desquartes, father and son, and their presumed relationship to Pierre Descartes, father of Joachim, see Grandmaison, "Nouvelles recherches," 426–32. It is possible that Grandmaison's identification of Pierre Desquartes, the *marchand-bourgeois* of Tours in 1531, with Pierre Descartes, the Doctor of Medicine of Châtellerault in 1543, may conflate two generations, father and son. It is also possible that the Descartes of Châtellerault did not go back to the Desquartes of Tours, and for that reason I begin only with Pierre; see n.12.

11. Barbier, *Trois médecins poitevins*, documents on 139–45, discussion on 33–48.

12. Poor Baillet, as ever the copyist to a fault, depended on the recently ennobled Descartes of his own day for genealogical information and got a lot, most of it bad. See his *Vie*, 1:xxiii, 2–4: "Monsieur Descartes came from a House that had been considered before his time one of the most noble, most ancient, and best founded in the Touraine." The *érudits* of the nineteenth

century, especially the Poitevins, heaped scorn on him, as if the blunders had been his own. See, for instance, the acerbic remarks in Barbier, *René Descartes*, 21–23: "Such inventions are regrettable, even grotesque."

Barbier championed the claims of Poitou in his *René Descartes* (1901), doing his best to defeat old claims on behalf of Tours updated by Louis de Grandmaison in "Nouvelles recherches" (1899). The republican consensus seems now to be that we cannot reach further back than Pierre Descartes, the *bourgeois-gentilhomme* doctor of Châtellerault (Adam, *Vie et oeuvres*, 1–8). Having reviewed the relevant evidence and the arguments of Barbier and Grandmaison, I tentatively support the latter. In any case, the two Gilles are not important to my argument.

13. Barbier, *Trois médecins poitevins*, 8–34, 90–92; *René Descartes*, 49.

14. Most of the important work is Barbier's in his *Trois médecins poitevins*. For a table with formal references, see Thouverez, "La famille Descartes," 14 (1901): 99.

15. For the Ferrand family more generally and the two daughters' marriages to nonlawyers, see the articles s.v.v "Ferrand de Janvry," "De la Vau (Barthélemy)," and "Desmons de la Salle (Antoine)" in vols. 2 and 3 of the Beauchet-Filleau *Dictionnaire historique et généalogique des familles de Poitou*, 2d. ed. (Poitiers, 1895 and 1905). The parentage of Barthélemy Delavau or de Lavau is not certain, but the names, dates, and places do fit the Barthélemy Delavau who was *greffier* in the *sénéchaussée* at Châtellerault in 1538—more law. The daughter of Barthélemy Delavau and Martine Ferrand, Claude, married François Lucas, *écuyer*, seigneur de Vaugueille, and *lieutenant général* at Châtellerault. Antoine Desmons was the cadet son of a noble family of Châtellerault.

16. Charlotte de Moulins, René's aunt, did her best to intertwine the branches in 1599, when, as Claude Brochard's widow, she married Isaïe Brochard, mayor of Poitiers in 1617 and also *conseiller d'État*.

17. Beauchet-Filleau, *Dictionnaire historique et généalogique*, 2:6–8.

18. Pierre or René Descartes to Jeanne Sain from La Flèche, year unknown, in Leroy, *Descartes*, 2:169, 172–73. See n.6 for cautionary remarks.

19. René Descartes to Joachim Descartes, 24 June 1625, summarized by Baillet in the *Vie de Monsieur Des Cartes*, 1:129.

20. The Sain line, like the Descartes line, was deformed by neo-aristocratic mythohistory. Both Barbier and Thouverez were too trusting: see the former's *Trois médecins poitevins*, 119–20, and the latter's "La famille Descartes," 12 (1899): 527–28 and 14 (1901): 101. Grandmaison's documentation establishes beyond any possible doubt this reconstruction of descent from merchants; see "Nouvelles recherches," 454.

21. Saulnier, *Le parlement de Bretagne*, 1:xx–xxi. In or shortly after 1607,

Joachim purchased a townhouse of his own in Rennes; Sigismund Ropartz, "La famille Descartes en Bretagne," 50–51.

22. Isambert, *Recueil général des anciennes lois françaises,* 14:234.

23. Jean Bacquet, *Du droict d'anoblissement,* in *Oeuvres* (Rouen, 1616), 79–83; François Bluche, *L'anoblissement par charges avant 1789,* in *Les cahiers nobles* 23–24 (1962), especially 23:8–9 and 24:15–18, 24; Roland Mousnier, *The Institutions of France under the Absolute Monarchy 1598–1789,* 2 vols. (Chicago, 1979–84), 2:324, 368.

24. Barbier, *Trois médecins poitevins,* 36 n.3, 139–45, 202. The one documentary reference to Pierre Descartes as a noble *"écuyer"* comes in an informal annotation in his father-in-law's hand on the *reverse* of the marriage contract. Baillet reports that Pierre Descartes, the doctor of Châtellerault, successfully defended his right to an exemption from the *taille* in a case resolved by the Cour des Aides of Paris on 4 September 1547, and he cites the register of that court and "the original papers of the case." However, no modern researcher has ever been able to find evidence of the matter in the records of this court. See *Vie de Monsieur Des Cartes,* 1:4.

Louis-Auguste Bosseboeuf has pursued the matter furthest in the archives. He found his way to the registers of the Cour des Aides, where he discovered that volume 241 did record acts from 1 October 1540 to 1 October 1546; unfortunately, the next volume, numbered 242, contained only the records from 1561–66. See Bosseboeuf, "Les ancêtres de René Descartes," *Bulletin de la Société archéologique de Touraine* 12 (1900): 56–57 and n.1, 248.

25. Barbier, *René Descartes,* 33.

26. Ropartz, "La famille Descartes en Bretagne," 174–75. In 1668, there were *two* persons named Joachim Descartes of Chavagne in the Parlement, the son and grandson of the patriarch. Ropartz wrote as if the special commissioner were the younger man. This must be a confusion of the like-named father and son. It would have made little sense to entrust this very responsible and very delicate task to the son, a very junior *conseiller* who was still in his early thirties and who had served on the court for less than ten years. The man for the job was his well-respected father, a man approaching seventy years of age, with forty years of service on the court.

27. Mousnier, *La vénalité des offices sous Henri IV et Louis XIII* (Paris, 1971).

28. The two principal authorities for the Breton dynasty are Ropartz, "La famille Descartes en Bretagne," and Saulnier, *Le Parlement de Bretagne,* especially 1:295–99. Xavier d'Haucourt offers a synoptic review in his paper "Une dynastie de 'non-originaires' au Parlement de Bretagne: la famille Des-Cartes (1585–1736)," *Annales de Bretagne* 44 (1937): 408–32 and 45 (1938): 3–24.

29. Saulnier, *Le Parlement de Bretagne,* 1:356–57; 2:734–35, 769, 776.

30. Ropartz, "La famille Descartes en Bretagne," 29, 52, 52 n.1, 54, 62–63; Barbier, *René Descartes,* 56–58; Saulnier, *Le Parlement de Bretagne,* 1:296–97; Camille Couderc, "Nouveaux documents sur la situation de fortune de la famille de René Descartes," *Bibliothèque de l'École des chartes* 78 (1917): 278–92.

31. Ropartz, "La famille Descartes en Bretagne," 92–95; Saulnier, *Le Parlement de Bretagne,* 1:295, 297.

32. Ropartz, "La famille Descartes en Bretagne," 49–50, 53; Saulnier, *Le Parlement de Bretagne,* 1:56–61, 288–89, 382–83.

33. Ropartz, "La famille Descartes en Bretagne," 67–71; Saulnier, *Le Parlement de Bretagne,* 1:234–35.

34. Ropartz, "La famille Descartes en Bretagne," 98–99, 164, 205–6; Saulnier, *Le Parlement de Bretagne,* 2:711–12.

35. Ropartz, "La famille Descartes en Bretagne," 54–55; Saulnier, *Le Parlement de Bretagne,* 2:766–70, 767 n.3.

36. Baillet, *Vie,* 1:15; Ropartz, *La famille Descartes,* 102–3.

37. George Huppert, *Les Bourgeois Gentilshommes: An Essay in the Definition of Elites in Renaissance France* (Chicago, 1977), 6–15, 31, 55, 87, 106, 118, 141; Mousnier, *La vénalité des offices,* 72–92, 455ff., 529ff. The star witness for Mousnier was Charles Loyseau, author of the *Cinq livres des offices* and the *Traité des ordres* (Cologne, 1613) and a very close contemporary (b. 1564) of Joachim Descartes (b. 1563). Loyseau shared others' criticisms of the veritable *archomanie* or mania for offices, but he also represented the phenomenon as an *avocat* become *lieutenant* and *bailli* and as a legal theorist of the new official class.

38. Adam, *Vie et oeuvres,* 40, presents arms for the cadet in a matter-of-fact sentence, without attempting to document this supposed paternal intention. The source is Baillet, whose language strongly suggests mere inference, which must have been all the easier in 1691, when the Descartes had retrospectively transformed themselves into an old noble family, supposedly as distinguished for the sword as for offices. See Baillet, *Vie,* 1:35. For the social discrimination between robe and sword in this crucial respect, see Huppert, *Les Bourgeois Gentilshommes,* 40–46, 48, 99–102.

39. Baillet, *Vie,* 1:106, 118, 129; 2:460. René Descartes to Pierre Descartes, 3 April 1622, AT, 1:1.

40. For identification by this *métairie,* see Descartes to Beeckman, 24 January, 26 March, 20 April, 23 April, 29 April 1619, in Isaac Beeckman, *Journal,* 4:57, 61, 63, 64; compare *Journal,* 1:257, 258, 263, 269, 270, 306, AT, 1:1; 10:555. On the property, see Grandmaison, "Nouvelles recherches," 426; Barbier, *René Descartes,* 22, 36–37, 42–43.

The particular beauty of the designation "Monsieur du Perron" had little or nothing to do with the insignificant piece of land, which Descartes sold with another parcel in 1623 for a grand total of only 3,000 *livres*. The great attraction was that this name suggested that of Jacques Davy du Perron (1556–1618): bishop, archbishop, cardinal, Grand Almoner, savant, courtier, *conseiller d'État*, representative of Henri IV to Clement VIII, commander in the Order of the Holy Spirit, director of the Collège de France, member of the Council of Regency, and president of the Assembly of Notables. In the words of the Chancellor du Vair: "He is the one man of our times whom I admire the most." See Georges Grente's sketch, with bibliography, in the *Dictionnaire des lettres françaises: Le seizième siecle* (Paris, 1951), 271–76.

41. René Descartes to Joachim Descartes, 22 May 1622, reported in Baillet, *Vie,* 1:106; 2:460

42. Ibid., 1:118. Baillet almost certainly misidentified the man in question as "the husband of his godmother." This husband must have been Jean Sain, the widower of Jeanne Proust. The Jean Sain who had been a *contrôleur des tailles* at Châtellerault, as Baillet states, had dictated a testament from his deathbed in 1619. See Barbier, *René Descartes,* 44.

43. Thouverez, "La famille Descartes," 14 (1901): 101.

44. Baillet, *Vie,* 1:118.

45. Ibid.

46. Ibid., 1:129–30.

47. Huppert, *Les Bourgeois Gentilshommes,* 34–39, 49–50.

48. Mousnier, *La famille, l'enfant, et l'éducation en France at en Grande-Bretagne du XVIe au XVIIIe siècle* (Paris, 1975). The report on crocodile parenting, which I have not attempted to verify, comes to me from an anonymous naturalist who published on a box of Celestial Seasonings Herbal Teas.

49. Charles VIII, "Ordonnance sur l'administration de la justice," Paris, July 1493, article 71, updated by Charles IX (Orléans, 1560, article 32, and Moulins, 1566, article 85), Henri III (Blois, 1579, article 116), and Henri IV (Rouen, 1597, article 6). See Isambert, *Recueil des anciennes lois françaises,* 11:217; 14:71–72, 212, 410; 15:122; La Roche Flavin, *Treize livres des Parlemens,* 378–80.

50. Saulnier, *Le Parlement de Bretagne,* 1:xxviii, with references.

51. Ibid., 1:296; Ropartz, "La famille Descartes," 115, 137–40.

52. The main point to be made about the finances of the Descartes in this generation is that there was much less money than there would be in later generations. The rosy retrospect encouraged by Borel, *Vitae Cartesii compendium,* 2, is deceptive. See Couderc, "Nouveaux documents," 276–79.

53. The modern authority is Mousnier, *La vénalité des offices,* 356–69. For the Parlement of Brittany, see Saulnier, *Le Parlement de Bretagne,* 1:xxxvi-xl.

54. Alfred Hérault, *Histoire de Châtellerault* (Châtellerault, 1928), 3:129–34.

55. On the présidials and their functions, see Ernest Laurain, *Essai sur les présidiaux* (Paris, 1896), and Roland Mousnier, *The Institutions of France,* 2:253–54, 263–64. For questions of status, see Laurain, *Essai,* 192–200, 244–55, and Mousnier, *Institutions,* 2:315–20, 350–56.

56. The lieutenant-generalcy at Caen, for instance, had risen in value from 30,000 *livres* in 1603 to 80,000 in 1634. See Mousnier, *La vénalité des offices,* 363.

57. Ibid., 349–54.

58. A problem: if Baillet's source on all this was the letter of 24 June 1625 *from Poitiers,* how did he learn about the subsequent events, René's departure from that city before hearing from Joachim, his arrival at Paris after Joachim's departure, and so on? There must have been a letter, but was it actually written from Poitiers, or only promised from Poitiers? I suppose that René must have gone on to Paris to plead his case in person, then sent the letter *from Paris,* explaining everything, including his promise to others that he would write to his father from Poitiers.

59. La Roche Flavin, *Treize livres de Parlemens,* 337–39; Saulnier, *Le Parlement de Brittany,* 1:xxviii–xxix.

60. Mousnier, *The Institutions of France,* 2:345, 350.

61. AT, 6:26. It is interesting that René's great and lasting ire, especially after the death of his father and the subsequent division of properties, was directed against Pierre, not Joachim II. See Descartes to Abbé Picot, 7 December 1648, AT, 5:234–35. A quick lesson in primogeniture might help explain such bitterness on the part of the cadet: see Mousnier, *The Institutions of France,* 1:72–74 and 170–73, and Emmanuel Le Roy Ladurie, "Système de la coutume: Structures familiales et coutume d'héritage en France au XVIe siècle," *Annales, économies, sociétés, civilisations* 27 (1972): 835–36. The ennoblement of Joachim and the Breton Descartes gave legal basis for a property settlement assuring advantages for the eldest son that he could not have enjoyed as a Poitevin commoner.

62. AT, 9:38, 39, 40.

63. Ibid., 2:56, 94; 3:228–29.

64. *De la sagesse* (1621), 659.

65. Ibid., 659–60. Charron's "wisdom" on fathers and children was only common sense, as we can see by comparison with the work of contemporaries. Albert Chérel includes representative selections from Jean Bodin, Olivier de Serres, and Guillaume du Vair in his *La famille française: le moyen-age et le XVIe siècle* (Paris, 1924), 173–200. Pierre Ayrault also deserves particular recognition for having stated the father's case with the barely restrained passion

proper for a *lieutenant criminel* whose grown son had disappeared into the Society of Jesus without paternal consent. This angry father explains how the laws of God, of man, and of nature support his claims to be sole accuser, witness, and judge of his disobedient son. He needed help only with the Jesuits. Ayrault brought suit against the rector of the Collège de Clermont in the Parlement of Paris just as Joachim Descartes was leaving that court. Then he laid down the law: *De la puissance paternelle,* in *Opuscules et divers traictez* (Paris, 1598), 231–356.

66. The anecdote comes from a manuscript record made in the eighteenth century by Eustache de Rosnyvinen, Joachim's great great-grandson. The filiation of the anecdote on Joachim's vexation, to call it that, is unexceptionable. The eighteenth-century "copyist" of other family records says that he had it from his father, Christophe, who had it from his stepfather's father, Joachim Descartes de Chavagne (d. ca. 1680), who heard it from Joachim the patriarch (d. 1640). Christophe had married into the family in 1676. See Ropartz, "La famille Descartes," 100. Any historical use is obviously subject to caution. However, Adam takes caution much too far when he suggests only two relatively innocuous explanations for the anecdote: either it was only a sudden burst of ill-temper, or, alternatively, it was only "the joke of a genial old man who was, after all, proud of his son's books" (Adam, *Vie et oeuvres,* 7–8).

The sixteenth-century *bourgeois gentilshommes* so well described by George Huppert did esteem letters, but even this esteem was qualified. Montaigne was *the* model of the gentrified magistrate as Renaissance man of letters, but even he took great pains to distinguish himself from bookish pedants and left important passages in the concluding essays of both the 1580 and the 1588 editions of his great book to the effect that he was *not* to be mistaken for "a maker of books." See the *Oeuvres complètes,* ed. Maurice Rat (Paris, 1962), 764 and 1088.

On a humbler level, Descartes's great-grandfather, the physician Jean Ferrand, had published a medical work in 1570. His heirs republished it in 1601, but only in a way that betrayed their own social aspirations and their admiration not so much of the author's learning as of the princely and royal patronage that he had enjoyed. On this book, see Alfred Barbier, *Trois médecins poitevins,* 11–13, 28–31. By the 1630s, sixty or seventy years after Ferrand's book, the family itself had changed, as had its social and cultural context. No representative of the Descartes parlementary dynasty in Brittany ever published a book.

On the eve of his long-awaited first book, even René Descartes was reluctant to be thought a "maker and seller of books"; see Descartes to Mersenne, end of May 1637, *Correspondance,* 1:350. In *La recherche de la vérité,* he presents a gentleman-savant as his beau-ideal and philosophical voice; this Eudoxus is an agreeable conversationalist but not characteristically a reader, let alone a writer; see AT, 10:495ff.

Chapter 6

1. Saulnier, *Le Parlement de Bretagne*, 1:295–96.

2. René's residence at Chavagne is known from two baptismal records, 22 October and 3 December 1617: see Pierre Grégoire, "La famille Descartes à Sucé," *Bulletin de la Société archéologique de Nantes* 12 (1873): 171. The date of his arrival at Breda must be calculated from the known duration of his residence there, fifteen months (Schooten Ms., AT, 10:646), and the known date of his departure at the end of this period, the end of April, 1619 (Descartes to Beeckman, AT, 10:162, 164). Neither Borel nor Baillet had access to any of this documentation, but they can be trusted on Descartes's status as an unenrolled volunteer, which was in perfect accord with common practice: Borel, *Vitae Renati Cartesii compendium*, 3–4; Baillet, *Vie de Monsieur Des Cartes*, 1:41.

3. *Compendium musicae*, AT, 10:141; Isaac Beeckman, *Journal*, 4:56.

4. Descartes to Beeckman, 26 March and 23 April 1619, AT, 10:158–59, 162; AM, 1:9–10, 13–14; *Journal*, 4:60, 62.

5. *Discourse*, AT, 6:11.

6. Descartes to Servien, 12 May 1647, AT, 5:25; AM, 7:317. Compare Descartes to Huygens, 3 October 1637, after the first publication but before anything like persecution. As he described it in this earlier letter, what distinguished the Breda period from later years, nominal soldiering from actual searching for truth, was the "great leisure" of the young volunteer: AT, 1:431; AM, 2:31.

7. Descartes to Pollot[?], 1648[?], AT, 5:556; AM, 8:119. See also Descartes to Wilhem, 15 June 1646, AT, 4:435; AM, 7:80.

8. Beeckman, *Journal*, 1:24. See also 10, 24–25, 44, 61, 101, 104–5, 117, 132, 157, and 167, all prior to the first encounter with Descartes. Beeckman realized that this was more than a passing aperçu; it was a fundamental principle.

Now compare the sentence with which Alexandre Koyré begins a chapter on "Galilée et la loi d'inertie" in *Études galiléennes* (Paris, 1966), 161: "The finest and most glorious claim to be made for Descartes-the-physicist is unquestionably to have given the principle of inertia a 'clear and distinct' formula and to have established it in its place." Koyré is well aware of Beeckman's priority; he argues for Beeckman's superiority on the problem of falling bodies: ibid., 107–36.

9. Beeckman, *Journal*, 1:58–59. The discovery of this law is commonly but mistakenly credited to Torricelli.

10. Ibid., 1:26, 46–47, 69–72, 78–79, 117, 200.

11. Ibid., 1:225, 228.

12. See de Waard's invaluable "Vie de l'auteur" and "Note sur le manuscrit," in Beeckman's *Journal*, 1:i–xxiv and xxv–xxxiv.

13. For the fourteen entries, see, respectively: Beeckman, *Journal*, 1:237, 242–43, 244 (twice), 246, 247 (twice), 255–56, 257, 258–59, 262–63, 269, 269–70, 270.

14. Ibid., 4:49–56.

15. Ibid., 4:56–65; AT, 1:151–69; AM, 1:1–23.

16. Beeckman, *Journal*, 1:237.

17. Ibid., 1:242–43; compare 1:30–32.

18. See the letters of Descartes to Beeckman, especially those of 24 January and 23 April 1619, and the response of Beeckman to Descartes dated 6 May 1619: AT, 10:151, 162–64, 167–69; AM, 1:1, 14, 21; *Journal*, 4:56, 62–63, 64–65.

19. Beeckman, *Journal*, 1:244.

20. Ibid., 2:377; 3:354. For Descartes's abuse of this privilege, see his letter to Beeckman, 17 October 1630, AM, 1:151–54; *Journal*, 4:197–98.

21. Rodis-Lewis, *L'oeuvre de Descartes*, 2 vols. (Paris, 1971), 1:37.

22. Stockholm Inventory, AT, 10:7.

23. AT, 10:219–28; *Journal*, 1:360–64.

24. De Waard, "Note sur le manuscrit," *Journal*, 1:xxv and nn.6–8, xxvi and n.1.

25. Ibid., 1:26–28.

26. Ibid., 1:xxvii–xxviii, xxix–xxx; see also de Waard's documentation in his "Vie de l'auteur," especially the character sketch on pp. 1:xxii–xxiii.

27. Descartes to Beeckman, 24 January 1619, AT, 10:151–53; AM, 1:1–4; *Journal*, 4:56–57.

28. Descartes to Beeckman, 26 March 1619, AT, 10:154–60; AM, 1:5–11; *Journal*, 4:58–61. See also Schuster, "Descartes's *Mathesis universalis*: 1619–1628," in *Descartes: Philosophy, Mathematics, and Physics*, ed. Gaukroger, 41–55.

29. AT, 10:159; AM, 1:10; *Journal*, 4:60.

30. AT, 10:157; AM, 1:8; *Journal*, 4:60.

31. AT, 10:159–60; AM, 1:10–11; *Journal*, 4:60–61.

32. Descartes to Beeckman, 20 April 1619, AT, 10:161; AM, 1:13; *Journal*, 4:61.

33. AT, 10:158; AM, 1:8–9; *Journal*, 4:60.

34. De Waard, "Vie de l'auteur," xi–xiii.

35. Ibid., xii–xvii.

36. Descartes to Beeckman, 23 April 1619, AT, 10:162–64; AM, 1:13–15; *Journal*, 4:62–63.

37. AT, 10:162–63; AM, 1:14; *Journal*, 4:62.

38. AT, 10:164; AM, 1:15; *Journal*, 4:63.

39. De Waard, "Vie de l'auteur," xiii, xiv, xvii, xix; Beeckman, *Journal*, 3:94; Descartes, *Discourse*, AT, 6:28.

40. Descartes had referred to the *Ars brevis* in the letter to Beeckman on 26 March 1619: AT, 10:156; AM, 1:7; *Journal*, 4:59. He would again make the same reference, more surprisingly, in the *Discourse* (AT, 6:17), where it seems quite clear that he recalls the old man's discourse in Dordrecht, not any old or new readings of his own; see Gilson, "Commentaire historique," 185–86. For Llull, the "art," and later Llullism, see Ramon Llull, *Selected Works*, ed., trans, and intro. Anthony Bonner, 2 vols. (Princeton, 1985), with further bibliographical references in 1:xix–xxix. The *Ars brevis* itself makes astounding reading for anyone accustomed to orienting Descartes forward toward the enlightenment; see *Selected Works*, 1:571–646. For Agrippa's commentary, see Henricius Cornelius Agrippa, "In artem Raymundi Lullii Commentaria," *Opera* (Hildesheim, 1970; reprint of Lyon, 1600[?]), 2:319ff. Finally, for the "keys" and the tradition to which Descartes's talkative old man belongs, see Paolo Rossi, *Clavis universalis: Arti Mnemonische e logica combinatoria da Lullo a Leibniz* (Milan, 1960), and "The Legacy of Ramon Lull in Sixteenth-Century Thought," *Medieval and Renaissance Studies* 5 (1961): 182–213.

41. Descartes to Beeckman, 29 April 1619, AT, 10:164–66; AM, 1:16–18; *Journal*, 4:63–64.

42. Ibid.

43. Beeckman to Descartes, 6 May 1619, AT, 10:167; AM, 1:19–20; *Journal*, 4:64.

44. Ibid., AT, 10:167–68; AM, 1:19–21; *Journal*, 4:64–65.

45. Ibid., AT, 10:168–69; AM, 1:21; *Journal*, 4:65.

46. Ibid.

47. *Journal*, 1:237, 242–43.

48. The text from the *Experimenta* certainly betrays Descartes's weakness for a (wonderful) book, Giovanni Battista della Porta's *La magie naturelle ou les secrets et miracles de la nature*, first published in Latin in 1558 and in French in 1612. Descartes's French text shows borrowings from this French version; I have consulted a reprint: *La magie naturelle* (Paris, n.d., ca. 1910), 278–88.

49. AT, 10:505. For further references and discussion, see Geneviève Rodis-Lewis, "Machineries et perspectives curieuses dans leurs rapports avec le Cartésianisme," *XVIIe siècle* 32 (1956): 461–74. Descartes still toyed with such matters in 1629 and perhaps later. See his letter to an unknown correspondent, tentatively dated September 1629: "There is a part of Mathematics

that I call the Science of Miracles, because it teaches us to use air and light so cleverly that we can reproduce by these means all of the same illusions that they say the Magicians perform with the help of Demons" (AT, 1:20–21; AM, 1:47). Even in the restrained *Discourse,* the mature Descartes was to promise near-miraculous health and effortless bounty in utopian visions of a scientifically-sophisticated medicine and agriculture; see AT, 6:62.

50. Gassendi to Fabri de Peiresc, 21 July 1629, in Beeckman, *Journal,* 4:153. Context limits the comparison to the other Dutch savants that Gassendi met in the course of his travels. Nevertheless, this is high praise, especially given that Gassendi never had a chance to consider the remarkable contents of Beeckman's manuscript notebooks, his only written work.

51. For several reasons, Beeckman's science has been easy to underestimate. He never published. He had never spoken to anyone else about his interests before Descartes, and that relationship ended very badly, with Descartes vehemently denying any obligation. As for his manuscripts, only three contemporaries, Descartes first among them, were ever given a look. It was not until 1905 that his *Journal* was recovered for serious study, and publication was not "complete" until 1953; meanwhile, the archives had been damaged in wartime bombardments; the now-published text remains relatively disorderly, and much of it is in Flemish, the rest in Latin, without translation into any of the most widely used modern languages. Finally, even when Beeckman's conceptions are more modern, his physical-mathematical formulations remain archaic.

As if the other problems were not enough, there is the additional task of trying to sort out how much credit goes to Beeckman and how much to Descartes for their work on free-fall during the honeymoon of their scientific partnership. For contrasting perspectives on the contributions of Beeckman and Descartes to mechanics see Alexandre Koyré, "La loi de la chute des corps: Descartes et Galilée" *Études galiléennes* (Paris, 1966), 107–36; John Schuster, *Descartes and the Scientific Revolution, 1618–1634: An Interpretation* (Ph.D. diss., Princeton, 1977), 53–111.

R. Hooykaas has offered two nontechnical and quite favorable overviews: "Science and Religion in the Seventeenth Century: Isaac Beeckman (1588–1637)," *Free University Quarterly* 1 (1951): 169–83, and "Isaac Beeckman," in *The Dictionary of Scientific Biography,* ed. Charles Gillispie (New York, 1970), 1:566–68. I quote from the latter. For the documentary evidence on this "meteorological station," see *Journal,* 3:85–86. For the studies of air pressure, see the indexed references, too numerous to cite, in the *Journal,* 4:331–32. For more technical assessments, see the most learned annotations by Cornelis de Waard in his editions of Beeckman's *Journal* and Mersenne's *Correspondance* and relevant pages in his *L'expérience barométrique* (Thouars, 1936), 75–91, 145–68.

Finally, E. J. Dijksterhuis offers a brief, balanced, broadly conceived, and technically competent assessment in *The Mechanization of the World Picture* (Oxford, 1961), especially 329–33. Dijksterhuis praises Beeckman for his "keen interest" and "his great scientific gifts." Comparing him to Leonardo da Vinci, he then criticizes him for failures with respect to "the tenacity of purpose and powers of concentration required to systematize, finish, record, and publish their inquiries, even if only in one field" (see *Mechanization*, 330).

The comparison of Beeckman with Leonardo is instructive. On the one hand, Beeckman was for a time one of Holland's greatest teachers, while Leonardo is still one of the world's greatest painters. On the other hand, Leonardo's science has been overvalued precisely because of his artistic genius, and he produced no truly distinguished pupil even as a painter, while Beeckman's scientific accomplishments were more substantial, and he did provide the initial impetus for Descartes.

We honor him for having written "Dat eens roert, roert altijt, soot niet belet en wort [that which once moves, moves always, if it is not prevented]." Would even Descartes or Mersenne, two of the three contemporaries shown the *Journal*, have read and understood this statement of the principle of inertia?

52. Descartes to Beeckman, September or October 1630, AT, 1:154–56; AM, 1:144–46; *Journal*, 4:194–95 and nn.5 and 6.

53. Descartes to Beeckman, 17 October 1630, AT, 1:156ff.; AM, 1:147–63; *Journal*, 4:195–202. The sentence quoted is from AM, 1:149–50; *Journal*, 4:196.

54. Cohen, *Écrivains français en Hollande*, 148.

55. *Discourse*, AT, 6:28.

Part Four: Particular Dream Elements

1. Consider Dream I and Interpretation I: Descartes offers what amounts to one vague association (moral evil or spiritual sin) for one particular element in the street scene (DE I.2). I suppose that Descartes was very selective in what he recorded from his thoughts in the two hours of wakefulness and that Baillet was to be at least somewhat selective in what he paraphrased or translated. Interpretation I does provide a "before-the-fact" association for the single element of Dream II. Even if Interpretation III.3 does offer more on the dream melon and the contrary wind from the school scene, that is not much.

2. Foulkes, *A Grammar of Dreams*, 33ff.

3. AT, 6:18.

Chapter 7

1. *Regulae,* AT, 10:360, 361, 364–65, 366, 370, 371–72 (rule IVa), 375. For a very perceptive paper on the implications of Descartes's two favorite images, the "firm foundation" and the "straight road," see Nathan Edelman, "The Mixed Metaphor in Descartes," *Romanic Review* 41 (1950): 167–78.

2. AT, 10:371–74.

3. Even in the *Discourse on the Method,* the first paragraph presents *le droit chemin* as "the right way" or "the direct route" for any philosopher-traveler, clearly symbolizing the Cartesian method itself, but the third paragraph uses *certains chemins* for "paths through life" that lead this one philosopher-traveler by way of reflections and maxims in his youth to "a method" as something further, something distinct. This paragraph clearly concerns Descartes's fortunate choice of "the search for truth" as his own "solidly good and important occupation"; see AT, 6:2, 3.

4. Freud, *Interpretation of Dreams,* 369–70, 382–83, 439, 563; Grinstein, *Freud's Rules of Dream Interpretation,* 30–31, 218. Laboratory researchers distinguish sharply between the manifest content of the successive dreams in a single night, which are not continuous, and latent meaning, which does often seem quite consistent: William Dement and Edward Wolpert, "Relationships in the Manifest Content of Dreams Occurring in the Same Night," *Journal of Nervous and Mental Disease* 126 (1958): 568–78; Harry Trosman, et al., "Studies in the Psychophysiology of Dreams: IV. Relations among Dreams in Sequence," *Archives of General Psychiatry* 3 (1960): 602–7; William Offenkrantz and Allan Rechtschaffen, "Clinical Studies of Sequential Dreams," *Archives of General Psychiatry* 8 (1963): 497–508; Allan Rechtschaffen, et al., "Interrelatedness of Mental Activity during Sleep," *Archives of General Psychiatry* 9 (1963): 536–47; Milton Kramer, et al., "Patterns of Dreaming: The Interrelationship of the Dreams of a Night," *Journal of Nervous and Mental Disease* 139 (1964): 426–39; David Foulkes, *The Psychology of Sleep,* 63–98; Rosalind Cartwright, *Night Life: Explorations in Dreaming,* (Englewood Cliffs, N.J., 1977), 15–31.

5. Antoine Furetière, *Le dictionnaire universel* (La Haye, 1690), s.v. "Droit."

6. Ibid.

7. Richelet, *Dictionnaire françois* (Geneva, 1680), s.v. "Droit."

8. Furetière, *Dictionnaire universel,* s.v. "Droit."

9. For a very long list in what is otherwise a concise reference, see Cotgrave, *A Dictionarie of the French and English Tongues* (London, 1611), s.v. "Droit."

10. Richelet, *Dictionnaire françois,* s.v. "Droit."

11. Beeckman recognized in himself a tendency to follow his older brother, Jacob, which the biographical record does confirm. Jacob's teaching had

already begun in 1611; Isaac's first formal appointment would come on 27 November 1619. See de Waard, "Vie de l'auteur," *Journal*, ix, xiii, xxii.

12. Antoine Furetière, *Dictionnaire universel* 1690), s.v. "N."

13. Montaigne, "Of Experience," in *The Complete Essays*, trans. Donald Frame (Stanford, 1965), 846.

14. Marc-Antoine Saint-Amant, "Le melon," in *Oeuvres*, ed. Jacques Bailbé (Paris, 1971), 1:18, lines 88–89 and note. This poem shows what could be done poetically in the way of a purely gustatory appreciation of Angevin melons. It was first published in 1631. The maréchal de Brézé is reported to have set aside a command when the campaigning season of 1638 conflicted with the melon season in Anjou. See François de Paule de Clermont, marquis de Montglat, *Mémoires*, in Michaud-Poujoulat, *Mémoires pour servir à l'histoire de France*, 3d ser. (Paris, 1838), 5:68–69.

15. La Curne de Sainte-Palaye, *Dictionnaire historique de la langue françoise jusqu'au siècle de Louis XIV*, 10 vols. (Niort,[?]–1882), s.v. "Melon." I have searched the great dictionaries of the late seventeenth century: Furetière, Richelet, and the Académie française. Neither Edmond Huguet's nor Frédéric Godefroy's dictionaries of older French usages are helpful. The Abbé Lalanne's *Glossaire du patois poitevin*, in the *Mémoires de la Société des antiquaires de l'Ouest* 32, part 2 (1867): 184, does list two curious provincial usages, but they seem wholly irrelevant. Descartes simply cannot have had a buzzing horsefly or a dessicating south wind in mind for his gift melon!

Dictionaries of the more modern language and of slang offer meanings that seem to have been unknown in the early seventeenth century. The size and shape of many melons suggest the human head, and this similarity, in turn, has led to wonderfully extended meanings: melon → head → imbecile → first-year cadet at the military school of Saint-Cyr. Given Descartes's intellectual aspirations and his recent experience as a raw volunteer, the notion of the melon as a dumb-head or a dumb recruit might appear apt, but the earliest such usages seem not to antedate the July Monarchy. For *melon-recrue*, see the discussion of hazing customs at Saint-Cyr in Eugne Titeux, *Saint-Cyr et l'école spéciale militaire en France* (Paris, 1898), 329–30. Of course, Saint-Cyr came into existence even as a *girls'* school only after Descartes's death. Even for boys, there were no military schools whatsoever in France in 1619, so there could hardly have been either the hazing or the slang for first-year cadets.

16. Cotgrave, *A Dictionarie of the French and English Tongues*, s.v. "Melon." In short, "a good woman is as hard to pick as a good melon."

17. Oudin, *Curiositez françoises pour supplément aux dictionnaires ou Recueil de plusieurs belles propriétez, avec un infinité de proverbes et quodlibets* (Paris, 1640). Oudin has nothing at the word *melon* itself.

18. Pellisson[-Fontanier], *Histoire de Louis XIV depuis la mort du Cardinal Mazarin en 1661 jusqu'à la Paix de Nimègue en 1678*, 3 vols. (Paris,

1749), 2:293. Descartes routinely referred to *paquets* of letters, but never, apparently, to *melons* in this sense.

19. Mermet, *Le temps passé* (Lyon, 1588), 43–44. The Bibliothèque Nationale also lists editions of 1585 and 1601. Because contexts play an important part in my argument, I have searched for Mermet's poem in other collections. The standard bibliographical guide is unhelpful on this point: Frédéric Lachèvre, *Bibliographie des recueils collectifs de poésies publiés de 1597 à 1700. Tome Premier: 1597–1635* (Paris, 1901). *Le temps passé* includes closely associated and historically suggestive poems on false friendship. Very similar themes also happen to have been closely associated in the collections of proverbs by Garnier and Cats, which I discuss later in this chapter.

20. Garnier, *Thesaurus Adagiorum Gallico-Latinorum . . . Trésor des proverbes françois expliqués en Latin* (Frankfurt, 1612), 31.

21. Cats, *Spiegel van den Ouden ende Nieuwen Tijdt*, 3 vols. in 1 (The Hague, 1632), 3:98–99.

22. Descartes's memory of Mermet's long poem could have prompted the images of the street scene and the encounters from the school scene of Dream I.

> La Pierre de Touche du Vray Amy avec la Manire
> de Cognoistre la Noblesse par la Vertu

> Ie m'esmerueille amy Factin,
> Me pourmenant parmy la rue,
> Quand quelque amy feinct ie salue,
> Le rencontrant soir ou matin.
> De tant loin qu'il me peut choisir,
> Il me faict vne barretade,
> Vne reuerence en gambade,
> M'approchant tousiours à loisir.
> Et puis quand il est près de moy,
> Il me dit en si beau langage,
> Ne te chaille amy, pren courage,
> Car tout mon bien n'est pour toy.
> Le voyant si prompt, et dispos,
> A me présenter son service,
> Son corps, son bien, sans avarice,
> Ie me repos en son propos.
> Pour caresser un bon repas
> Rien qu'honneur, Monsieur en présence,
> Mais par derrière, en mon absence,
> Ie croy qu'il ne me connoit pas.
> Mais quand ie pers force, et auoir,

265

Si ie luy veux faire request,
Mon gallant tourne un peu la teste,
Et fait semblant de ne me voir. . . .

The poet goes on to describe the true friend, who helps before having been asked and without regard to time or cost. See Mermet, *Le temps passé*, 11–13; compare Garnier, *Thesaurus Adagiorum*, 22–32.

23. Beeckman to Descartes, 6 May 1619, AT, 10:167–69; AM, 1:19–23; *Journal*, 4:64–65.

24. See Dijksterhuis, *The Mechanization of the World Picture*, 329–33; Koyr, *Études galiléennes*, 107–36; Schuster, *Descartes and the Scientific Revolution*, 53–111.

25. The uncertainty of identifications is only a special case of what Freud called "over-determination," the principle by which one manifest dream element can be traced back to many different latent dream thoughts, and of the contrary phenomenon, which Freud described but did not label, by which one dream thought finds expression in many different dream elements. See Freud, *The Interpretation of Dreams*, 318, 351, 353, 355–58; Foulkes, *A Grammar of Dreams*, 62–63, 215–19.

26. See Robert A. Moses, "Entoptic and Allied Phenomena," in *Adler's Physiology of the Eye*, 6th ed. (St. Louis, 1975), 545ff., especially 551–54; John C. Cavender, "Entoptic Imagery and After-images," separately paginated as chap. 20 in *Biomedical Foundations of Ophthalmology*, ed. Thomas D. Duane and Edward A. Jaeger (Philadelphia, 1982), 1ff., especially 9–13.

Among these phenomena are "Moore's lightning streaks," first described scientifically in 1935: "The symptoms are the occurrence of flashes of light, almost always compared to lightning, seen periodically for a few weeks or a month or two . . . ; they are most conspicuous . . . in the dark, and are either accompanied or followed by the appearance of spots before the eyes." Moore thought that the phenomenon was "fairly common," especially in older women, and innocuous. See R. Foster Moore, "Subjective 'Lightning Streaks,' " *British Journal of Ophthalmology* 19 (1935): 545–47 (quoted material from 545); "Subjective 'Lightning Flashes,' " *American Journal of Ophthalmology* 23 (1940): 1255–60; "Subjective 'Lightning Streaks,' " *British Journal of Ophthalmology* 31 (1947): 46–50. Others have suggested that Moore's lightning streaks may be either more common or less innocuous than Moore himself implied: F. H. Verhoeff, "Moore's Subjective 'Lightning Streaks,' " *American Ophthalmological Society Transactions* 39 (1941): 220–26; Conrad Berens, et al., "Moore's Lightning Streaks: A Discussion of Their Innocuousness," *American Ophthalmological Society Transactions* 52 (1954): 35–63. Verhoeff emphasized that ocular motion is the necessary and sufficient cause of such subjective lightning streaks.

See also Bernard R. Nebel, "The Phosphene of Quick Eye Motion," *Archives of Ophthalmology* 58 (1957): 235–43. "The 'flick phosphene' is best observed in the dark-adapted well-rested eye, i.e., before dawn after a restful sleep. Then if one flicks the eyes, e.g., from left to right [vertical flicks "require much practice but otherwise conform to the general scheme"], with the lids closed, one observes in each monocular field the short-lived appearance of a bright pattern" (236–37). With eyes open, the "flick phosphene" is reproducible but "usually less prominent and less brilliant."

Chapter 8

1. De Waard, "Note sur le manuscrit," *Journal*, 1:xxv. Descartes to Beeckman, 23 April 1619: AT, 10:162–63; AM, 1:14; *Journal*, 4:62.

2. De Waard, "Note sur le manuscrit," 1:xxx; Beeckman, *Journal*, 1:244.

3. Beeckman, *Journal*, 4:62; AT, 1:162; AM, *Correspondance*, 1:14.

4. *Journal*, 4:65; AT, 1:168–69; *Correspondance*, 1:21–23.

5. Descartes to Beeckman, 26 March 1619, *Journal*, 4:59–60; AT, 1:156–58; *Correspondance*, 1:7–8; *Regulae*, rules II, III, IVb, (AT, 10:362–70, 374–79).

6. Especially rule I: AT, 10:359–61.

7. Beeckman, *Journal*, 4:59–60; Baillet, *Vie*, 191–92. Rule IVa is of particular interest in that the philosopher of a regular, infallible, and universal method contrasts himself so insistently with the unphilosophical wanderer and treasure-seeker. See AT, 10:371.

8. Baillet, *Vie*, 2:545.

9. AT, 6:17–21.

10. Freud, *Interpretation of Dreams*, 347, 351–53.

11. Freud, *Interpretation of Dreams*, 182–83, 253n, 317–18, 341–43, 344n, 365, 527, 543.

12. Freud, *The Interpretation of Dreams*, 562–63; "The Employment of Dream Interpretation in Psychoanalysis" (1912), in *Therapy and Technique*, 99–100; "Some Additional Notes on Dream Interpretation as a Whole: The Limits to the Possibility of Interpretation" (1925), in *Therapy and Technique*, 219, 221–22.

13. *Black's Law Dictionary*, rev. 4th ed. (St. Paul, 1968), s.v.v. "Corpus juris civilis," states that "the name is said to have been first applied to this collection early in the seventeenth century." *The National Union Catalog* does bracket this title scrupulously for editions into the 1580s. Then, the edition of Denis Godefroy (d. 1621) uses as its title *Corpus juris civilis in IIII partes distinctum*, 4 vols. in 1 (Geneva and Lyon, 1583). This title, which may have been suggested by the first publication of the complementary *Corpus juris canonici* in 1582, quickly became the standard reference.

14. The teaching of French law as such was to be an innovation under Louis XIV. See Alfred de Curzon, "L'enseignement du droit français dans les universités de France au XVIIe et XVIIIe siècles," *Revue historique de droit français et étranger* 43 (1919): 209–69 and 305–56. There is a full and recent list of relevant literature in Christian Chêne, *L'enseignement du droit français en pays de droit écrit, 1679–1793* (Geneva, 1982). For the program at Poitiers, see M. Audinet, "La Faculté de droit de l'ancienne Université," in *Histoire de l'Université de Poitiers, 1432–1932*, ed. Paul Boissonnade (Poitiers, 1932), 138–79.

15. Adam, *Vie et oeuvres*, 40 and note a.

16. Charles Du Fresne, sieur Du Cange, *Glossarium mediae et infimae Latinitatis* (Niort, 1882), s.v.v. "Corpus juris"; J.F. Niermeyer, *Mediae Latinitatis lexicon minus* (Leiden, 1954), s.v. "Corpus." The dictionaries of Richelet (1680), Furetière (1690), and the Académie (1694) all list the French phrase, *corps de droit civil*, but not, naturally enough, the Latin *corpus*. The best dictionaries of modern French do show the eventual adoption of the latter term; *Le corpus* is now an acceptable abbreviation for *Le corpus juris* or *Le corpus juris civilis*. See *Trésor de la langue française: Dictionnaire de la langue du XIXe et du XXe siècles* (Paris, 1978), s.v. "Corpus."

17. St. Antony's example was very important for Augustine. Antony had happened to enter a church during this reading from Matthew 19:21: "Go, sell all that thou hast, and give to the poor, and thou shalt have treasure in heaven, and come and follow me." That was enough for Antony. But aleatory book opening would later be particularly associated with Augustine; see *The Confessions*, trans. Rex Warner (New York, 1963), bk. 8, chap. 12:182.

18. Ibid., 182–83.

19. Alternatively, Descartes may have known of the less celebrated chapter on the choice between ways of life in *The Divine Institutes* of Lactantius, even if he had never read it. The Christian Father works the old pagan topos of a youthful choice between "two ways" of life, right and left representing virtue and vice, into a little exposition of moral theology on the routes to heaven and hell. See *The Ante-Nicene Fathers* (Grand Rapids, 1951), 7:164–65. It is quite plausible that Descartes's Jesuit instructors at La Flèche might have glossed the poets with this chapter in mind.

20. Mousnier, *The Institutions of France*, 2:34–35.

21. Ropartz, "La famille Descartes," 11; compare 63, 93, 138, 165.

22. Adam, *Vie et oeuvres de Descartes*, 40 and note a; Audinet, "La Faculté de Droit de l'ancienne Université," 146–47.

23. Leibniz, "Notata quaedam G.G.L. circa vitam et doctrinam Cartesii," *Philosophische Schriften*, 4:310; *Cogitationes Privatae*, AT, 10:216; Adam, *Vie et oeuvres*, 49.

24. For the education and its principles and practices at La Flèche, with particular regard to Latinity, the poets, and pedagogy, see especially Camille de Rochemonteix, S.J., *Un collège de jésuites aux XVIIe et XVIIIe siècles: le Collège Henri IV de La Flèche* 4 vols. (Le Mans, 1889), 3:1ff., particularly 40–43, 61–75; François de Dainville, S.J., *La naissance de l'humanisme moderne* (Paris, 1940), 101–104, 118ff., 142ff.

According to the *Ratio studiorum,* "The [exclusive] use of spoken Latin will be maintained above all else and very severely, except in the [lowest grammar] classes in which the pupils do not [yet] know Latin. The use of French should never be permitted with respect to anything related to class-work." Students in the humanities were most honored for public recitations of Latin texts learned by heart. Teachers devoted the greatest care to explications. See the *Ratio atque institutio studiorum societatis Jesu,* trans. and ed. H. Ferté (Paris, 1892), 86–87, 91–92; Allan P. Farrell, S.J., *The Jesuit Code of Liberal Education: Development and Scope of the Ratio studiorum* (Milwaukee, n.d.), 172–75, 265, 344–49, 404.

25. Freud's review of the earlier literature on this topic is remarkably full and respectful; see *Interpretation of Dreams,* 44–55.

26. *Meditations,* AT, 9:71.

27. Des Brosses edited them as Ausonius's *Idylls* (numbered 15 and 17), just as the dreamer remembered. It is of some interest, given the theme of finding and seeking in the dream, that the two verses appear on either the same page (1603) or facing pages (1611): Pierre des Brosses, ed., *Corpus omnium veterum poetarum latinorum* (Lyon, 1603, and Geneva, 1611), 2:655 and 655–56 (first edition); 2:658–59 and 659 (second edition).

28. Given the emphasis on son-father relations in my historical inquiry and in psychoanalytical theory, it is worth mentioning that book 7, eclogue 1, was not anthologized with the other idylls by des Brosses. The poem is addressed by the father, Ausonius, to his son, Drepanius, and concerns the gift of a book, but it is completely irrelevant to my inquiry.

29. Ausonius, *[Works] with an English translation by Hugh G. Evelyn White,* 2 vols. (Cambridge, Mass.: Harvard University Press, 1919), 1:162–65. The Latin text:

Ex Graeco Pythagoricum de Ambiguitate Eligendae Vitae

Quod vitae sectabor iter, si plena tumultu
sunt fora, si curis domus anxia, si peregrinos
cura domus sequitur, mercantem si nova semper
damna manent, cessare vetat si turpis egestas;

5   si vexat labor agricolam, mare naufragus horror
infamat, poenaeque graves in caelibe vita
et gravior cautis custodia vana maritis;
sanguineum si Martis opus, si turpia lucra
faenoris et velox inopes usura trucidat?

30. Ibid., 1:170–73. The Latin text:

Nai kai ou Pythagorikon

Est et Non cuncti monosyllaba nota frequentant.
His demptis nil est, hominum quod sermo volutet.
Omnia in his et ab his sunt omnia, sive negoti
sive oti quidquam est, seu turbida sive quieta.

5   alterutro pariter nonnumquam, saepe seorsis
obsistunt studiis, ut mores ingeniumque
ut faciles vel difficiles contentio nancta est.
si consensitur, mora nulla intervenit "Est Est,"
sin controversum, dissensio subiciet "Non."

10   hinc fora dissultant clamoribus, hinc furiosi
iurgia sunt circi, cuneati hinc lata theatri
seditio, et tales agitat quoque curia lites.
coniugia et nati cum patribus ista quietis
verba serunt studiis salva pietate loquentes.

31. It is possible that the waking reflections of Interpretation II, which concern entoptic phenomena misinterpreted as self-generated night-lights, may have become a sort of night residue that helped to recall to mind Ausonius, *Eclogue* 4, lines 18–22.

32. Evelyn White's "Introduction," 1:xxv–xxvii. These judgments are widely shared. See Marie Joseph Byrne, *Prolegomena to the Works of Decimus Magnus Ausonius* (New York, 1916), 20, 41ff., 65–66.

33. It is possible that the explicit reference to Pythagoras was a bit of learning or pedantry added by Baillet.

34. Schuster, *Descartes and the Scientific Revolution*, 92.

35. S. K. Heninger, Jr., *Touches of Sweet Harmony: Pythagorean Cosmology and Renaissance Poetics* (San Marino, Calif., 1974) 256–84.

36. CP lines 39–46 do imply that Descartes experienced some depressive symptoms, but I would not make too much of them.

37. Heninger, *Sweet Harmony*, 269–72. A first qualification: Pythagoras is not apparent in what must have been the best-known passage from the poets on this theme; Virgil confronts his hero with an end-of-day choice between a *right* way of virtuous conduct to Elysium and a *left* way of vice to Tartarus (*Aeneid* 6.539–543). A second qualification: the wonderful en-

graving of Hercules at the Pythagorean Y-intersection, directing young travelers to the *right,* was published just about a century after the dreams (as the frontispiece to an edition of the Pythagorean *Carmen Aureum,* Dresden, 1720). A third qualification: however well Descartes knew the Latin poets, he may or may not have known the *locus classicus* for the Pythagorean Y from the patristic moral theologians; see Lactantius, *Divine Institutes,* 6.3, in *The Ante-Nicene Fathers,* ed. Alexander Roberts and James Donaldson, 7:164–65.

38. Persius, *Satires,* 3.52–62.

39. Persius, *Satires,* 5.19–51.

40. *Professors of Bordeaux,* 11.4–5; *Technopaegnion,* 13.9.

41. Thomas H. Thomas, *French Portrait Engraving of the XVIIth and XVIIIth Centuries* (London, 1910), 21–22; Eugène Bouvy, *La gravure de portraits et d'allégories en France au XVIIe siècle* (Paris, 1929), 4–5, 76.

42. Bouvy, *La gravure de portraits,* 12–16, 78. Saulnier's *Le Parlement de Bretagne* includes many such portraits of proud judges. How better to grace a candidate's thesis than with a portrait of one of them? It was a society of patrons and clients, and with the right patron, the client's ascent was easier. See the "Table des gravures: portraits des magistrats et dessins," *Le Parlement de Bretagne,* 2:891–92. I have not seen M. le comte de Palys, *Les thèses bretonnes illustrées* (Vannes, 1890).

43. Gouhier, *Les premières pensées de Descartes,* 32–41; *La pensée réligieuse de Descartes,* 2d ed., 313.

44. *Premières pensées,* 86–103.

45. I summarize the Cartesian manuscripts and published works that can offer support to Gouhier's theory. It is not much: Leibniz (CP 109–12) and Baillet (VDC 273–82) document the bare fact that Descartes did resolve to complete and publish an unspecified "treatise." Baillet alone is the authority that the resolution was dated on 23 February 1620 and was appended to the dream record of the *Olympica,* but he also reported that the disorder of the Olympian materials seemed to him to preclude the identification of *this* as the "treatise" and confessed that *he* had no idea what "treatise" Descartes can have meant.

Of the three known Cartesian cogitations on spiritual symbolism (CP 88–91, 115–19, 131–35), only the first seems by its sequence in Leibniz's notes to have preceded the late-February resolution. Only the second cogitation explicitly refers to "Olympian things," and, of five "perceptible things" mentioned, only one can be related convincingly to specific dream elements ("wind"), whereas two are so general that it is hard to tell ("motion in time" and "instantaneous activity"), and another two seem quite irrelevant to the dream narratives as we have them ("light" and "heat"). None of the three so much as hints at a larger writing project, much less sketches even the most preliminary plan for a "treatise" on any such subject.

The first argument against the Gouhier hypothesis is that it is too easy to suggest a much better identification for the "treatise," namely, the *Regulae*. Argument based on the internal evidence of the *Regulae* seems to have established that this writing project was begun even before the climactic day(s) of 10–11 November 1619 and that Descartes referred to it in his drafts as a "treatise." For chronology, see Jean-Paul Weber, *La constitution du texte des Regulae*, 3–47; for "treatise," see rules IVa, VI, VII, VIII, in AT, 10:373, 381, 392, 399. The *Experimenta* and the *Olympica* also help document the early interest in scientific method: see CP 5–9, 29–38; VDC 158–159, 183–192. Finally, the entire second part of the *Discourse* provides the strongest support for wintertime work on the development and testing of a mathematically inspired method, not the hypothesized philosophical treatise on spiritual symbols.

The second argument against the Gouhier hypothesis is that it is almost impossible to imagine that an ambitious and independent thinker who began the winter with a sense of wonderful scientific discovery that remained fresh a year later—and seventeen years later—could have decided in the course of this season that his mission was to explain to others that "wind signifies the spirit" (CP 116). Even Gouhier discounts these cogitations as so many "schoolboy thoughts"; see *Premières pensées*, 103.

The third argument against the Gouhier hypothesis, developed in the text that follows, is that the dream materials as we have them do not serve the purposes supposed. The first and second interpretations, especially, are obscure and inconsistent. They are not spiritually symbolic. And the third concerns quite particular dream elements, which are given what seem to be nongeneralizable explanations.

It is curious that so distinguished a scholar can have pursued this line of argument. I suggest two contributory factors that have nothing to do with the preceding evidence so quickly reviewed: first, Gouhier, who knew so much else, was ignorant of modern dream psychology, which meant that he tended to discount or hurry past the dream narratives and interpretations as such; second, he focused on the early manuscripts very soon after the esotericist Paul Arnold had advanced his unfortunate argument, based on misreadings of a generally unfamiliar literature, that the Olympian "dreams" were not real dreams but only Rosicrucian allegories. See appendices 2 and 3.

46. Leibniz's CP 93–101 is virtually identical to Baillet's VDC 163–72, which is part of Interpretation III.1. *If* it were certain that Baillet followed Descartes's sequence unfailingly, *then* it would be virtually certain that Leibniz's CP 88–91 belongs here, too, because Foucher de Careil presents CP 88–101 as a coherent block. But it is not certain. Indeed, we have to be particularly suspicious at just this point.

As Gouhier has already argued, Descartes's presumption of sleep for VDC

154–178 is reason enough to call into question the apparent place of these materials (see *Premières pensées*, 79–81). Descartes might possibly have *dreamed* the rest of this part of Interpretation III, which consists solely of altogether arbitrary assertions. However, having made due allowances for thoughtlike NREM mentation during sleep, I doubt that Descartes could have *dreamed* anything like this: "Just as the imagination uses figures to conceive physical things, so the intellect uses certain perceptible bodies, like wind or light, to represent physical things. Philosophizing in a more elevated way . . ."

Baillet seems to have felt the need to provide some defense or explanation for the hero-philosopher's remarkable assertion that the dream anthology of the *poets* "represented in particular and in a more distinct way the union of Philosophy and Wisdom." He found materials for a brief and authentically Cartesian defense/explanation in the passage that also caught Leibniz's eye, trimmed it of irrelevancies ("like wind or light, . . ." which have nothing at all to do with Dream III), and used it to patch one of the holes in the philosopher's nighttime thinking-cap.

The upshot is that the passage on figures known only from Leibniz (CP 88–91) must have been entered into the Little Notebook only after the dream narratives and interpretations proper, presumably at some later date, quite possibly much later, as is more obviously true of all other related passages.

47. The best layman's dream book in Descartes's day was that of Scipion du Pleix, *Les causes de la veille et du sommeil, des songes, et de la vie et de la mort* (Paris, 1609), 84, 86, 88, 111–17. There was a venerable spiritual tradition, starting with cautionary texts in the Scriptures, particularly Ecclesiastes 34:1–8. The great patristic authority for demonic dreams was Gregory, *Dialogues*, 4:50. For a useful collection of traditional essays on related problems and a bibliography, see Nicolas Lenglet Dufresnoy, *Recueil de dissertations anciennes et nouvelles sur les apparitions, les visions, et les songes*, 4 vols. in 2 (Avignon and Paris, 1751), especially 2:250–54.

48. Du Pleix, *Causes de la veille et du sommeil*, 145–50. Augustine, *Confessions*, 10:30.

49. Du Pleix, *Causes de la veille et du sommeil*, 82–84.

50. See chap. 7.

51. David Foulkes and Gerald Vogel have done the most important laboratory research on hypnagogic hallucinations. Their relevant findings after 212 experimental awakenings of nine subjects can be summarized in the following four points: first, over the entire hypnagogic period (into descending stage 2 sleep but not beyond), 202 of 212 awakenings yielded reportable mental content; second, sensory imagery predominated, primarily visual and secondarily auditory; third, individual differences were very large, some subjects never reporting auditory imagery upon being awakened from descending stage 1 or stage 2, others always reporting such imagery on being awakened;

fourth, intense affect was found to be quite rare. See Foulkes and Vogel, "Mental Activity at Sleep Onset," *Journal of Abnormal Psychology* 70 (1965): 231-43.

It would fit these experimental data better and also help make sense of his own Interpretation II if Descartes had reported *visual imagery before awakening* and *perfect calm after awakening*. However, the extant texts of Dream II and Interpretation II have him doing neither. The assertions are quite clear: Descartes *heard a dream noise,* then, *terrified, awoke to see "real" sparks*. There are several possibilities: first, Descartes's actual dream—or hypnagogic hallucination—may have been experienced or remembered as reported, without visual imagery; second, he may have experienced visual as well as auditory imagery but recorded only the former; third, he may have experienced and reported both, leaving Baillet to reduce the dream to the noise alone. The second and third possibilities both require accepting the historicity of things unseen in Baillet's text. The first does not.

52. CP 5-9, 29-38; *Regulae,* rules I-X; *Discourse,* part 2.

Conclusion

1. AT, 9:71.

2. Speculation that there must have been real winds outside the heated chamber to account for dream winds inside (Dream I) or real noises to account for the real noise (Dream II), for instance, reflects a fundamental discomfort with the fact of unconscious thinking. See Leroy, *Descartes,* 1:84; Sebba, *The Dream of Descartes,* 21.

3. Descartes had not been capable of anything so sophisticated in the *Discourse,* where the best that he had been able to do in roughly parallel passages was, first, to defy anyone else to find any rigorous distinction between dream images and sense perceptions and, second, to posit his own still-crude distinction between dream thought and waking thought: "Our reasonings are never either so evident or so entire during sleep as they are during wakefulness . . ." (AT, 6:38, 40).

If he did not have the elegant criteria from the *Meditations* in mind even when he published the *Discourse* in 1637, he could hardly have used them to fabricate the perfectly dreamlike set of narratives in the *Olympica* in 1619.

4. AT, 9:71-72.

5. *Discourse:* AT, 6:32, 38-40; *Meditations:* AT, 9:14-15, 21-22, 56, 61, 71.

6. For reconsideration of the work of Henri Gouhier and Paul Arnold, see the preliminary remarks in my introduction and the fuller discussion in appendices 2 and 3. It could have been no part of Arnold's intentions to save

the thinker from himself; more than anything else, he wanted to claim this hero-thinker for the esoteric tradition as he understood it. Gouhier's motivations in his qualified endorsement are another matter; he was quite ready to substitute Cicero's quasi-Platonic pseudodream for the Rosicrucian allegories as Descartes's supposed model, but he would not take the dreams seriously as dreams.

7. See chap. 5.

8. See chap. 6.

9. See chap. 3.

10. See chap. 3.

11. See chap. 4.

12. See chap. 4.

13. See chap. 7.

14. See chap. 7.

15. The *manifest* incoherence of Dream II as the central narrative in this set of dreams and its *manifest* irrelevance to the rest of the dreamer's life are both obvious. The dream winds had abated in the school scene (DE I.13), and there is nothing stormy or noisy about Dream III. Furthermore, when Descartes awakened from Dream II, it required an exercise of ingenuity for him to reason away his fears (VDC 90–102), which must mean that there was not a freak beginning-of-winter thunderstorm raging outside the heated chamber on the night of 10 November.

16. See chaps. 5 and 7. All teachers of Christian morality interpreted the commandment to honor parents as a commandment to obey one's father in the most extended and the most absolute senses.

17. See chaps. 6 and 8.

18. See chaps. 3 and 8.

19. See chaps. 4 and 8.

20. See chaps. 3, 5, and 8.

21. See chaps. 3, 6, and 8.

22. Freud, *Interpretation of Dreams*, especially chaps. 4 and 6.

23. On Freud's personal identification with the psychoanalytical movement, see his *Autobiographical Study*, trans. James Strachey (New York, 1963), chaps. 4 and 5, and his *History of the Psychoanalytical Movement*, trans. Joan Riviere (New York, 1963), 41–42: "Psychoanalysis is my creation. . . . No one can know better than I what psychoanalysis is. . . ." Like the young Descartes (CP 10–12), the mature Freud used marital imagery to represent the intimacy, fidelity, and exclusivity of his relationship to the new science (*History*, 49). Freud was especially jealous with respect to dream studies; he confessed that his great dream book was bound up with his most traumatic experience, his father's death, as well with his heroic self-analysis and his discovery of the principal doctrines of psychoanalysis: *Interpretation*, prefaces to the 1st ed.,

2d ed., and 3d English ed., xxiii–xxvi, xxxii; *Autobiographical Study,* 81–93; *History,* 53–58.

24. These sources are Beeckman's *Journal,* Leibniz's *Cogitationes Privatae,* and the earliest strata of the *Regulae.* See my introduction.

25. The most prominent are Charles Adam, *Vie et oeuvres de Descartes,* 49; Gustave Cohen *Écrivains français,* 397; Jacques Maritain, *The Dream of Descartes,* 15–16.

26. Freud to Leroy, in Leroy's *Descartes,* 1:90; for sexuality in dreams, see the *Interpretation of Dreams,* 195, 216–21, 385–432. Freud tended quite generally to emphasize the place of evil inclinations in unconscious mental life as revealed in the course of dream analysis; see *Introductory Lectures,* 142–43, 146–47, 201–6, 210–11.

27. AT, 6:11, 33; AT, 9:21–22, 26.

28. AT, 6:11–13.

29. AT, 6:13.

30. Ibid.

31. The cautious savant in his middle years, acutely aware of Galileo's troubles and anxious to win a better hearing for his own new thought, would hardly have invented so radical a moment.

32. AT, 6:13–14.

33. AT, 6:18.

34. D'Alembert, "Discours préliminaire des éditeurs," in Diderot, et al., *Encyclopédie ou dictionnaire raisonné des sciences, des arts, et des métiers* (Paris, 1751), 1:xxvi.

35. AT, 10:362–70.

36. AT, 6:32–33.

37. AT, 7:7–8.

38. It is true that Descartes defined "thinking" quite broadly in the *Meditations,* but it is also true that, before the duc de Luynes' translation of a subordinate passage, he found no place in this conception of the self as thinker even for such elemental if nonrational mental activities as loving and hating; see AT, 9:21, 22, 27.

Appendix 1

1. Adam, *Vie et oeuvres de Descartes* (Paris, 1910), iv, 49; AT, 10:171–88.

2. AT, 10:174–75.

3. "Bajuletian" is the wonderful pejorative for this sort of thing. See Antoine Boschet, S.J., *Réflexions sur les Jugemens des Savans,* ed. Guy de la Monnoye, in Adrien Baillet, *Jugemens des Savans* (1725), 7:303–4. For the critical magic, Boschet seems correct in discerning a more-than-moralistic

médisance, expressed at the expense even of Descartes himself; see *Réflexions d'un académicien sur la Vie de Monsieur Des Cartes,* in *Jugemens des Savans,* 7:359, 361, 363. See also Sebba, "Adrien Baillet," 24–25, 27, 50, 59.

4. Baillet, *Vie,* 1:i, ii, viii, x, xxii–xxiii; 2:476–77.

5. See appendix 2 for a discussion of dream psychology with respect to the doubly imponderable question of Descartes's accuracy as a dream reporter in the lost report.

6. Milhaud, "Une crise mystique de Descartes en 1619," in his *Descartes Savant* (Paris, 1921), 47–63, especially 50–54, where Adam's unfortunate concessive sentence is pulled from context and more unfortunately extended. Jacques Maritain's brilliantly rhetorical and widely read attack on Cartesianism, couched in the form of a discussion of the dreams, accepted Milhaud's opinion as a last word on the subject and dripped tar heated for the proud Descartes onto his humble biographer: *The Dream of Descartes,* trans. Mabelle Andison (New York, 1945), 13–14, 21, and 189, n.4. Gustave Cohen also repeated the master's word on Baillet's alleged amplifications: *Écrivains français,* 397.

7. AT, 10:175, with Adam's references to his vol.1, pp. 217–18, and vol. 10, pp. 49–50. The corresponding passages in Baillet's *Vie de Monsieur Des Cartes* come in vol.1 at pp. 160–64 and 42–44, respectively.

8. For a profile, see R. Hooykaas's article in *A Dictionary of Scientific Biography,* ed. Charles Gillispie (New York, 1970), s.v.v. "Beeckman, Isaac." C. de Waard has edited Beeckman's scientific *Journal,* contributing a learned "Vie de l'auteur," 1:i–xxiv. Descartes enters the *Journal* proper for the first time on 10 November 1618, 1:237.

9. Adam, *Vie et oeuvres,* 94–98.

10. Lipstorp, *Specimina Philosophiae Cartesianae* (Lyon, 1653), 76–77. Borel, *Vita Renati Cartesii* (Paris, 1656), 4–5. Baillet, *Vie,* 1:xiii–xvi, and 160–64, 42–44, respectively.

11. For these memoirs, see Augustin Frion, "Abrégé de la vie de Mr. Baillet," in Baillet, *Jugemens des Savans* (1725), 1:xxxvi: "Mr. l'Abbé Legrand and some other interested persons engaged him to arrange in order the memoirs that he [Legrand] had gathered on . . . Mr. Descartes." Frion was Baillet's nephew. On the one hand, he was very well informed, and we must accept that Baillet took over a project that had languished in the hands of better qualified Cartesians. On the other hand, he well knew how controversial the Cartesian philosophy and so the Cartesian life-story had become, and we must suspect that he minimizes Baillet's own role ahistorically.

12. Borel, *Vita,* 4–5; AT, 1:217–18.

13. Baillet, *Vie,* 1:50–51, 81–86.

14. Adam, *Vie et oeuvres,* iv.

15. AT, 10:175.

16. For references documenting the immediate (Milhaud and Maritain)

impact of Adam's concessive sentence, see the preceding n.6 and add Cohen, *Écrivains français*, 397. For the lasting impact, see Gouhier, *Premières pensées*, 31 and n.1. Gouhier, the ranking student of the *Olympica*, closely follows Adam in his suspicion that Baillet's "more or less paraphrased" version was only "approximate," having been "ornamented" or "amplified." He does not add new evidence or argument; see Gouhier, 32, 40, 78, 117.

17. Sebba's last word on Baillet's characteristics as Descartes's biographer is cautiously favorable. See Sebba, "Adrien Baillet," in Lennon, *Problems of Cartesianism*, 23 n.45, 48 n.94, 51, 59.

18. AT, 10:217, note a, and 184, note a.

19. Henri Gouhier's useful distinction between the "suspect historian" who recklessly filled gaps and the "meticulous" or "conscientious scholar" who carefully assembled his documentation applies here. See *Premières pensées*, 20, 124.

20. Ibid., 145.

21. AT, 10:215 and note a.

22. Gouhier, *Premières pensées*, 142, 146–47.

23. There is amplification and perhaps even invention in Baillet's incorporation of learned references to Calapino, a fifteenth-century lexicographer, and Evander, traditionally honored for having brought the alphabet to Latium. However, this is just the sort of book-learning that *does not* appear in Baillet's version of Descartes's *Olympica*, with the notable exception of the tags from Ausonius, for which there is the independent evidence of Leibniz's *Cogitationes*.

24. AT, 10:352–53.

25. Descartes, *Regulae ad directionem ingenii*, crit. ed. G. Crapulli (La Haye, 1966), 106, 108.

26. For Baillet's favorable judgment on Le Nain de Tillemont, see his "Discours sur l'histoire de la vie des saints," in *Vies des Saints*, 1: col. 57. For his discussion of his sources for the stories of the paired saints celebrated on 7 March, Perpetua and Felicity, see his *Vies des Saints*, 1: March, cols. v–vi. Baillet's French version of the great dream vision follows Le Nain de Tillemont's earlier version almost verbatim; see the latter's *Mémoires pour servir à l'histoire ecclésiastique des six premiers siècles* (Paris, 1701), 3:143–44. Where Baillet seems to add inventive details to the modern translation, in fact, he had returned to the ancient original; see the *Passio Sanctarum Martyrum Perpetuae et Felicitatis*, in Migne, *Patrologia Latina Cursus Completus* (Paris, 1844), 3: cols. 25–26.

27. Baillet, *Vies des Saints*, 1:xv.

Appendix 2

1. Gouhier, *Premières pensées de Descartes,* 2d ed., 33. The second paragraph break is mine. This passage reproduces the same argument, based on the same authorities, and presented in almost the same words that the author appended to the *Pensée réligieuse de Descartes,* 313. "The psychologists" clearly means Foucault and his named predecessors, Egger and Tannery, too.

2. *Premières pensées,* 33.

3. *Pensée réligieuse,* 313.

4. Ibid., 311–12.

5. Maury, *Le sommeil et les rêves* (Paris, 1861), 133–34.

6. Egger, "La durée apparente des rêves," *Revue philosophique,* 40 (1895): 41–43.

7. Ibid., 41.

8. It is not known when Descartes recorded his dreams. If we could trust Baillet's assertion that "his enthusiasm left him a few days afterward," which we certainly cannot, the record would have to have been made within days. If we could trust Baillet's assertion that Descartes made a vow to leave his heated chamber for a pilgrimage to Loretto "before the end of November," which we almost certainly can, the record would have to have been made within two or three weeks at the very latest. So much for Baillet's assertions. Historically and psychologically, by far the most likely date for the written record of narratives and interpretations is the day after, 11 November 1619.

9. Egger, "Le sommeil et la certitude; le sommeil et la mémoire," *La critique philosophique, politique, scientifique, littéraire,* 1 (1888): 345.

10. Paul Tannery's collected works fill seventeen octavo volumes under the general title *Mémoires scientifiques,* ed. J. L. Heiberg and H. G. Zeuthen (Toulouse, 1912–1950). The papers on dreams are relatively slight, even unimportant: "Sur l'activité de l'esprit dans le rêve," *Revue philosophique,* 38 (1894): 630–33; "Sur la mémoire dans le rêve," *Revue philosophique,* 45 (1898): 636–40; "Sur la paramnésie dans le rêve," *Revue philosophique,* 46 (1898): 420–22. For Tannery's disclaimers as a nonauthority on dream psychology, see the beginnings of the first and third of these papers.

11. Tannery, "Sur l'activité de l'esprit dans le rêve," 630–31.

12. Ibid., 630–31; Tannery, "Sur la mémoire dans le rêve," 640.

13. In 1905, Tannery responded to a questionnaire distributed by a mathematician, not a psychologist, to fellow mathematicians, not psychologists. The questioner sought evidence of formal mathematical reasoning accomplished in dreams or inspired by dreams. Tannery responded somewhat impatiently, confessing "only very vague memories" of his dream studies from the 1870s and professing a vigorously Cartesian conviction that it is a waste of time to look for mathematical thinking in nighttime dreaming. See Edmond

Maillet, "Les rêves et l'inspiration mathématique," *Bulletin de la Société philomathique de Paris* 7 (1905): 24–25.

14. Foucault, *Le rêve* (Paris, 1906), 48–49; compare 80–81, 140–42, 168–70, 297–301.

15. *Le rêve*, 8–9.

16. *Le rêve*, 12.

17. In addition to the previously quoted passage, see *Le rêve*, 9–19, 130–33, 140.

18. *The Interpretation of Dreams*, 85.

19. Ibid., 556.

20. Freudians and anti-Freudians alike agree with Freud on the fundamental importance of the dream book. See Freud, *Interpretation of Dreams*, xxxii and 154 n.1. Among Freudians, I mention only Ernest Jones, *The Life and Work of Sigmund Freud* (New York, 1953), 1:287, 319–20, 324, 350–51, 356, and that self-styled "post-Freudian," Erik Erikson, "The First Psychoanalyst," in *Insight and Responsibility* (New York, 1964), 19ff. Anti-Freudians typically object to theoretical presuppositions, constructions, and applications, not to the analytical methods of dream interpretation; see, for instance, Robert W. McCarley and J. Allan Hobson, "The Neurobiological Origins of Psychoanalytic Dream Theory" and "The Brain as a Dream State Generator: An Activation-Synthesis Hypothesis of the Dream Process," *American Journal of Psychiatry*, 134 (1977): 1211–21 and 1335–48; David Stannard, *Shrinking History: On Freud and the Failure of Psychohistory* (New York, 1980).

21. Egger condescended in words from a bygone epoch: "Let us grant to common opinion that dream life is life in the American manner (*à l'américaine*), the dreamer like someone fevered or pointlessly agitated . . ." (Egger, "La durée apparente des rêves," 46).

Tannery compared the deeply sleeping brain to disengaged, unproductive machinery, then added: "The dream is a period of starting up, with its jerkiness and its accidents; when the gears are fully engaged once again, we have awakened" (Tannery, "Sur la paramnésie dans le rêve," 421).

Finally, Foucault began his first publication on the law of logical evolution with a favorable reference to a paper in which L. Marillier had effectively added dream reporters to a longer list of untrustworthy types, namely, "women, clerics, soldiers, businessmen, all types of people who are not accustomed to scientific criticism . . ." (Marillier, "La suggestion mentale et les actions mentales à distance," *Revue philosophique*, 23 [1887]: 415). Egger and Foucault both respectfully referred to Marillier's paper as part of the current literature on the question of the accuracy of dream reports. See especially Foucault, "L'évolution du rêve pendant le reveil," *Revue philosophique* 58 (1904): 459; *Le rêve*, 3.

22. The first generation of Chicago researchers included William Dement,

David Foulkes, and Allan Rechtschaffen. All have published accessible and authoritative accounts of the work accomplished largely by the end of the 1960s: Dement, *Some Must Watch while Some Must Sleep* (San Francisco, 1974); Dement and Merrill Miller, "An Overview of Sleep Research: Past, Present, and Future," in the *American Handbook of Psychiatry,* 2d ed. (New York, 1975), 6:130–91; Foulkes, *The Psychology of Sleep* (New York, 1966); Foulkes and Gerald Vogel, "The Current Status of Laboratory Sleep Research," *Psychiatric Annals* 4:7 (1974): 7–24; Rechtschaffen, "The Psychophysiology of Mental Activity during Sleep," in *The Psychophysiology of Thinking: Studies of Covert Processes,* ed. F. J. McGuigan and R. A. Schoonover (New York, 1973), 153–206.

23. Frederick Baekeland and Richard Lasky, "The Morning Recall of Rapid Eye Movement Period Reports Given Earlier in the Night," *The Journal of Nervous and Mental Disease* 147 (1968): 570–79.

24. Ibid., 573–74, 576.

25. Ibid., 575.

26. Ibid.

27. C. A. Meier, et al. (including C. S. Hall), "Forgetting of Dreams in the Laboratory," *Perceptual and Motor Skills* 26 (1968): 551–57. With respect to the heroism of the subject, it is only honest to admit that he took off every other week from the laboratory routines of repeated awakenings for what must have been better sleep in his own bed.

28. Ibid., 554–55.

29. Ibid.

30. Ibid., 553. Hall's extensive collections of dream reports antedate the era of laboratory REM research. See, for instance, "What People Dream About: In which 10,000 dreams are statistically investigated with respect to setting, cast of characters, plot, emotions, and coloring," *Scientific American,* 184 (May, 1951), 60–63. On the comparability of home dreams with laboratory dreams, see Robert Weisz and David Foulkes, "Home and Laboratory Dreams Collected under Uniform Sampling Conditions," *Psychophysiology* 6 (1970): 588–96.

31. In addition to other papers cited in this appendix, see Donald R. Goodenough, et al., "Repression, Interference, and Field Dependence as Factors in Dream Forgetting," *Journal of Abnormal Psychology* 83 (1974): 32–44.

32. J. Trinder and M. Kramer, "Dream Recall," *American Journal of Psychiatry* 128 (1971): 296–301.

33. David Cohen, "Toward a Theory of Dream Recall," *Psychological Bulletin* 81 (1974): 138–54; "Remembering and Forgetting Dreaming," in *Functional Disorders of Memory,* ed. F. Kihlstrom and F. J. Evans (Hillside, N. J., 1979), 239–74.

34. Cohen and Gary Wolfe, "Dream Recall and Repression: Evidence for an Alternative Hypothesis," *Journal of Consulting and Clinical Psychology* 41 (1973): 349–355.

35. For easily accessible illustration and discussion, see Foulkes, *The Psychology of Sleep*, 63–85, and Rosalind Cartwright, *Night Life: Explorations in Dreaming* (Englewood Cliffs, N. J., 1977), 15–31. For scholarly papers, see William Dement and Edward Wolpert, "Relationships in the Manifest Content of Dreams Occurring in the Same Night," *Journal of Nervous and Mental Disease* 126 (1958): 568–78; Harry Trosman, Allan Rechtschaffen, et al., "Studies in Psychophysiology of Dreams: Relations among Dreams in Sequence," *Archives of General Psychiatry* 3 (1960): 602–7; William Offenkrantz and Allan Rechtschaffen, "Clinical Studies of Sequential Dreams: A Patient in Psychotherapy," *Archives of General Psychiatry* 8 (1963): 497–508; Allan Rechtschaffen, et al., "Interrelatedness of Mental Activity during Sleep," *Archives of General Psychiatry* 9 (1963): 536–47; Milton Kramer, et al., "Patterns of Dreaming: The Interrelationship of the Dreams of a Night," *Journal of Nervous and Mental Disease* 139 (1964): 426–39.

36. Gouhier, *Pensée réligieuse*, 313–15; *Premières pensées*, 32–37.

37. Allan Rechtschaffen to the author, 4 February 1986. My inquiry raised Gouhier's doubts as questions: Too much detail? Too much logic? Rechtschaffen worked from my translation of Baillet's version of the Olympian narratives and interpretations. I am particularly grateful for this assistance, knowing that he would not presume to speak for "the psychophysiologists," let alone "the psychologists," but that all informed readers will respect the weight of his carefully chosen words. His publications include a notable summary of psychophysiological research and several contributions to the studies of dream recall and of sequential dreams. See n.35 of this appendix.

38. Adrien Baillet, who is the last man known to have seen and used the original manuscript, offered this as his last word on the subject: "But there is so little order and connection in the materials of the *Olympica* in his manuscripts, that we can easily see that M. Descartes never planned to make a regular and coherent treatise of them, let alone to publish it." See *La Vie de Monsieur Des Cartes,* 1:86

Appendix 3

1. Arnold, "Le 'songe' de Descartes," *Cahiers du Sud* 35 (1952): 274–91. Arnold revised this paper only inconsequentially before republishing it in the *Histoire des Rose-Croix et les origines de la Franc-Maçonnerie* (Paris, 1955), 273–99. His later restatements suffer from the same problems that afflict the original publications: "Descartes et les Rose-Croix," *Mercure de France,* no.

1166 (October, 1960): 266–84; *La Rose-Croix et ses rapports avec la Franc-Maçonnerie* (Paris, 1970), 158–63.

2. Gregor Sebba, *Bibliographia Cartesiana: A Critical Guide to the Descartes Literature 1800–1960* (The Hague, 1964), 20. Sebba's review of Arnold's "careful historical study" headed a bibliographical section that he defined by the categories of Arnold's hypothesis: "Descartes's 'dream' and 'Rosicrucianism.'" Sebba himself clearly knew little or nothing about the supposedly influential (and nominally Rosicrucian) allegory, Andreae's *Chymische Hochzeit: Christiani Rosenkreuz* (1616), which he cited as the "*Noces chymiques de Christian Rosenkrantz* (1616)." It is important that the first French version of Andreae's work was published only in 1928, not 1616; Andreae himself was a perfectly orthodox Lutheran pastor, not an esoteric author as imagined by the French translator in 1928; his hero was an allegorical Christian Rosenkreuz, not a comic Rosenkrantz.

Compare the better-qualified judgment of John W. Montgomery in *Cross and Crucible: Johann Valentin Andreae (1586–1654), Phoenix of the Theologians* (The Hague, 1973), 1:286, and 2:494–95. Montgomery's bibliographical notices on Arnold denounce his "careless scholarship, . . . crippled by lack of depth contact with the entire corpus of primary sources bearing on Andreae" (512, 556). Cartesians who have accepted the Arnold hypothesis uncritically should consult Montgomery, 1:269–70 and 2:512, 555–56.

3. "Le 'songe' de Descartes," 287–88.

4. Ibid., 290. Montgomery has established beyond any possible doubt that Andreae was an orthodox Lutheran Christian, not a "Rosicrucian Illuminist" or a "medieval mystic." See his *Cross and Crucible*.

5. For a well-introduced and well-annotated facsimile, see Montgomery, *Cross and Crucible*, 2:288–487.

6. Arnold, "Le 'songe' de Descartes," 287.

7. Ibid., 288.

8. The alleged parallels for DE I.4 (if this claim is intended), DE I.5, 6, 8, 9, and 10 all refer to Andreae's Day II; the alleged parallel for DE I.11 refers either to one narrative element from Day III or to another from Day VI—Arnold cannot quite decide which one it is.

9. Rosenkreutz's "night of reflection, of terror, and of prayer, just like [Descartes's] two hours of reflection, of terror, and of prayer . . ." (Arnold, "Le 'songe' de Descartes," 288).

10. Ibid., 287.

11. Ibid., 288.

12. Montgomery, *Cross and Crucible*, 315 n.5.

13. Sebba, *Bibliographia Cartesiana*, 20.

14. Arnold, "Le 'songe' de Descartes," 289: "The evident parallel that we have just discovered between the first [two dreams] and the *Noces* authorizes

and even obliges us to conclude that in this case [the third dream], too, it is a matter of a version of some allegory placed or replaced in circulation by the German doctrinaires of the Rosy-Cross. I don't know which one."

15. Gouhier, "Descartes a-t-il rêvé?" 203–4.

16. Ibid., 206–8.

17. Ibid., 205.

18. "Rhodophilos Staurophorus," *Raptus philosophicus* (N. p. 1619), 5. In Latinized Greek, the pseudonym identifies the author as a "Lover of the Rose" and "Bearer of the Cross," and, lest the reader miss the Rosy Cross, the author refers twice more to the "Fraternity of the R.C." on the title page alone. "Ecce Crucis Rosae . . ." recurs four times in the brief Latin "Ad lectorem," and the German text itself variously flags the "FRATERNITET R.C." and the "FR. R.C." at the beginning and the "FRATERNITET des R.C.," the "FRATERNITET des H. Ordens R.C.," and the "FR. R.C." at the end, not to pause longer over such references as this: "B.B.H.H.G.G.H.H.B.B.D.H.O.R.C." (pp. 3–5, 14–15). In short, whatever else may be left mysterious in this peculiar little work, a Rosicrucian (or nominally Rosicrucian) imprint is unmistakable. Descartes's Olympian dreams differ in this respect as in others.

For my inquiry, the *raptus* is the crux. In his first, tentative article on the subject, Arnold explicated the *raptus* as a "pretended dream ravishment." Although he quietly corrected himself—and Gouhier—on the point in a subsequent article, when he dropped the reference to dreaming and made it only a "pseudo-ravishment," Gouhier had already carried off what he wanted, "a dream." For Arnold's successive versions, see "Le 'songe' de Descartes," 289; "Descartes et les Rose-Croix," 277. For Gouhier's notion of the *raptus* as dream, see "Descartes a-t-il rêvé?" 205; *Premières pensées,* 139.

In classical Latin, a *raptus* is "a snatching away, a plundering, an abduction." For persons, it is properly "a rape." There are no connotations of sleeping or dreaming, but Cicero himself extends the proper meaning of sudden and forceful snatching away when he uses the verb for the actions of contemplatives who "withdraw" themselves from carnal influences, standing the "rape" on its head to get something like our spiritual "rapture" or "ravishment." See *De divinatione,* 1.xlix.111, where this sort of divination by natural inspiration is clearly distinguished from the divination by artful dream interpretation already discussed (*Div.* 1.xviii.34, xx.39ff., xlix.110).

In biblical Latin, the term denotes an overwhelming spiritual experience in which an individual is raised up by God. Paul tells of a time when he was "caught up into the third heaven, whether in the body or out of the body, I do not know" (2 Cor. 12:2 and 4; compare 1 Thess. 4:17 and Apoc. 12:5). Nowhere in any of this is there a suggestion of sleeping or dreaming. Augustine discusses these matters authoritatively in *De Genesi ad litteram,* 12.5.13, 26.53–54, 27.56, 28.57.

A modern German can use *Raptus* as a colloquial equivalent for *Rappel,* "tantrum, fit of madness, mad whim," and a Frenchman can use *raptus* for "a violent movement of the soul under the impulse of an ardent emotion," but neither Rhodophilus Staurophorus nor René Descartes could have made the leap from *raptus* to dream that the Arnold hypothesis supposes.

19. *Raptus philosophicus,* 5, 11.

20. Ibid., 11–13.

21. CP 13–16.

22. Descartes to Beeckman, 29 April 1619, AT, 10:164–66; AM, 1:16–17; Beeckman, *Journal,* 4:63–64.

23. Gouhier, "Descartes a-t-il rêvé?" 204, 206. Compare his *Premières pensées,* 38, 39, 119, 120, 133, 135.

24. Gouhier, "Descartes a-t-il rêvé?" 208; *Premières pensées,* 41; *Pensée réligieuse,* 2d ed., 315.

25. Arnold did restate his position, attempting to take Gouhier's work into account. His restatements still suffer from the problems that afflicted the original publications: "Descartes et les Rose-Croix" and *La Rose-Croix et ses rapports avec la Franc-Maçonnerie.*

One example illustrates what has changed and what has remained the same. With respect to the *Chymische Hochzeit* and Dream I, Arnold now claims: "Just as Rosenkreutz dreams that on top of the tower he advances with difficulty because he alone limps on both feet [N.B.] and is ashamed of it, so, too, Descartes can advance only by limping along on one side [N.B.], and he is astonished and ashamed that he alone is so afflicted" (*La Rose-Croix et ses rapports,* 158). In fact, Rosenkreutz dreams that he "together with a *numberless multitude* of men lay fettered with great Chains in a *dark Dungeon . . .*" within a symbolic Tower of Babel. He is lifted up from this *lowly estate* by God's grace, but he still feels "the Wounds which the fetters had caused" him and presumably *every other sinner,* and this prevents him from going forward and forces him to "halt on both Feet" (CH 7, 10, 13; HR 9, 13, 16 [Foxcroft's emphases in quotations]). In the dream, he receives heavenly reassurance, and, after awakening, he is able to advance with ease, even to hasten toward the castle for the wedding, apparently unimpeded by his wounds (CH 16, 18, 19, 22; HR 20, 25, 26, 29–30). Properly speaking, his physical lameness represents his spiritual sinfulness, which he guiltily shares with all others. This is very different from a bodily infirmity, which could have distinguished him shamefully in comparison with others (CH 37, 43–44; HR 28, 33).

In short, what has changed is the definition of "similarities," the quondam "parallels" perceived by Arnold. What has not changed is his slipshod argumentation without formal documentation and his determination to demonstrate Descartes's indebtedness to Rosicrucian literature. Although he has been undeterred with respect to the former by Gouhier's hesitations, he has become visibly more assertive with respect to the latter after Gouhier's support.

26. Macrobius, *Commentary on the Dream of Scipio*, translated with introduction and notes by William Stahl (New York, 1952), 61–62.

27. Gouhier, "Descartes a-t-il rêvé?" 206–7; *Premières pensées*, 38–39; *Pensée réligieuse*, 315. This is perhaps the point to remark that the Latin title for *this* true pseudodream is the *Somnium Scipionis*, not the *Raptus Scipionis*.

28. Macrobius, *Commentary*, 1.2.7–11.

29. The following theoretical studies of allegorical literature have helped me greatly, although in the text, which is already freighted with heavy cargoes from ancillary disciplines, I have tried to stay close to the sources and scholarship most directly relevant to the historical analysis of Descartes's dreams: Angus Fletcher, *Allegory: The Theory of a Symbolic Mode* (Ithaca, 1964); Edwin Honig, *Dark Conceit: The Making of Allegory* (New York, 1966); Maureen Quilligan, *The Language of Allegory* (Ithaca, 1979); Morton Bloomfield, ed., *Allegory, Myth, and Symbol* (Cambridge, Mass., 1981).

Fletcher: "In the simplest terms, allegory says one thing and means another. . . . For the most part [it] springs from the natural desire to conserve some idea which, owing to its age, has come to be regarded as sacred. . . . Somehow the literal surface suggests a peculiar doubleness of intention, and while it can, as it were, get along without interpretation [by the reader], it becomes much richer and more interesting if given interpretation. . . . Someone does see that [secondary, non-literal, allegorical] meaning, and once seen, it is felt strongly to be the final intention behind the primary meaning. . . . The strengths of the mode are . . . clear. . . . [A]llegories are the natural mirrors of ideology" (*Allegory: The Theory of a Symbolic Mode*, 2, 3 n.9, 7, 8, 368.

Honig: "The concept of allegory assumes a subject sacred to belief or revered in the imagination. . . . Allegory is a rhetorical instrument used by strategists of all sorts in their struggle to gain power or to maintain a system of beliefs" (*Dark Conceit*, 28, 179).

Quilligan: "Actual allegorical narratives . . . [take] place in a specialized, dreamlike landscape peopled by personified abstractions. . . . Personification manifests the meaning as clearly as possible by naming the actor with the concept [so "Christian Rosenkreutz" but not "René Descartes"]. Allegories do not need *allegoresis* [literary criticism of texts] because the commentary, as [Northrup] Frye has noted, is already indicated by the text. . . . Allegorical protagonists often find themselves in scenes which simply reenact the details of that other book, the first text, the original pretext of all Christian allegory. I term the Bible the 'pretext' not simply to emphasize the fact of the Bible's anterior originality for allegory, but to stress as well the covert nature of that relationship. Allegories do not state but discover the nature of that book . . ." (*The Language of Allegory,* 31, 97).

    30. Baillet, *Vie,* 1:51.

Index of Descartes's Life, Thought, and Works

Index of Historical Persons and Authors (Pre–1800)

Index of Scholarly Authorities
(post–1800)

A Note on the Author

JOHN COLE, professor of history at Bates College, Lewiston, Maine, received his Ph.D. from Harvard University. His previous publications include articles on Greek history and literature.

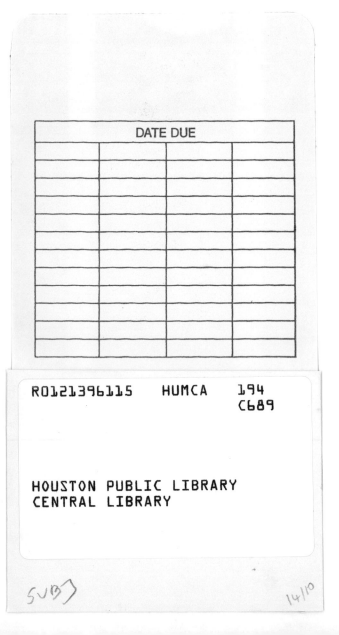